OUR LITTLE HOUR

Bernard Anson King

B. A. King

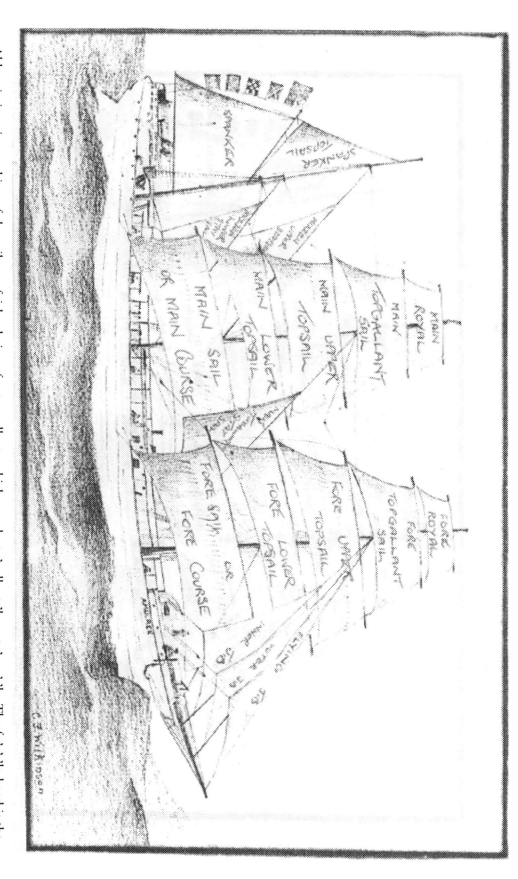

Abbreviations in speaking of the sails are fairly obvious for topgallants which may be to'gallants'ls or to'gan's'ls. The fo'c's'le-head is the raised deck right for'ard under which the fo'c's'le in earlier times accommodated the crew; the poop is the similar deck right aft where the officers lived; hence, perhaps, the half-deck, a raised cabin on the main deck usually abaft the mainmast where the apprentices were.

Our little hour, how swift it flies
When poppies flare and lilies smile;
How soon the fleeting minute dies,
Leaving us but a little while
To dream our dream, to sing our song,
To pick the fruit, to pluck the flower,
The Gods - They do not give us long,
– One little hour.

Leslie Coulson
("But a short time to live")

Copyright © 2002 by Bernard Anson King

Published by Stephen King

ISBN: 0-9542509-0-7

Printed in the United Kingdom by TandemPress · www.tandempress.co.uk

DEDICATION

This book has been produced specifically for the benefit of the extended King/Bloomfield family. In its production, special thanks are due, in the first instance to Cathy whose perseverance was responsible for the job being started and for subsequent encouragement. Secondly I'm indebted to Stephen for all the practical assistance received in producing the paperwork and for the printing costs. My thanks also go to Marion for proof-reading and correcting and eliminating incorrect English so as to render the work sufferable, whereafter Captain Simon Waite kindly agreed to contribute the foreword. The real thanks are due to the man whose writing of his experiences form the major part of the story and which thoroughly deserve the attention of posterity; I only hope he would have approved of what I have done.

AUTHOR'S NOTE

I have used the sketch of "Amulree", as depicted by my mother some years before her marriage, to illustrate sails etc. referred to in the log. It may also help if I explain some other mysteries, such as: Standing rigging (stays, shrouds, similar stationary ropes or wires, footropes and the like) were, where appropriate, given protection by way of spun-yarn filling between strands (worming) and canvas wrapping (parcelling) which was secured by yarn wound or "served" tightly around the work. Footropes for sailors to move along up aloft were attached to the yards, those heavy horizontal spars to which the sails were secured. The shrouds were permanent mast support wires; buntlines were sail fastenings - the bunt being the baggy part of the sail; the keelson was a box-shaped structure inside the ship at the bottom, running fore and aft over the keel; dunnage is waste timber, mostly softwood, indispensable when loading cargo which stands on it and is separated by it. It creates air space to assist in ventilation. Other nautical terms are generally self-explanatory within the text and, of course, the Red Duster is the Merchant Navy flag, the Red Ensign. At the end of the book I have appended a copy of Dad's commendation in the London Gazette together with such of his verse as survives and I hope this will give some insight into the thoughts and feelings of one whose life was largely one of self-imposed exile.

CONTENTS

LIST OF ILLUSTRATIONS

FOREWORD

by Captain S.T. Waite, Master of "Cutty Sark".

I was appointed Master of "Cutty Sark" in November 1989 and met Bernard King when he was interviewed for the position of Second Mate in 1990 when he was looking for employment before "real" retirement two years later.

Although older than me, Bernard and I shared many similar experiences during our seafaring days and we also shared a common interest in 19th Century merchant sailing ships, music and family history. Bernard's interest in sailing ships obviously came from his father, while mine came from the age of about eleven when a teacher could tell me nothing about the Dutton prints of sailing ships that we had around the class room walls. I was determined to find out more and then I became hooked.

Bernard approached me to comment on the manuscript of this book, which I found absolutely fascinating, and although it could be considered something for a niche market, I believe that there are sufficient "old sea dogs" still around who will love the book, as I did, but also I believe that it will be of great interest to social historians.

To many, the long periods of separation from loved ones must seem alarming and unacceptable, but to a substantial number of families in Britain at the time it was normal, not only for Merchant Seamen but men of the armed forces and the Colonial Service.

For anyone interested in our maritime heritage, and in particular our merchant shipping in the first half of the 20th Century, this book is an essential read.

PROLOGUE

It occurs to me that boys up chimneys belong with the dinosaurs and such skills as they may have learnt are not mourned in their passing. We are reconciled to the changes wrought by the march of time and happily allow chimney boys and dinosaurs to slip away never dreaming that a day will come and with it the stark realisation that one has oneself become a dinosaur.

At this point comes the unpleasant awareness that a familiar way of life and all that goes with it is about to disappear with very little trace. The question now arises as to whether in a generation or two anyone will really care and therefore whether I am justified in bending the listener's ear or straining the reader's eyes with tales of an outmoded way of living, my father's and mine.

I claim justification on two counts: firstly I have been told I must and secondly, since Dad and I won the second world war with a little help from some of our friends, I feel I have the right.

Where to start? To highlight the similarities in our careers or to point out areas of total disagreement and separateness of experience? One thing we had in common and with all the seafarers of our day; the dichotomy which had the power to imprison and in many cases to destroy even the strongest of men. This was engendered by the fact that once a man became accustomed to seafaring no other way of living could compare, or in the event of a shore job coming along, compensate for the lost vocation.

The opposing aspect that created the problem was the separation from home and loved ones and at the time of which I write a six-month voyage was considered a short trip, something of a plum job, most voyages continuing for any length of time up to, say, eighteen months. Home and family had initially to be pushed to the back of the mind subsequently to emerge as a tantalising distant dream and as a result every seaman one ever met roundly cursed the sea and whatever circumstances led him to it in the first place. At times the advice given to the new recruit to get ashore while the going was good became extremely wearisome.

As the son of a seaman I had better reason than most to heed the warnings but only became fully aware of the fact after serving a year as junior cadet; this formative period was also the most eventful of my life, my metamorphosis time.

More of this later though, as it is necessary to try to establish the origin of the seafaring tradition in our family, a matter for which a knowledge of the background provides clarification if not the full story.

Dad was born in January 1896, a time before contraception became widespread and when infant mortality occurred at a frightening rate. Parents` attitude towards children was markedly different then, in self-defence it had to be. If the little ones survived they threatened to grow sufficiently numerous to keep the family poor and the bread-winner`s nose to the grindstone but if they died they had to be written off and the experience smothered as well as it could be.

Little wonder the youngsters were kept at arms length to be seen, not heard and introduced to the housework as early as possible to reduce the load on an ever increasingly exhausted Mum.

In the King family case one of the more vicious twists of fate greeted the arrival of Dad, the eldest survivor. He would have been number four but for the death of the second born, a son, shortly after birth and the subsequent passing of three- and one-year old daughters on successive days from whooping cough while his mother was heavily pregnant and shortly to give birth.

There is no record as to how premature his arrival was but he was small enough to be cradled in a shoe-box and we are told that for his first year he was washed only with oil, no water being allowed to touch his skin.

At all events, Dad developed a life-long respect for his mother who from all accounts was given a hard time by my grandfather who worked as a clerk at Surrey Docks and was presumably

Grandma`s social inferior, she having been a school teacher. They successfully reared another daughter and two more sons after Dad and when he had reached the age of sixteen he may well have decided that by apprenticing himself to John Stewart & Co. he would be reducing the burden on his parents, sparing them the expense of assuaging at least one very healthy appetite.

Before leaving home Dad had been a model student (another instance of being helpful and setting an example?) and had an astonishing loyalty towards the "old school". How times have changed. He had no explanation for his decision to go to sea, but when this was made it was with the proviso that nothing but sail would do.

His indentures stipulated a minimum of four years servitude and these were spent on the three masted barque "Amulree" under Captain George Anson Cooper. Where the Anson came from is anybody`s guess but as a mark of respect to the man who he admired so much Dad passed it on to me and thereby started another family tradition.

His first voyage lasted fourteen months and was recorded in his personal log, a luxury which was denied me on my first trip as under war-time conditions such records were strictly forbidden to crew members. Fortunately, now in command, Dad did not abide by these regulations as presumably he would have disposed of personal logs together with all other secret documentation in the event of emergency. Flag code books, ship`s logs, crew discharge books, anything indicating ports of origin or intended destination would go into the holed and weighted bags kept by the ship`s safe for disposal overboard should the ship be disabled or captured.

Thanks to his logs and retained correspondence, in particular that with his schoolgirl sweetheart whom he married in 1920, it is possible to reconstruct much of Dad`s career first on the "Amulree" and subsequently on Ellerman & Bucknall`s steamships.

Various records of my seafaring past have gone astray and the most reliable source for the early part is contained in pay-off slips which give both voyage dates and ports of call. In addition

I can say with absolute certainty all the contributory factors which determined me to take a life afloat.

In spite of Dad's repeated protestations that no son of his would go to sea, he made the mistake of having his whole family on board the "City of Khartoum" for Christmas when she was laid up off Southend Pier together with surely a dozen other ships in 1935. He was lucky to retain employment as watchman living on board and serviced by the agent's motorboat that plied from the end of the pier.

The "...Khartoum" of 6127 tons, formerly the "Karroo", was built in 1913 and was therefore reaching the end of her normal life anyway by that time and the depression settled her fate. This ship meant a great deal to Dad and he made sure that he was the last Englishman to leave her when she was handed over to Italian buyers in January 1936. It is an interesting fact that the company's official records show her as being scrapped, perhaps a discreet blurring of the truth as the Italians were definitely not flavour of the month at that time.

The ship had rod and chain steering gear which means that lengths of chain lay on the surface of the rust covered steel decks, an extra item of clutter to add to the steam piping that snaked around the hatches and all the paraphernalia of winches, weather boarding and what have you. The most extraordinary aspect that makes her unique in my memory is that she had no mast ladders. To reach the cross-trees one climbed ratlines as on sailing ships and this of course I did at nine years of age and got severely told off afterwards in view of the prevailing wind strength.

My activity was regarded for some odd reason as dangerous and I was thereafter relegated to the duty of scraping sheets of rust from the decks. The holiday receded and was no doubt slotted into my subconscious mind, probably influencing my reaction some five years later when I lay in bed one stormy night in Knebworth where we had fled from the blitz. I was listening to the wind howling through the poplars outside and I knew at that moment that I would follow in my father's footsteps and dedicate my life to the sea.

CHAPTER ONE

UNDER SAIL

Dad's early years are very well covered by his logs and letters supplemented by documents and some material from other sources enabling a very clear picture to emerge. The die was cast when father and son attended the Fenchurch Avenue offices of John Stewart & Co. on 24th June 1912 and signed the Ordinary Apprentice's Indentures which:

"Witnesseth that the said Arthur Ernest King voluntarily binds himself Apprentice unto the said John Stewart & Co .... for the term of four years from the date hereof".

The Indenture further binds the apprentice, the company and the apprentice's guarantor each to fulfil the terms of the agreement in the penal sum of £10.00, the apprentice to provide his own clothing and bedding, the ship's master to provide food and medical care. The apprentice was paid nothing until his four years were completed, thereafter he was required to stay by the ship until the voyage end at a wage of £2.10s per month. The Indenture was drawn up on linen paper and was endorsed on the back '6th October 1916', with a hand-written certification to the effect that the said apprentice served his time on board the barque "Amulree" of London to everyone's entire satisfaction. It does not say that it took only two voyages to fulfil this task, the logs for which speak for themselves thus:

"Record of a voyage in the barque "Amulree" of London

Commencing from 1st of July 1912 —
Arthur E. King, Apprentice

From Liverpool to Durban with general cargo.

LOG BOOK

Monday 1st July:

Goodbye to dear old England. Left Brunswick Dock Liverpool at midnight, turned in 2.45am (Tuesday). Towed by "W.T. Joliffe". Calm sea and rather cold with slight breeze from NW.

Tuesday 2nd July:

Tug left us at 2.30pm, calm sea NW wind. Seasick, so feeling very happy, sighted White Star training ship "Mersey" bound for Liverpool. Our speed about 7 knots.

Wednesday 3rd July:

Watches chosen. Starboard under 2nd Mate (Mad Alec) and Old Man (Georgie). Slight N wind, speed about 5 knots. Sickness over thank goodness.

Thursday 4th July:

Turned out at 4.00am for four hours. Helped to loose main royal. Sighted a shoal of porpoises and a number of steam trawlers. Dog watch 6-8.00pm, we played cricket. Wind rather gusty NNE. 5-7 knots.

Friday 5th July:

Course SSW speed about 9 knots. Helped to put new serving on footropes. My chum (Thompson) and I reckon we are just off Cape Ortegal (NW Spain).

Saturday 6th July:

Fine day, almost a dead calm. Deck cricket in second dog watch. Speed about 2 knots.

Sunday 7th July:

The day of rest. Did our washing (Oh! What a game it was!) Sighted a French yawl, which hove to and sent a boat to barter fish for bread. Light breeze, calm sea, speed about 3 knots. Saw shark on starboard bow.

Monday 8th July:

Washed down decks during morning watch. Painted new starboard lifeboat. The Old Man came and took my brush just before I started and proceeded to show me how it should be done. Light breeze, SSE course.

Tuesday 9th July:

Slight rain during early morning. Hot day afterwards. Footropes taken off tops'l yards and tested on weather capstan. Sighted steamer on port bow. Breeze still holds and course still the same.

Wednesday 10th July:

Hot day. Odd jobs on deck. Still the same course. Played cricket on deck in 2nd dog watch with a spun-yarn-and-canvas ball and weather capstan as wicket.

Thursday 11th July:

Sighted lights of a steamer about four bells in the middle watch. Helped ABs serve new footropes. 2nd Mate says our position is about 39 N, 11 W. Doing about 5 knots all day.

Friday 12th July:

Wind from the NW. Tramp steamer "Salvadora" of Monte Video, heading northward, passed on port side about 100 yards distant. She couldn't have had any cargo for she was rolling like a ball. Also sighted a three-masted barque homeward bound, but not within signalling distance. Wind shifted to the NE during the first dog watch. Speed increased to about 8 knots.38.38N,13.08W.

Saturday 13th July:

Have caught the NE trades. Wind strong and heavy sea running. Unbent fores'l and bent fresh one in our fore-noon watch on deck. Sighted a tramp steamer this afternoon who promised to report us.

Sunday again, 14th July:

Wind from NNE, sea dropping. Washed some more gear. 2nd Mate rigged a horizontal bar from mainmast to weather shrouds and we indulged in some gymnastics.

Monday 15th July:

We unbent mainsail, main lower and upper topsails and fore to'gallant and royal and bent fresh ones. Speed about 4 knots. 3rd Mate's gramophone on the after hatch this evening-had a regular sing-song. Some of the songs made me feel jolly homesick.

Tuesday 16th July:

Scrubbing wire ropes and brace wires, also oiled them. Dead calm and a blazing sun. Slight rain in first dog watch.

Wednesday 17th July:

Hot day with slight rain and a light breeze. Chipped and scraped topgallant rail. Lime juice for first time with our sea-pie.

Thursday 18th July:

Fair breeze dead aft. Doing about 7 knots on SSW course. Very hot. Finished chipping topgallant rail and painted it.

Friday 19th July:

Very hot again with very light breeze. Washing paint-work and overhauling buntlines. Doing about 4 knots. Course SSW.

Saturday 20th July:

Baking hot day; doing 5-6 knots. Course still the same. Washed decks at 2.00pm. Songs on the main hatch in the evening.

Sunday 21st July:

Had a cold water bath and washed some more gear. Started teaching Thompson (Tommy) the semaphore.

Wednesday 24th July:

Nothing much in the way of work to do since last Sunday-just odd jobs about the deck and aloft. Sighted a German three masted ship today on same course as ourselves but she went ahead faster and gradually disappeared.

Tuesday 30th July:

Have got the SW monsoon.

Wednesday:

Passed out of the Doldrums today.

Thursday:

Wind from SW. Close-hauled and continually tacking ship. Sighted two homeward bound wind-jammers.

Friday:

Sighted homeward bound tramp steamer. Wind still the same.

Monday:

Wind shifted to SSE Getting the SE trades.

Wednesday:

Wind blowing harder. Took in royals, first sails to come in since leaving home.

Thursday:

Sighted island of Trinidad about 20 miles away on port bow. Also saw a wooden Peruvian barque.

Saturday 17th:

Bent our storm canvas today.

Wednesday 21st:

Had our first hard blow today. Shortened down to 3 tops'ls this afternoon. Plenty of water coming aboard through scupper holes.

Thursday 22nd:

Set to'gallants in morning, took them in again this afternoon and in the evening set them again, also the foresail. Fair wind now for two or three days.

Wednesday:

Another hard blow with sharp lightning and thunder. Took in royals and to'gallants.

Thursday:

Fair wind again. All sail set and making good way.

Thursday 5th September:

Sighted Africa today but got blown off again and passed Friday out of sight of land.

Saturday 7th:

Approached land again and saw the Bluff lighthouse, Durban at 10.15pm.

Sunday 8th:

Outside Durban at 7.30am having passed the night in tacking up and down outside. Taken in tow at 8.00am and finished making fast at 9.30am.

Durban. Very beautiful town but there is nothing for us to do but stroll about West Street each evening. Everything very dear here so we can't be millionaires on 5/- a week. Weather pretty hot and Kaffirs very amusing. Have made good friends here- American vice-consul (Mr Hood) and family. Have got to write to Beatrice Hood which means more scribbling to add to my already immense correspondence list. Met old school chum Gilbert England on "Clan McGillivray".

Saturday 28th September:

Left Durban with a little general cargo for Lourenco Marques as well as 780 tons of wet sand ballast.

Sunday 29th September:

Heavy gale blowing this afternoon. Fore lower tops'l split right down the bunt as we were going aloft to take it in. Sighted the light at the entrance to Delagoa Bay at 10.00pm. Head winds set in however, which destroyed all chance of getting in for a day or two.

Wednesday 2nd October:

Have been trying since Sunday to get in and at last, at 12.0'clock (midday), succeeded in entering Delagoa Bay and at 4pm were anchored off Lourenco Marques. The "Clan McGillivray" is already here but I don't expect I shall see anything of Gilbert England.

Thursday 3rd October:

Portuguese tug "Magul" towed us farther in to our moorings. We passed Friday and Saturday in getting everything ready for discharging cargo and painting ship. Saturday was the anniversary of the Portuguese Revolution so the town was all decorated, the Portuguese war-ship in the bay fired salutes and rockets were sent up in the evening.

On Thursday 10th October we finished cargo and got everything ready for sea.

Friday 11th October:

Towed into the bay and dropped anchor there.

Saturday 12th October:

Heaved our anchor at 5am by means of the donkey engine but the wind dropped and we had to anchor in the bay again.

Sunday 13th October:

At 4.30am we again hoisted our anchor and this time we succeeded in getting out. A glorious breeze got up and we commenced the passage to Newcastle at a rate of about 9 knots per hour. We had hardly got clear of the bay when the youngest apprentice, Tom Hodgkinson, fell down the fore-hatch from the tween decks, missing the keelson by about 6 inches, so we just escaped a funeral.

Monday 21st October:

One week gone and nothing of importance has happened. We get an occasional bit of work aloft as the Old Man wants to make a smart passage and hangs on to his canvas as long as possible, so making hard work of taking in sail.

Tuesday 22nd October:

Wind from the NE with slight rain. Chipping and scraping the bulkheads and beams in the hold all day.

Wednesday 23rd October:

Rather rainy and wind very unsteady, blowing almost a gale at times, then suddenly falling calm. Chipping in the hold again.

Thursday 24th October:

Had plenty of rain last night but the weather was fine by 8am. Strong breeze from the SE. No work today; have been standing by under the fo'c's'le-head.

Friday 25th October:

Wind blowing strongly from the S with plenty of sun. Chipping and painting in the holds.

Saturday 26th October:

Very cold today. Wind is just the same but not much sun. Took in both the to'gallants this evening in 2nd dog watch.

Sunday 27th October:

Not much wind and plenty of sun. No work all day. Food is improving; we got corned beef and apple pie instead of preserved mutton and duff for dinner. Sang a few hymns in 2nd dog watch which made me think of Evening Service in St. Andrew's at home.

Monday 28th October:

Bright sunny day with a very strong wind blowing. No work on deck. Passed St. Paul's Island on starboard side but not near enough to distinguish anything ashore.

Tuesday 29th October:

Light wind blowing with occasional rain. Chipping and painting in the hold.

Wednesday 30th October:

Sunny with a light fair wind. Work the same as yesterday.

Thursday 31st October:

Light, fair wind with slight rain and a heavy mist.

Friday 1st November:

Wind still the same with plenty of sun. Commenced stowing dunnage today.

Saturday 2nd November:

Very little wind today and a bright sun; quite warm. Continued stowing dunnage this morning. Washed down at 2pm then knocked off.

Sunday 3rd November:

Lovely day but no wind at all. It looks as if we should spend Christmas in Newcastle after all for we shan't be there much before then at this rate. Had a few more hymns this evening.

Monday 4th November:

No wind at all and a little rain in the afternoon. Still stowing dunnage.

Tuesday 5th November:

No wind but sun quite warm. Have only done six degrees these last four days. Slow but sure! I guess they're having some fun at Home tonight (Guy Fawkes Day).

Wednesday 6th November:

A little bit of wind at last. Port watch took the royals in at 10pm but that seemed to be the sign for the wind to drop. Shan't be sorry to get a good fair wind again.

Thursday 7th November:

Fair wind at last blowing from N by E. Warm and bright all day. Port watch set the royals and gaff tops'l at 5.30am. Have been going along at rate of 8 knots all day.

Friday 8th November:

Wind shifted round to the WSW blowing strongly and inclined to increase to a gale. Heavy rain squalls at times. Starboard fore royal sheet carried away at the yard-arm this afternoon. Tommy and I went aloft and took in the sail and the sheet was spliced and sent up again by Port watch in first dog watch. Took in the main royal in 2nd dog watch and once had to stand by to'gallant halliards but didn't take the sail in.

Saturday 9th November:

Wind blowing moderate gale from WSW. We are well in the Australian Bight now. Did 243 knots from noon yesterday till noon today.

Sunday 10th November:

Gale blowing from SW, very heavy sea running. Sunny on the whole but inclined to rain. Under 4 tops'ls and fores'l but set main to'gallant in 1st dog watch. Have run 256 knots from noon yesterday to noon today, the record day's run this voyage.

Monday 11th November:

Breeze dropping very quickly. Sun bright but the glass is falling and what wind there is, is inclined to go round to the N.

Tuesday 12th November:

Light breeze from the N, very warm. Doing about 3 knots.

Wednesday 13th November:

Still fine and very warm. No wind. Rather cloudy this afternoon.

Thursday 14th November:

No wind. Rain all day. The only work has been an occasional trimming of the yards to some faint suggestion of a breeze.

Friday 15th November:

Fair wind with plenty of rain. May be able to get through Bass Straits before night-fall.

Saturday 16th November:

Weather very warm with stiff breeze. Passed through Bass Straits at midday.

Sunday 17th November:

Fine day with light breeze till 4pm when a heavy white squall struck us nearly driving us on a lee shore S of Cape Howe. Squall over at 5.30pm and we tacked ship later to a breeze from the NE.

Monday 18th November:

Breeze increased to a moderate NE gale.

Saturday 23rd November:

Have spent the last five days in attempting to clear Cape Howe and have not yet succeeded in getting round.

Sunday 24th November:

Breeze has shifted and is now blowing very lightly from the S. Rounded Cape Howe at 4am. Doing about 5 knots.

Monday 25th November:

Sighted Sydney Heads at about 7am. 3pm 15 miles N of Sydney, the Newcastle tug "Heroic" took us in tow and we dropped anchor in Newcastle at 9.30pm.

NEWCASTLE

I am enjoying myself here; am a regular visitor at the Mission to Seamen and have found good friends in everybody there. On Christmas Day a large party of us went to Tomago (9 miles up the Hunter River) in the Mission's motor launch and on Boxing Day to Raymond Terrace (18 miles up the river). I also experienced the pleasure of a shave at the hands of "Father Neptune" at a concert held in aid of the Mission aboard the Norwegian ship "Hiawatha". Shall be sorry to leave Newcastle.

Monday 3rd February:
Towed out to buoys. 11am- 5.30pm we shifted some of the coal in the after hatch.

Tuesday 4th February:
Out on the "briny" again. Towed out 3pm by tug "Victoria". Moderate gale blowing, set tops'ls, t'gallant, fores'l, inner jib and mizzen stays'l.

Friday 7th February:
Wind dropping slightly, set the other t'gallant and both royals.

Monday 10th February:
Very heavy gale: shortened down to tops'ls. Bitterly cold and large seas coming aboard. Sharp hail squalls occasionally.

Saturday 15th February:
Dead calm, all sail set, very cold.

Sunday 16th February:
Wind gets up again; blowing a heavy gale this afternoon. All hands on deck to shorten down to lower tops'ls. Both upper tops'ls split while taking them in. Wind and hail almost unbearable.

Monday 17th February:

Heavy gale still blowing; inner jib blown clean out of the bolt ropes. Part of taffrail smashed, ports stove in and man nearly washed from the wheel by huge sea at 8pm. Rounded the S of New Zealand about 8 bells in the middle watch.

Tuesday 18th February:

Sea and wind going down; set all sail. Fair wind from the NW.

Wednesday 19th February:

Breeze still holds. Bright sun and slightly warmer. Wind shifted to the N , doing about 8 knots and shipping small seas.

Thursday 20th February:

Bright sunny day with a light head wind.

Friday 21st February:

Stiffer breeze from the NW, making more headway. Crossed meridian of 180.

Friday 21st February:

Second Friday this week. Wind and sea rising in preparation for a very dirty Sunday. Took in royals, to'gallants and mains'l at 4pm.

Saturday 22nd February:

Wind blowing hard from the N. We are now under tops'ls having taken in the fores'l at 8am. Doing about 5 knots.

Sunday 23rd February:

Sea and wind gone down considerably but what there is, is right ahead so we haven't set more sail.

Monday 24th February:

Running out of dirty weather now.

Laid up in my bunk for three weeks with salt-water boils so have had to stop keeping a log. After a month of light winds and warm weather we arrived in Taltal on 31st March 1913.

April 16th 1913:

Norwegian barque "Dorade" of Kristiania left Taltal with full cargo of nitrate homeward bound for Dunkerque; lucky beggars! I'm afraid its Capetown for us.

May 2nd 1913:

London barque "Gladys" arrived at last to take saltpetre to Capetown.

On Friday 8th May we learnt that the "Gladys"'s arrival had just saved us and that we were homeward bound at last for Dunkerque. We all shouted ourselves hoarse on hearing the news and every ship in the harbour knew what had happened by the noise we made.

Saturday 17th May:

Left Taltal at 8am in tow of the tug "Taltal".

16th June:

Rounded Cape Horn doing 12 knots an hour under main lower tops'l, spanker and two jibs. Did 263 knots in 24 hours, our best day's run throughout the whole voyage.

18th July:

Crossed the Line; once again in the northern hemisphere after nearly a year in the southern.

23rd July:

Spoken by German steamship "Aldeah" in 10 N 27 W. She will probably report us, so good news for the people at home.
Caught the NE trades about 10 N. Wind about N by E (Heading about NW by W).

30th August:

Passed the Lizard also the "Dorade" who left Taltal over a month before we did. Drifting about off Beachy Head in a thick fog for two days and nights. Picked up the London tug "Doria" off Dungeness on Monday 1st September and towed into Dunkerque at about 3pm on Tuesday September 2nd 1913.

So finishes the first voyage of exactly 14 months. The homeward bound passage took 107 days, the smartest passage of the year from the West Coast."

His final sentence may perhaps have tempted providence: after all it took a mere 14 months to achieve a straightforward circumnavigation; the second voyage was a rather different kettle of fish.

The ship sailed from Dunkerque for Buenos Aires and thereafter seems to have accomplished a tramping voyage. Unfortunately the log only covers to arrival at B.A. but a subsequent 22 page letter to his parents gives some indication of the ordeal undergone in this second circumnavigation of the globe which lasted some five weeks less than three years.

The lack of further record from Dad is unfortunate indeed as the voyage became extraordinary in many respects not least of which was an outbreak of beri-beri on board that very nearly ended his life. Captain Cooper nursed Dad back to health dosing him with bottled stout for a substantial period of time. I'll let him tell the eventful 64 day passage to Buenos Aires as follows:

"Record of my second voyage in the Barque "Amulree"

Commencing Tuesday 4th November 1913
Arthur E. King, apprentice

From Dunkerque to Buenos Aires with a cargo of iron pipes.

LOG BOOK

Monday 20th October 1913:

Rejoined the ship at 6am having left London at 9pm on Sunday, 19th October. We now spent a very miserable fortnight in Dunkerque unable to sail owing to contrary winds in the Channel. Heavy SW gale blowing up-channel with continual rain and fog. Our new crew are mostly Danes and Scandinavians with a Yankee in the port watch and a New Zealander in the starboard watch. Thompson has gone into the port watch and Hodgkinson has come into the starboard watch; the rest of us are in the same watches as last voyage. Of the two new apprentices Collins (Londoner) is in the port watch and Lind (a Swede from Stockholm) is in our watch. Hambling is now 3rd Mate and the new 2nd Mate, Mr Walker, is a New Zealander and a jolly decent fellow.

Tuesday 4th November:

Left Dunkerque at 3.30pm in tow of the London tug "Guiana". The wind is going round to the N so we may be able to beat down-channel at last. Tug left us off Beachy Head at about 10am Wednesday as her coal supply had given out.

Tuesday 11th November:

After a week spent in trying to force our way down-channel against wind and sea we are at last clear of the Channel. Since the tug left us we have been continually tacking across the Channel under tops'ls and fores'l with the mains'l set occasionally. Last night (Monday) at 8 bells in the 2nd dog watch all hands were called out to shorten down to lower tops'ls in a very heavy squall. This morning, just before 8am we set our upper tops'ls again. During the night the cargo has started to shift and we can hear a faint rumble in the holds every time the ship rolls. We shall be in a tight fix if this shifting increases. The weather is pretty dirty, very squally and chilly with a big sea coming aboard occasionally. Off the Scilly Isles at noon yesterday we sighted the tramp steamer "Westhampton" who promised to report us. Today we are doing about 3 knots on a W $\frac{1}{2}$ S course with the wind about S by W.

Wednesday 12th November:

Yesterday afternoon our watch went down into the main hold and succeeded in re-stowing the pipes that had broken loose. Today they are worse than ever. Several of the biggest pipes have broken loose and are charging about and kicking up the deuce of a row. We shall be lucky if some of them don't succeed in knocking a hole in the side. During the night we made more sail, as far as the to'gallants; today we are shortened down to tops'ls and fores'l in a very heavy blow. A large 4-masted barque, probably Norwegian, has passed us with double to'gallants set and is just disappearing ahead. The wind has gone round again to W by S and we are doing about 6 knots on a S by W course.

Thursday 13th November:

Yesterday evening at 3 bells in the 2nd dog watch, all hands on deck to haul the fores'l up as the weather was getting steadily worse. We were absolutely scooping the water aboard – plunging into it by the head and settling down aft, full up from stem to stern. The wind and sea are every bit as bad as they were off Cape Horn in mid-winter last voyage. Each watch is working below, watch on deck, day and night trying to re-stow the cargo that has broken adrift. Last night the mate was working with us when he should have been asleep, for $2\frac{1}{2}$ hours, re-stowing 20 of the biggest pipes which had broken loose.

Today they broke loose again but the port watch have just succeeded in putting everything straight once more- I wonder for how long? The sooner we get into decent weather the better it will be for the ship and everybody aboard. We are now under tops'ls and fores'l heading SW by W. The wind and sea have gone down slightly. Doing about 4 knots.

Friday 14th November:

Yesterday afternoon the weather cleared a little and we set the mains'l and main to'gallants'l. Last night it began blowing and raining again as hard as ever; we are now under tops'ls and fores'l again heading SW at 5 knots. The cargo has started shifting again and the mate says if a heavy gale springs up now we shan't come through it. If we don't run into better weather soon we shan't see Home again. Our position today is 45 51N 8 16W.

Saturday 15th November:

Last night the sunset gave promise of better weather; today the wind and sea have gone down considerably and we have set the mainsail and both to'gallants. Doing about 6 knots on SSW course with every sign of a fine day tomorrow. My violin is in great demand and hardly a dog watch passes without the singing of all the latest songs "accompanied by the orchestra".

Sunday 16th November:

Beautiful day, warm and clear with a light breeze. Doing about 3 knots with every sail set except the royals. Course SSW. Position about 80 miles SSW of Cape Finisterre. This afternoon the second mate spent his watch below on the fo'c's'le head teaching Hodgkinson and me how to use a sextant. There is every sign of coming fine weather. In the dog watch the breeze dropped, a dead calm lasting right through the night. Rain in the middle watch.

Monday 17th November:

Dead calm; trimming to every visible suggestion of a breeze.

Tuesday 18th November:

Occasional light flickers of a breeze. Squared yards to light breeze aft. Doing about 3 knots. Set the main royal in the first dog watch.

Wednesday 19th November:

Almost dead calm again; set fore-royal at 7.30am. Light breeze on port quarter. Doing 2 knots. Breeze freshened in 1ˢᵗ dog watch and went ahead. Doing about 5 knots close-hauled on starboard tack.

Thursday 20th November:

Breeze has dropped a lot and we are doing about 2 knots. Very hot. Running into tropical weather already. Should catch NE trades soon. Breeze freshened at the end of afternoon watch ; doing about 6 knots throughout night. Course SW.

Friday 21ˢᵗ November:

Breeze dropped considerably by end of morning watch. Doing about 3 knots close-hauled on starboard tack. Course SW. Fine day and fairly hot. Breeze stiffened in the afternoon and we did about 5 knots till about midnight.

Saturday 22nd November:

Breeze dropped early in the middle watch and today there is a dead calm. Very hot and not a breath of wind. Bracing the yards all day; mostly on starboard tack. Breeze stiffened in the afternoon and we did about 5 knots all through the night.

Sunday 23rd November:

Heavy rain at 2 bells in the morning watch lasting till nearly 4 bells. Last night at 6 bells in first watch we took in the royals, wind blowing from all directions. The Old Man is puzzled about the reason for this unusual occurrence. Breeze continued steady all through today; doing about 5 knots. Set royals in the afternoon. Course SSW.

Monday 24th November:

Bent and set flying jib in forenoon watch. Doing about 4 knots close-hauled on starboard tack. Took my first wheel this afternoon. Course SW ½ S, wind about NW ½ W. (My wheel 1ˢᵗ dog watch).

Tuesday 25th November:

Bent and set a new spanker also unbent outer and inner jibs and fore topmast stays'l , but did not set them. Stiff breeze coming up on port quarter in the afternoon. Course SW by S. Doing about 8½ knots. 32 32 N 19 16 W.

Wednesday 26th November:

Blowing hard on port quarter with occasional squalls. Fairly big sea getting up . Set jibs and stays'l. Doing9 knots, course SW by S 29 32N 20 50W.

Thursday 27th November:

Still blowing stiff but wind going ahead a little. Doing 9 knots on course SW by S. Took the wheel again 2 to 4pm. Have got to take regular wheels and look-outs as have Jock and Weller also. 26 32 N 22 45 W.

Friday 28th November:

Kept look-out from 2 to 4am. Yards squared in a little this afternoon. Took the wheel from 10 to 12pm still doing 9 knots, course SW by S ½ S. 24 11N 23 00W.

Saturday 29th November:

Blowing up very hard at 4am. Took in royals, to'gallants, mains'l and gaff-tops'l. Light rain and continual lightning. Weather cleared in the forenoon. Set to'gallants, main royal, mains'l and gaff tops'l. Doing 10 knots. Course SW by S ½ S.

Sunday 30th November:

Went to the wheel 2 to 4am. Breeze dropped this morning but this afternoon it freshened up again; now doing about 5 knots almost close-hauled on port tack 50 miles due west of Cape Verde Islands at noon. Course SSW.

Monday 1st December:

Went to the wheel 6 to 8am. Squared the yards a little this morning. Doing about 6 knots, course due S. Kept the second dog watch look-out. Breeze stiffened in the evening; did about 9 knots throughout the night.14 27N 26 52 W.

Tuesday 2nd December:

Breeze still holds; doing about 8 knots. Went to the wheel 10am to 12, noon. Course at 10am S ½ E, altered at 11.30 to S.

Wednesday 3rd December:

Very hot; went to the wheel 2 to 4am. Doing about 7 knots, course S. Lightning and heavy rain in 2nd dog watch, clewed up gaff tops'l, royals and mains'l. Set mains'l and main royal in middle watch. Kept the look-out 2 to 4am (Thursday).

Thursday 4th December:

Blazing hot day with good stiff breeze dead aft. Unbent main lower and upper tops'ls and main to'gallant and bent fair weather ones; also bent a new main royal. Heavy rain squall at 11pm; clewed up royals and gaff tops'l. Went to the wheel 8 to10pm.Course S ½ E, doing about 6 knots.

Friday 5th December:

Almost dead calm. Set royals and gaff tops'l in morning watch.

Light breeze coming up in forenoon watch, doing about 4 knots. Course S ½ E. Blazing hot day. Heavy rain squall in 2nd dog watch; clewed up royals and gaff tops'l and mains'l. This is probably the commencement of the Doldrums. Kept the look-out 12 (mid-n't) –2am.

Saturday 6th December:

Pouring rain all day and no wind. Has not stopped raining since 7pm yesterday. Went to the wheel 10am to 12. Close-hauled on port tack, head SSW.

Sunday 7th December:

Rain has stopped; very light breeze and very hot day. Doing about 3 knots. Course SW, breeze about SE. Went to the wheel 2 to 4pm.

Monday 8th December:

Very hot day with no wind. Kept the look-out 2 to 4am. Head WSW, light breeze in the afternoon. Doing about 3 knots Went to the wheel 8 to 10pm. Head SSE (8pm), SE by S (10pm). Close-hauled on starboard tack.

Tuesday 9th December:

Very hot day; close-hauled on port tack to light breeze from SSE. Italian mail steamer passed about 1 mile distant on port side, bound for Buenos Aires and promised to report us. Doing about 3 knots steering by the wind and heading SW by S ½ S.

Wednesday 10th December:

Went to the wheel 12(mid't) to 2am. Steering by the wind and heading SW ½ S. Doing about 6 knots. During morning wind hauled round a little towards SE, course S by W.

Thursday 11th December:

Blazing hot day, light breeze, doing about 5 knots steering full and bye, heading SW by S. Should cross the Line tomorrow afternoon. Wheel 4 to 6am.

Friday 12th December:

Blazing hot day, fairly stiff breeze, doing about 6 knots; course SSW. Went to the wheel 8 to 10am. Crossed Line 3.30pm. Kept lookout 8 to 10pm.

Saturday 13th December:

Still very hot, heavy rain squall 6.15 to 6.45am. Went to the wheel 12 (noon) to 2pm. Course SSW doing about 6 knots. At noon an Italian mail-steamer bound for Buenos Aires passed on port side and a French Seven Star liner passed on starboard side.

Sunday 14th December:

Blazing hot day with good stiff breeze; kept look-out 12 (midn't) to 2am. Doing about 6 knots. 10am large Italian mail steamer, homeward bound, passed on starboard side. Went to the wheel

4 to 6pm, steering full and bye SW by S. 10pm. 3-masted ship, homeward bound, passed on port side about ½ mile away.

Monday 15th December:

Kept look-out 4 to 6am. Good stiff breeze, moderate sea. Doing about 6 knots. 3.45pm small 3-masted barque on NNE course passed on port side. Went to the wheel 2nd dog watch. Course SW by S ½ S.

Tuesday 16th December:

Blazing hot day, stiff breeze, doing about 5 knots. Abreast of Pernambuco at noon. Went to the wheel 10pm to midn't. Steering SW by S ½ S.

Wednesday 17th December:

Very hot day, breeze still holds; doing about 5 knots, course SW by S ½ S.

Thursday 18th December:

Very hot day; heavy rain squall at 10am. Doing about 4 knots. Went to the wheel 8 to 10am, course SW by S ½ S still braced sharp on port tack.

Friday 19th December:

Blazing hot day with breeze falling light. Went to the wheel 1st dog watch, course SSW, wind SE by E. Doing about 3 knots.

Saturday 20th December:

Blazing hot, light breeze, doing about 4 knots. Kept look-out 8 to 10pm. Course SSW.

Sunday 21st December:

Very hot day, no wind. 4.15pm squared yards to light breeze from NNE. Went to the wheel 2nd dog watch, course S by W.

Monday 22nd December:

Blazing hot day, no wind. 10am breeze sprang up on port quarter, commenced doing about 6 knots S by W.

Tuesday 23rd December:

Breeze shifted round to starboard quarter at 8am blowing about NE by N, heavy seas aboard. Braced sharp up on starboard tack at 3pm, wind shifting round to SW. 7.45pm all hands on deck to shorten down to tops'ls; blowing hard with heavy rain all night. Went to wheel 12noon to 2pm, course SW.

Wednesday 24th December:

Very light wind with heavy rain all day. Heading ESE (by the wind). Being Christmas Eve we passed the 2nd dog watch in singing Christmas hymns and carols played by me on the violin; the mate and 2nd mate came into the half-deck and joined in the singing. 7.40pm.

Port watch tacked ship placing us on SW course (by the wind). Kept the look-out 8 to 10pm. Rain ceased about 10.30pm.

Thursday 25th December, Christmas Day 1913:

Went to the wheel 6 to 8am, course (by the wind) SW by W. Blazing hot day with bright sun and very light breeze. Being, of course, a holiday, we hardly knew what to do with ourselves all day. Bolton, Billy Edington and I used the puddings we brought from home for a half-deck feed at dinner and tea. 6.30pm Bolton took photos of all us boys, the 2nd and 3rd mates and the sailmaker grouped round the capstan on the forecastle-head. 7 to 8pm. I played some hymns while the rest of the boys and the mate sang them.

Friday 26th December:

Hot day with no wind. Port watch got anchors over the side and cables shackled on this afternoon. Went to the wheel 10 to 12pm. Head SW.

Saturday:

Hot day- no wind.

Sunday 28th December:

Breeze still wanting. Went to the wheel 8 to 10am, heading SW by S. Kept look-out 8 to 10pm. Breeze freshening up right astern at 10pm.

Monday 29th December:

Weather much cooler. Stiff breeze from NE by N, doing about 7 knots on course SW ½ S. Went to the wheel midn't to 2am (Tuesday).

Tuesday 30th December:

Breeze still holds; weather fairly cool. Doing about 6 knots. Course SW.

Wednesday 31st December:

Breeze still holds, doing about 7 knots on course SW by S.

Thursday 1st January 1914:

New Year's Day. Another holiday. Hot day, breeze much lighter. Doing about 4 knots on course SW by W.

Friday 2nd January:

Very hot day. Breeze gone. Head about SW.

Saturday 3rd January:

Very hot day. Fair breeze on starboard quarter. Doing about 3 knots (12noon). Wind hauling round to SSE. Took in to'gallants, fores'l and mains'l. Hove-to close-hauled on port tack. 5pm tacked ship wind hauling round to SW. Went to the wheel 8 to 10pm. Heavy gale and fairly big sea. Head (by the wind) S ½ W. The black cat died today.

Sunday 4th January:

Breeze has gone again. Saw a turtle and a seal this morning. 7pm land all along starboard side and right ahead. 12(mid't) Cape Santa Maria light on port bow; burnt 2 blue flares for a pilot.

Monday 5th January:

Wind very light and unsteady until 10am then hauled aft. Doing 3 knots SW by W ½ W. Went to the wheel 10 to 12 noon. Steamers continually passing. Passed St. Ignatio light 6pm, sighted pilot cutter on starboard bow. 7.15pm took pilot aboard. 8pm passed Lobos Island and light 10pm. Kept look-out 10pm to mid't.

Tuesday 6th January:

Wind dropped in the middle watch and left us to drift down-stream again with the tide. Off Punta Negre at 8am breeze sprang up but the enormous force of the ebb tide prevented us from heading up-stream again. Head SSE till 12 noon. Tide then turned and strong breeze came up. Doing about 9 knots NW ½ N up the river all the afternoon and night. Passed Monte Video at 6pm. 30 miles from Buenos Aires at midn't, close-hauled on starboard tack. Went to the wheel 10am to 12 noon.

Wednesday 7th January:

Still making good way up the river. In sight of the anchorage at 10am Norwegian wooden 3 masted barque outward bound passed about a mile away to starboard".

And there the journal stops. Clearly arrival in port took precedence over the log but for whatever reason it was never resumed and I am left to supply matters of fact concerning the next part of the voyage without benefit of graphic details.

After discharge of those all but lethal pipes, the ship sailed in ballast to Newcastle, New South Wales via Sydney and loaded coal for Caldera, Chile. On arrival 11th August 1914 they learnt of the outbreak of war.

Another ballast passage ensued, the ship returning to Newcastle for more coal, re-crossing the Pacific to Guayaquil and on again to Portland, Oregon. At this point the story is covered by a letter Dad wrote to his parents thus:

"Barque "Amulree",
At sea, 56. 40 S 71. 13 W
Monday 25th October, 1915.

Dear Mother and Dad,

As this is the day on which we ought to get our first sight of land since leaving Portland, I am also making it the day on which to start another letter to you. Already we are 81 days out from Portland and in that time have seen nothing but one steamer bound for some West Coast port. The 90 day passage which we at first expected is looking rather sick now for we are not more than two-thirds of the way to Algoa Bay yet. The winds as usual have been having a game with us for we have not yet had a breeze worth taking in to'gallant-s'ls for, although for caution's sake and on account of weak canvas we have occasionally spent a day or two under tops'ls and fores'l and on one occasion we ran for a day under main tops'ls fore-lower tops'l and fore-s'l. The NE Trades were rather weak and we crawled down to the south'ard managing to pick up the SE Trades without experiencing the usual discomforts of the Doldrums.

The Old Man originally intended to sight the Pitcairn Islands in 25 S 130 W, the home of the descendants of the "Bounty" survivors. This would have made an interesting break in the passage for the inhabitants come off in small boats to any passing ship for news of the outside world and for books and papers and any other odds and ends they might be able to get. The skipper said that if we passed close enough he would heave-to for a short time and we had quite a big collection of old magazines and newspapers but, after all, the SE Trades held us too far to the west'ard and we passed the Pitcairns in 132 W. After we lost the SE Trades at about the same time as we passed the Pitcairns, we picked up the westerlys and north- westerlys with occasional breezes from the south and steered E by S and ESE in order to cut down our 60 degrees or so of westing as much as possible by the time we reached the latitude of Cape Stiff (i.e. Cape Horn). As you will see we have just managed this nicely for we are now in 56 40 S 71 13 W and the Horn is in 55 58 S 67 17 W and with a strong westerly poking us along at about 11 knots, we are steering E by N.

We've had a fine weather passage all the way so far and even now, with a westerly its fairly warm although, of course, the decks are full of water and we have to make a jump every now and then for the breakwater or the lifeline to dodge an unwelcome and very malicious visitor in the shape of a hefty, roaring, racing sea But life is not quite so pleasant when the breeze shifts to the south'ard, for then the biting wind and occasional snow, hail or sleet squalls make two hours at the wheel seem rather less pleasant than two hours in a flooded refrigerator. In the evenings, though, we have a way of dealing with cold weather which is highly satisfactory and very warming. At 6 o'clock as soon as tea is over we boys all congregate in the half-deck on the chests farthest from the door and proceed to create what we call a "Cape Horn fug". We close all the ports and the skylight, light the lamp and drop the canvas curtain over the door; then out come the pipes and all hands light up.

In about ten minutes anyone entering the house would find himself enveloped in a thick, blue, scorching-hot mist or "fug" which hides the further end of the half-deck and through which the lamp shines dimly, like a street-lamp in a London fog. From the depths of the fug my violin squeals while half a dozen figures in oilskins and sea-boots roar all the songs, comic and otherwise that they ever knew with an occasional interval for the re-filling of pipes. Thus the dog watch passes till the striking of eight bells breaks up the fug party. Some time between 6.30 and 7 o'clock this evening, according to the latest news from the cabin, we shall sight the Diego Ramirez Islands in 56 31 S 68 43 W. We have never seen land so far south before as we were two degrees farther to the south'ard when we came round here last voyage, so we are rather anxious to see it.

Tuesday 26th October 1915:
At 6.40 o'clock last night we sighted the Diego Ramirez and

passed about 10 miles to the south'ard of them. We are still roaring along at about 10 knots with a good westerly breeze. We rounded the Horn some time about midnight and are now once more in the Atlantic after 18 months spent in the Pacific. The Old Man expects to sight Staten Island before sunset.

7pm. After midday the breeze slacked considerably and we have been making about 8 knots all the afternoon. Staten Island is now visible away on the weather bow but as we are only making about 6 or 7 knots and the wind is easing down a bit, we shall only be about abreast of it at sunrise.

Wednesday 27th October 1915:

At 4am today Staten Island was on the port beam, just visible through a thick mist but at 5am the mist lifted and the island showed clear with Cape St. John in the foreground, backed by enormous, snow-covered peaks. The wind had fallen very light and finally came away on the port bow so that we can barely lay our course (NE) and it looks as if we are in for a head wind at last. That, of course, is just what we don't want for the weather on this side of the Horn is much colder than on the western side and if we get driven to the south'ard now things will be decidedly uncomfortable and we may not get off so lightly as we have up till now. We are well within the limit of drift-ice and the look-outs have standing orders to "keep a sharp look-out for ice and outward bounders".

4pm Thursday, 4th November 1915:

Here we are again! With a mug full of hot coffee, a pipe full of tobacco and feet as warm as two chunks of ice. What more inducements for letter-writing could any fellow want?

Of course we got our head wind and had to steer E by S for two or three days with occasional amusements such as taking in royals and to'gallants'ls and then setting them again. Then the wind began to free and we gradually worked back on course again.

Now the wind is round in the SSW and we are making about 10 knots E by N with all sail set. Today at noon our position was 46 04 S 28 54 W with 238 miles made good since noon yesterday. The voyage's record in noon-to-noon runs made off New Zealand on the way to Guayaquil is 299 miles.

The weather is slightly warmer on the whole but last Friday was the coldest day we have had since we came round the Horn in mid-winter last voyage. In addition to the cold there was a thick, wet mist all day and we had to take in sail in a heavy hail squall. I think we spent most of the day in making uncomplimentary remarks about the skipper for taking in sail, the fellow who first invented ships, all the fools that ever came to sea, etc. Such days as that are what make the sailor sing:

> "A life on the ocean wave!
> Oh, who put a name to the song?
> I'd like to tickle his ribs
> With a spike about 40 feet long"

Two years ago on Tuesday 4th November 1913 we left Dunkerque never thinking that two years and more would pass before we should see England again. We were only expecting a 14 month voyage and even that seemed an endless, miserable stretch to look forward to; for the memories of a six week holiday at Home were very fresh in our minds and the sudden change from Home with its dear ones and its luxury, to a crowded little hovel of a half-deck with no company but our own, had made us thoroughly miserable and ready to sell our souls for the ability to wipe out five years and go back to our school-days again.

But I suppose the spirit of the sea has just about soaked into us by now for we can look forward to every succeeding port as just one more step on the homeward road and the past two years have not seemed half as long and dreary as did the fourteen months of last voyage. Home always seems to gleam brightly just ahead and even big disappointments such as Algoa Bay and another prospective 14 months afloat, though they bite hard for a while, cannot push it any further away or lessen its glow. We know we shall get there some day and worrying won't ease the road.

Sunday 7th November 1915:

The weather is gradually getting warmer and the breeze still holds, shifting occasionally to S or W but always keeping within those limits. We are making about 6 knots E ½ S with everything set. Next Tuesday, so the Old Man expects, we shall sight Gough Island, an uninhabited rock in 40 19 S 9 57 W.

Monday 8th November 1915:

This morning the wind began to shift to the nor'ard and dropped till at noon we were just rolling about with no wind. This afternoon the breeze freshened up again in the North and we are now making about 5 knots and steering E ½ N. Our position at noon was 41 52 S 13 53 W. Algoa Bay for us some time before Christmas! 95 days out from Portland already!

Tuesday 9th November 1915:

Today the weather was beautifully warm and bright with a strong N'ly breeze. Gough Island appeared on the port bow about 10.30am and, making about 7 knots, we have passed about 20 miles to the south'ard of it and left it astern and out of sight at 5pm. The island is over 3,000 feet high so you can bet it looked a bit of a lump at 20 miles distance. That's about the last land we shall see before we get to the Cape.

Thursday 11th November 1915:

10.30pm. At present we are in a nice little blow under tops'ls. Yesterday morning the wind went ahead and we were making about E by S by the wind. In the afternoon as we were well off our course and the breeze was strengthening we took the royals in and ran about ESE making 8 or 9 knots all through the night. This morning the wind was still freshening and we took in the to'gallants'ls and, later on, the fores'l. The wind was coming along good and strong from the NE with driving rain and we were looking forward to a very pleasant night with upper tops'ls to take in, a good stiff blow and plenty of water aboard. About 7pm the main topmast stays'l sheet parted under the strain of the breeze in the canvas and before the watch could get the stays'l in it had flapped itself to ribbons. Of course that pleased the Old Man- another sheet to be made and practically another sail. After 8pm the wind commenced to shift and at 9 pm had gone round to the N, allowing us to lay our course, E by N again. It is still blowing too hard to set any more canvas but the breeze is slacking a little all the while and crawling round to the NW.

Saturday 13th November 1915:

We are still kicking along making about 7 knots E by N with the wind in the SW. Our position at noon was 38 28 S 3 28 E with 1105 miles yet to do. Yesterday at noon we were 0 28 E, so we crossed the meridian of Greenwich at about 8am.

Sunday 14th November 1915:

Today has been bright and sunny but the weather is still pretty cold; colder in fact than it should be seeing that it is summer-time and we are only in 38 S. All day we have been surrounded by an enormous flock of ice-birds, little white fellows about the size of a thrush. At noon we were in 37 46 S 6 57 E and 936 miles from Algoa Bay – less than a week's run if we can hold the breeze.

Saturday 20th November 1915:

Stuck! And practically in sight of port too! We slid along all right till the day before yesterday, making an average run of about 130 miles in 24 hours. But on Thursday morning the wind , which had been pretty steady between S and SW, went ahead and breezed up a bit at SE; ENE was as far easterly as we could make with that and we were in a current bearing us northward at 2 or 3 knots; we were one degree south and three degrees west of Cape Agulhas, so you can see an ENEly course and the set of the current combined would have carried us to the nor'ard and foul of Cape Agulhas. Consequently we had to keep tacking from ENE to SW and back again, losing a little to the south'ard and west'ard all the time. The wind still holds SE and we are still tacking; our position today was 36 44 S 19 18 E so we have gained a bit to the East'ard on the whole but not enough to carry us clear of Cape Agulhas while this wind lasts. If the breeze stiffens or lasts for three or four days things will be getting awkward for we have only about 8 days water left and other stores are getting low too.

Sunday 21st November 1915:

Fair wind again! At about 6 o'clock the breeze slacked and began to creep to the south'ard. At 8am it was blowing very gently from the south and we were making about 2 knots on course, E by N ½ N. In the forenoon it stiffened a little and we made 5 or 6 knots. At noon our position was 35 47 S 20 26 E, 280 miles from Algoa Bay and clear of Cape Agulhas, so the course was altered to ENE .With ordinary luck we shall spend Tuesday night in port. 108 days out today!

9.30am Monday 22 November 1915:

At 8 o'clock last night the breeze freshened considerably and went round to the west'ard and we made about 9 knots until daybreak. But at 4am today the weather had turned very dirty with the wind strong and very squally in the SSE and we took in the royals, fore to'gallants'l and mains'l. At 6.30am the weather was clearer and the breeze a bit lighter so we set the fore to'gallants'l and mains'l again; but at 8 o'clock all hands were called on deck again to take in both to'gallants'ls with a heavy squall driving our lee rail under water and showers of spray flying across the deck. We are now under tops'ls, fores'l and mains'l making about 7 knots and still on course E by N ½ N; the wind is yelling its battle song through the rigging and every now and then a sea comes lumping over the lee rail looking for somebody who wants to keep dry. Fortunately the weather is pretty hot now so dry or wet we don't mind.

At 8 o'clock the Old Man managed to shoot the sun and fixed our position as 35 07 S 23 06 E, 144 miles from Algoa Bay and 62 miles off the coast. If we can keep up our present speed and the breeze doesn't foul us we shall get in some time during tomorrow forenoon.

4pm. Stuck again! At 2 o'clock this afternoon the breeze shifted ahead to ESE and dropped fairly light, heading us off to NE. Our position at noon was 34 56 S 23 26 E about 120 miles from Algoa Bay and 50 miles off the coast.

The breeze is gradually working round to E so we have had to go about and stand out to sea again heading about SSE. We shall continue to tack running in towards land for a time then standing out to sea for a while till the wind frees sufficiently to enable us to fetch port. Its certain now that we shall spend another day at least at sea. Of course we ought to have expected this for this old packet usually has a good look at a port and then backs out again to think things over for a day or so before deciding that she would like a rest in port after all.

Last voyage we sighted Durban and then had to stand out to sea again for a couple of days; we got right up to the mouth of Taltal harbour and after signalling in vain for a pilot, had to stand out and beat up and down outside for a day and a half. Homeward bound we were hanging about becalmed in the Channel for two days; we were within three miles of Portland harbour when we were driven out again. So we are expecting two or three days of this little game.

2pm Tuesday 23rd November 1915:

We have had a little better luck since noon today. Since 2pm yesterday we had been tacking at intervals making SSE on the port tack and N by E on the starboard but at noon today the wind shifted a little towards the south so we tacked again and set the to'gallants'ls and are now heading NE at about 5 knots. That course won't take us to Algoa Bay although it's a change for the better, so we shall have to go about again before nightfall if the wind doesn't come fair. At noon we were in 25 02 S 23 55 E 107 miles from Algoa Bay and about 50 miles from the coast which is just visible now on our port beam.

10am Wednesday 24th November 1915:

At 8 o'clock last night we tacked again and stood away to the south'ard. After a while the breeze stiffened and at midnight was blowing hard enough to compel us to clew up and make fast the to'gallants'ls and mains'l. At 4am today we went about and stood in towards the coast again and are now making about 4 knots under tops'sls and fores'l and heading NE by N ½ N which is 1 ½ points worse than we were making on this tack yesterday.

Thursday 25th November 1915:

Still hanging about! At noon yesterday we were in 34 57 S 24 06 E 70 miles from Algoa Bay and hove-to under tops'ls heading SSE. At 3pm the wind hauled round to SE by S and we laid course E for 3 hours. Then we went about again and were hove-to all night under tops'ls heading S in a yelling gale and thunder storm with pouring rain and incessant lightning which made the night almost like day. Today at 7am the breeze went round again to S and dropped and now we are just rolling about heading E without a scrap of wind. The sun is very bright and hot and a few black squalls on the horizon form the only sign of a breeze.

1.30pm. Fair wind at last! At 10 o'clock I went to the wheel and then, of course, the breeze couldn't help coming fair!

At about 10.30 the first flickers of a breeze appeared and gradually strengthening shifted round through the S and W to NW. The rain came down in torrents all the while but with a fair wind we didn't care if it snowed ink. At noon our position was 34 53 S 23 58 E with Algoa Bay 100 miles distant bearing N 58 E. So we have lost 30 miles in the last 24 hours. We are now steering E making about 5 knots with every stitch set.

10am Friday 26th November 1915:

The end of the passage is now in sight after 113 days at sea the longest passage of our 3 ½ years. We are about 5 miles off the coast running up at 6 or 7 knots and Port Elizabeth lighthouse is now about 1 point on the weather (port) bow easily visible to the naked eye. We ought to make port in an hour and a half. Oh! For letters and fresh war news.

Port Elizabeth S.A.
8pm Friday 26th November 1915:

Dear Mother and Dad,
Here we are in port once more. We entered the Bay at about 11am and moored off Port Elizabeth just before noon. When we reached the lighthouse the breeze was blowing pretty hard and we had shortened down to tops'ls preparatory to picking up a tow boat. We passed the light very close, so close that we could recognise the features of the fellows standing by the signalling mast in the lighthouse grounds. Then as we rounded the small reef at the entrance to the Bay, from the lighthouse the signal fluttered out "You are standing in too close". The Old Man immediately jumped round to the lee side of the wheel and helped to head her off and as we swung out and headed for the centre of the bay the davits of some wrecked ship appeared sticking out of the water a short distance away on our port bow. But for lighthouse's timely warning we should have driven right on to the reef and torn the bottom clean out of the ship which would have been beastly awkward don'cherknow, with a big sea breaking on the rocks and sharks swarming all round.

Of course I am as happy as a dog with half a dozen tails tonight! Three letters from you, one from Else, one from Fred, three from Wilf and one from Harry Neale. Many thanks for the Magazine of the Old Scholars Association; it's a fine thing and I'm proud of the School that has got such a Roll of Honour. The list of the dead is very saddening, especially to one who knew well, as I did, every one of them. Thurston, Sidnell, Howard, Apps and Rangecroft. Poor, glorious, old school-chums, true sons of England and the dear Old School. Thank Heaven I shall soon be able, or so I sincerely hope, to do my bit for the honour of England, the family and good old Brownhill.

I am very sorry to hear of Fred's illness but the news that he is getting on all right makes up for that to a certain extent, so once again pride rules supreme. God bless our soldier boy. Good luck to Sergt. Wilf too! I'm jolly glad he managed to get a spell at Home after all.

By the way I must thank you too for enclosing those two letters for me, one as you know from Beatrice Hood and the other from another dear friend of mine Miss Irene Bethune of Newcastle, NSW.

We are chartered for Sydney with maize which probably means that our next cargo will be wheat from Sydney for Home; you know how we are praying that it may be so.

We are to unload 200 tons of our present cargo ourselves while lying out here in the bay and shall then haul in to the Town Wharf for a Kaffir gang to discharge the remainder so there is no prospect of shore leave before next Wednesday at the earliest. There is every up-to-date facility for discharging and loading in this port and consequently we hear we shall be at sea again in less than 12 days. What's the odds anyhow? The sooner at sea the nearer Home.

I am enclosing two photos; one taken in Portland in which unfortunately I don't appear as I was on the wharf tallying cargo when it was taken: the other is a photo of the Xmas (1914) picnic of Newcastle Mission. It was sent to me from 'Frisco by good old Folliot , third mate of the "Ville de Mulhouse". I guess it's a case of "Put me among the girls" for Arthur Ernest, eh! I am wearing a duck suit of Billy's borrowed for the occasion; Mrs Crothall is on my left hand and Miss Bethune on my right: Folliot, mon cher Auguste, is on the extreme right of the photo, wearing a serge suit and a badge cap. A typical Frenchman isn't he? His autograph appears on the back together with that of another deep-water chum, Emil Vandervekin, a young Belgian Count who, like me, is serving his time under John Stewart's flag, in the barque "Kilmallie". He stands at the back third from Folliot and is wearing a bowler hat.

I guess I'm out of news now so I'll heave to. Love to all my relatives and best wishes to my friends. If our limited stay in this port permits, I will write to Aunt Em, Uncle Fred and Harry Neale, beside of course, Wilf. Congratulations and kisses on the event of the Silver Wedding.

I will write again very soon. God bless and protect you all. For the present, with fondest love and kisses to Mother, Dad, Else, Fred and Bill and congratulations and best wishes to Wilf.

Goodbye from

Your loving son,

Arthur

PS Please give my kindest regards to Mr and Mrs Regan and all my former masters and mistresses at good old Brownhill and tell them how proud I am of the Old School."

From South Africa the ship sailed, not to Sydney after all, but to Rangoon for a cargo of rice for Liverpool where she arrived a further ten months from the time of the letter from Port Elizabeth. By that time Dad was time-expired and he left her for a spot of leave followed by the gruelling business of sitting for his 2nd Mate's ticket (Certificate of Competency as 2nd Mate of a foreign going sailing vessel). On passing the exam he then made the transition to a life on steamships; he may have had his fill of sail or he may have felt that steamers were now the way forward, bringing him into closer contact with the 20th century and giving him an opportunity to make his contribution to the war.

As for "Amulree", perhaps she should not have finished that mammoth voyage when she did but have gone on and on like the "Flying Dutchman" living in a world of her own entirely governed by the wind and weather.

The astonishing thing is that on her return home nearly half of a world war had run its course and by arriving at Liverpool she seemingly came through the wardrobe door into a completely new existence.

After discharge of her rice she loaded coal for Santos, crossed the Irish Sea and after a brief call at Belfast, sailed again only to be intercepted by a German U-boat. The ship was sunk by gunfire after the crew had been allowed to leave in lifeboats which succeeded in reaching the coast. Captain Cooper and his men were landed in Ireland April 26th 1917.

Any further comment at this stage would be superfluous.

CHAPTER TWO
INTERLUDE

Seafarers of my day were not a secret society but judging by the misconceptions and general perplexity of many landsmen of my acquaintance they might just as well have been. I think before proceeding with the story a few aspects of the life at sea should be clarified.

From the foregoing logs and letters, Dad will have opened a few chinks but a broader picture needs to be painted.

Firstly to go back to his early years we need to remember that the wrist watch was all but unheard of and the working man relied on whatever clocks were available to keep a check on the time. When the bell striking tradition started there were probably no clocks either hence it was necessary to keep watch-keepers in touch by the simple system of announcing every half hour of each four hour watch, hence: one bell at 12.30, 4.30 and 8.30; two bells at 1 o'clock, 5 o'clock and 9 o'clock and so on until eight bells at the end of each watch. Additional quirks arose with the one bell warning a quarter of an hour before the change of watch, seven bells at 7.20am to allow relief watch-keepers comfortable time for breakfast and sixteen bells at midnight New Year's Eve / New Year's Day.

Another apparent oddity was the custom of steering by compass points instead of degrees; this makes more sense when visualising the floating compass card swinging to the ship's perpetual motion. The marking of the compass card, the pattern of points, half and quarter points allowed the helmsman to latch on to a position on the card to try to hold against the ship's centre line mark to maintain the best average course that he could. Steering was an art dependent largely on anticipation of a combination of movements, the sea's, the ship's and the compass card's, complicated on the sailing ship by the vagaries of the wind.

It will pay to stop and consider the reason for and the

function of the cargo ship. It was (and no doubt still is) built for the express purpose of stowing and carrying as high a tonnage as possible of whatever goods were on offer to wherever in the world they would provide the highest profit. The seaman was a necessary adjunct to this purpose and a balance had to be struck between employment of the fewest number in order to keep wage costs down, and the safety and satisfactory maintenance of all the working parts and the structure of the ship to ensure the longest possible working life.

Crews fell into three categories of worker, namely those who made the ship go, those who navigated, controlled and decided movement and those who ministered to them all by feeding, cleaning and so on.

The first two categories were, in the main, the officers who worked continuously operating a shift system whilst the others were on day work. What appears on the surface a complex system was followed but in practice was quickly adapted to.

Deck officers and engineers worked usually a four hour watch duty followed by eight hours off such that certain ranks operated certain watches wherever they served at sea; the third mate usually worked from eight to twelve, very much under the Old Man's eye, partnered by the fourth engineer; the second mate and the third engineer had the graveyard watch from twelve to four when most of the rest of the ship slept both at night and to some extent during the day as well; the mate and the second engineer had the plum watch, presiding over sunrise and sunset on the four to eight.

Radio officers worked more civilised, usually daytime hours.

Officers' meals were taken in the saloon, each consisting of two half hour sittings with juniors relieving the bridge and engine room. Dress code was observed, meal-times constituting an important social event.

From this routine it emerges that different groups of men would be off duty at different times with variations in numbers being created by the duty hours of day workers; each man would have a quiet time to himself to carry out necessary every day chores, letter-writing, reading, relaxing etc. interspersed with periods of socialising – usually yarning or possibly setting up card schools and, depending upon weather conditions, sunbathing in the tropics or keeping in the warm in colder climes. The ship's response to the state of the sea made a full-time contribution to the activities followed and there were fairly few periods of complete monotony. On the ships on which I served experienced elders set an example of virtually no consumption of alcohol at sea. On the occasions when this sort of thing did happen it usually proved to be very costly one way or another.

In sailing ships watches were set differently with the crew split into two groups, each led by one of the officers, and a twelve hour system operated. This gave rise to the dog watch method of daily alternation of watches so that each man had one night duty followed by a night's sleep, assuming no emergency call-outs.

Spells at the wheel were taken either by crew members or by quartermasters whose employment was almost exclusively steering. Two hours was the optimum period for the required degree of concentration and in four quartermaster ships a somewhat weird time-share evolved: two hours on two off, two on four off, two on six off, two on eight off, giving a twenty eight hour rotation with adequate rest periods and convenient meal breaks.

At most times of the day someone was asleep and consideration always had to be given for others of one's shipmates; this stretched to the need for watch keepers to relieve each other in good time. It didn't take long for the newcomer to discover a very special kind of discipline, largely self generated, which was generally universally observed at sea. It was also quickly noted that locked doors were an extreme rarity, such was the need for trust on board. Its fair to describe the life style as unique and it was no doubt responsible for driving the sailor back to his life-long penury once shore leave was finished and disillusionment with life ashore had set in. The camaraderie was universal and without national barriers.

CHAPTER THREE

FIRST BLOOD

I have to read between the lines to begin to realise some of the contributory factors that formed Dad's attitude towards European crews, by which I mean the ABs and deck hands as opposed to the full ship's complement. On sailing ships these men were drawn, on the whole, from deprived or otherwise undesirable backgrounds and frequently included criminal elements evading justice ashore. At all events they were a hard-bitten lot and all too often proved to be trouble makers who had to be controlled with a very heavy hand.

His experience when he had to work alongside such men seems to have jaundiced Dad's outlook permanently and to what extent it led him towards native crew ships when he turned to steam I cannot say. I do know that he was infinitely more comfortable with the latter.

At the time of Dad's conversion from sail to steam, Ellerman was in the process of consolidating his shipping empire.

The City Line and the Hall Line were well-established when taken over by Sir John at the turn of the century while Bucknalls were just beginning; they were taken over when in financial difficulties in 1908. Between them the three lines formed what ultimately became the "City boats", City Line operating from Glasgow, Hall Line from Liverpool and Bucknalls from London.

The crews were Mohammedan Indians taken on aboard usually and for preference at Bombay except for the catering staff who were Goanese Christians. They were well paid by local standards, but with a pittance in comparison with their European counterparts. This inequity was balanced by the employment of more than twice as many men in the crew. Whereas they were subordinate to the officers, they took their orders from their own foreman or Serang through whom orders were transmitted.

In December 1916 Bucknall's ships still traded under their original names and in that month 3rd Officer King joined, of all ships, the "Karroo". She had been requisitioned in Australia to serve as an army transport and while in convoy carrying troops to the Dardanelles she intercepted a radio message from the "Emden".

"Emden" was a raider similar to the pocket battleships of the 1939 war and was responsible for the sinking of many ships in the Indian Ocean.

The "Karroo" duly passed her information to HMAS "Sydney", one of the escort vessels which some time later sank the "Emden" in a gun battle. Whether or not "Karroo"'s contribution actually affected the outcome of the fight is a moot point but there is no doubt that she had a nose for trouble. It took no more than four months since Dad joined her for him to earn his spurs and again I'll give it to you appropriately enough, directly from the horse's mouth. This is a letter he wrote to his schoolgirl sweetheart whom it appears he was beginning to court in earnest:

"Devonport,
Friday, 27th April 1917.

My dear Cath,
We arrived here all right on Monday and on Wednesday our mail came down. Your letter of March 29th was amongst my little pile and I was very glad indeed to get it. You see your other letter hasn't turned up yet, so you can guess how pleased I was to get this one; and it didn't take me very long to understand the meaning of your remark that "If I had not received your last letter I must guess the contents". Its not a bit of use my trying to tell you in a letter all that I have been thinking since I received yours. I couldn't do it so we must wait till we meet again. But oh, girl, I am glad!

I think April must be my lucky month for I'm going to tell you a bit of news which will surprise you. I've seen active service at last! Last Sunday afternoon from about the time the people would be coming out of church in dear old Catford till the time when most of them would be finishing dinner, we were in action with a submarine. Just before noon when my watch on the bridge was nearly over, I suddenly saw a streak of foam dart towards us and pass just astern of us. I realised at once that it was a torpedo and so did everyone that saw it; the helm was immediately put hard over and the ship swung on her heel as a second streak flew down towards us: it was a beautiful shot for our engine room and nothing but the swinging of the ship as a result of porting the helm saved her from the second torpedo. It ran level with us for an instant or two about 30 feet away. Of course the whole of the Engine Room Staff went down below and proceeded to get every inch of speed that they could out of the ship; the gun was manned and cleared for action and the Captain kept the ship away to try and bring the sub dead astern when she rose. She came up to the surface about ten minutes after the torpedoes missed us and we opened fire at once giving her half a dozen rounds in quick succession before she could reply. Then she started and kept us under a steady fire of high explosive and shrapnel shells throughout the whole action.

Her eighth shell, a high explosive landed in the Chief Engineer's room and completely wrecked it. Soon after another landed in the after deck, tearing the horse stalls to pieces and blowing 6 horses to eternity in small fragments. And of course, wherever a shell hit it started a blaze, and I was in charge of a small party flying around with the fire hose wherever a shell hit.

The sub fired between 180 and 200 rounds in the course of the fight and her shooting was excellent. Yet, thanks to the splendid manner in which the Captain handled and manoeuvred the ship we were hit only five times; though her worst misses were very nearly hits and, on the bridge as well as on deck, everybody was soaked with the spray of the shells that were dropping all round the ship. In fact my principal impression of the whole affair is of rushing around with my jacket off, soaked to the skin, dragging fire hoses about, carrying messages between the bridge and the gun and making a tour of the ship at intervals to ascertain if any of the men or officers had been hit.

The sub had every advantage for he carried two guns to our one, and both of heavier calibre and longer range than ours; and his surface speed was nearly twice our own. Yet the cowardly skunk was afraid to stay within range of us for he could see he had us out-ranged and was content to lie off and shell us from a distance at which he knew we couldn't reach him. Occasionally he did attempt to rush us and finish the fight but our gunners made such fine shooting that he got out of reach again in a deuce of a hurry. And so we only used 35 rounds in all, holding our fire, only opening on him when he attempted to rush us and driving him out every time.

We fought him for three hours, a running fight of about 40 miles, which I believe, is the longest fight that has yet taken place between a British ship and a submarine; and so you see we were shelled at the rate of one round in about 56 seconds. And at last a patch of smoke appeared on the horizon in answer to our wireless signals; the smoke soon resolved itself into two destroyers travelling down at full speed and after giving us several rounds very rapidly the sub dived and fled and the fight was over. But we fired the last shot of the action, for just an instant before the skunk submerged we gave him one shell as a last farewell.

Of course the end of the affair has been quite a little shower of congratulations for all on board. The two destroyers on returning from their search for the sub came up on either side of us and cheered us in great style. We received a wireless from the Admiral at Queenstown, "Very well done", our owners sent a telegram of thanks and congratulations, the admiral of this port has done the same and, best of all, our own Captain mustered the Deck and Engineer Officers, Petty Officers, Apprentices and Gunners on the lower bridge and having read us his report to the Admiral, said he himself thanked us "from the bottom of his heart for our splendid behaviour and great assistance throughout the fight. He would always be proud to remember that he had been shipmates with such a crowd and had commanded them in such a fine and successful action".

And it certainly was quite a success for us; we fought for three hours with an enemy decidedly superior to us in speed, armament and range, held him off until assistance arrived, and though badly knocked about in places, reached our intended port with a loss of only 14 horses and not one man was scratched, much less killed.

Of course, Cath, you must keep quiet about this for the present at any rate. But I'm going to tell you just a little more that I don't want you to mention ever. I know you will be pleased to hear it, so I don't think it will be boasting if I tell you. Several officers were mentioned individually in connection with their different jobs in the Captain's report to the Admiral in Command here and I was one of them. Certainly the only thing that saved us from the second torpedo was the quick use of the helm, but the skipper has attributed it to the "alertness and prompt obedience of my 3rd officer on the bridge to my order of "hard-a-port" and then again he remarks about the "splendid behaviour and great assistance" of the Chief Officer" and adds "as did also my Second and Third Officers". And some of my fellow officers have been trying to tell me what a lot I did. Of course its grand to have fellows ten years or so older than oneself shake hands with one after such a fight and remark that "You're one man, anyhow" but still I know that I didn't do a scrap more than anybody else.

However I have certainly come through the affair with a bit of advantage, for the other day at the breakfast table the Captain, after praising me in front of his wife and telling me that he was very pleased indeed with me (all of which, of course, made me feel rather red and uncomfortable) gave me his own sextant "in commemoration of the action fought by the "Karroo", and as an appreciation of the fact that you were wide awake and obeyed my orders instantly". That sextant will always be a treasure, more even on account of the man who gave it me than as a souvenir of the fight. Now please don't forget Cath.; don't say anything about our fight, for a while at all events. And don't mention this last portion at all. I've told you merely because I know you will be pleased.

PS Don't let the fact that we have had a dust-up with a sub worry you at all when we leave port again. Just remember that we came out on the winning side and that so long as we all stick together with the same skipper in command we shall come out on top every time.

Arthur."

Remarkably, the Admiralty paid prize money to the ship for her gallant action, the crew's share amounting to some £1150.00 of which £33.00 came to Dad.

The bigger reward from his point of view, was to be gazetted for "zeal and devotion to duty...." and thereby entitled to wear oak leaves over his war medal ribbons. His promotion to 2nd Mate of SS "Bechuana" early in 1919 was in all probability speeded as a result of the favourable reports and at all events the improvement in status and pay (such as it was) appears to have given him the confidence to proceed in his courtship to the extent that he married his "Cath" in May 1920.

It was a step not to be taken lightly in those days under any circumstances, but for an absentee sailorman husband doubly so. They were lucky that their relationship started so early in their lives and all the evidence suggests that they really were made for each other.

As a matter of interest the company, Ellerman & Bucknall, wrote an open letter to its personnel at the end of hostilities thanking them for their service and the courage shown. Appended was a list of 23 names of their men who had been decorated or gazetted, the highest award being presented to a Chief Steward named A.W. Furneaux. I am told that he refused to leave a sinking ship where one of his staff remained trapped by the foot. He returned to release his man by the only means available; taking a hacksaw he severed the limb without benefit of anaesthetic. His action saved the man's life but did irreparable damage to his own nervous system.

CHAPTER FOUR
BETWEEN THE WARS

Except for two or three outstanding incidents there is little enough to be said from the nautical point of view for the inter-war years.

This was the time when the young married couple was becoming established, raising a family with the handicap of an absentee father who strained every sinew to be present in spirit by the frequency and content of letters home.

It has to be remembered that the early 1920s preceded the advent of radio and only the wealthiest of homes boasted a telephone. This was a time of unrest and general poverty when a job was a job for life provided the employer survived the depression. It was a time when the employee did what he was told and patiently awaited dead mens' shoes.

It was also the time of idyllic childhood when the London streets and parks were safe and mothers knew that the kids would come home. Neighbours could be relied on in emergencies and could, for example, be called upon to run round to the doctor's house at any time of the day or night if called upon to do so.

Depending upon which collection time post was taken it was possible to anticipate at which time it would be delivered the following day, such was the importance of mail. The only alternative to cards or letters was the telegram or cable.

Few houses in our area had electricity, that and the telephone arrived in our house in the very late '30s. Even street lighting was by gas, the lamplighter arriving at dusk armed with a very long pole to pull down the chain to turn on the light.

The only transport was the bus, tram or train and the nearest bus stop was a ten minute walk away. It follows that we were brought up to do a great deal of walking and this required substantial stoking. Rose-coloured memory says that we ate like fighting cocks; certainly mothers whose place was the home were usually first class cooks and food was cheap - it had to be.

On her own for so much of the time, my mother managed the house, the budget, my two elder sisters and me with unbelievable efficiency not to mention stamina. Washing day, Monday, demanded a great deal of physical strength heating and carrying water, prodding sheets and the like in the copper with the appropriate weapon, wringing and mangling and so on.

Flat irons were heated on the gas on Tuesdays after the first of many shopping expeditions which involved walking a mile to the main shopping centre at Catford to find the cheapest meat available for tomorrow's lunch. Without a refrigerator she had to revisit more or less daily and carry home the purchases. In the '20s this would have involved pushing a pram and/or a push-chair as well.

Throughout this time we kids were presented with an idealised picture of our absent father who was a hero, almost a demi-god, to me at least. It was a red letter day when the mail arrived from abroad and we children received our own individual letters meticulously thought out and written, always with the intention of educating and improving, particularly the son and heir.

The great day would arrive when Dad's return was imminent and excitement mounted until his final arrival at which point it became a question of what's he brought me this time? For a few days the excitement continued until after a while it became apparent that my mother was less available to me than normal and as time stretched on and a sterner authority took charge of the house I became more and more miserable. This was exacerbated by the referral of any wrong-doing to male discipline - "Wait till your father comes home!"

It was always a relief when Dad went back to sea. After all his only interest in me was whether I was doing well at school and if not, why not? He clearly had no real love for me.

Well, that's how my child's mind worked things out and this unvoiced relationship persisted throughout my childhood, developing into a concealed dread as I grew older.

Against this background, Dad was establishing himself in Bucknall's; after leaving the "Karroo" in June 1918 to sit for Mate's ticket he served in sixteen other ships before, after twenty-three years service, he gained his command in October '39 and perhaps only then because the war was under way and there was a literal need to fill dead men's shoes.

Some of the highlights of this period are worthy of record as for instance the transmission of news of the arrival of a newly born to the ship's 2nd officer arriving in Baltimore. It was achieved by cable to the ship's agents in New York who had to contact the Baltimore office who in turn had to send a man down to the ship to spread the glad tidings. Cumbersome but effective. Return communication might well have been by letter to be despatched via New York in time to catch a particular sailing of one of the transatlantic liners.

It's a sobering fact that when sickness forced Dad ashore in 1931, Mum's, not his, he was immediately taken off the payroll. He had to cope with three young children while his wife fought for her life for quite a protracted period during which I contracted scarlet fever and was shunted off to a different hospital.

Now he had two girls to feed, a wife in Lewisham hospital, a son in the Brooke and no money with which to do anything about it. I can only say that we all survived.

At the time, Mum's younger sister, our Auntie Dorry, was living with us, which may have lightened Dad's burden a little, but the astonishing fact is that on returning from hospital visits Dad wrote, then posted, a letter which was delivered before his next visit the following day. Here is one which is not typical but otherwise special revealing one of his other talents:

"11pm Monday, 23rd November

Dear Love,
I expect you'll wonder why I'm starting tomorrow's letter tonight and at this hour too. As a matter of fact I've got to get something off my mind at once. Its this - and quite true.

Dorry bought some fish and chips on her way home tonight;
They packed 'em in a tiny bag, and packed 'em in too tight.
She was loaded up beforehand with packages and things
And the fish bag dangled corner-wise, the way a limpet clings.

She scuttled up from Brownhill with our supper in her charge;
The bag you know was very small, the chips were very large -
She turns around the corner, and past the police-box trips;
The policeman gave a sudden cough - and bang went all the chips

They tumbled right side up by chance, the paper underneath,
And some stuck to the paper, by the skin of a 'tater's teeth.
The streets are muddy, the night is wet, there's misery in the air:
She grabbed up the paper and some of the chips - the rest are Lord knows where.

We've had our supper of fish and chips before I started to write.
We've had our supper of fish and chips, all we shall get tonight,
I'm holding my pants up extra tight, for fear my waist-belt slips,
For we've had our supper of chish and fips but minus half the fips.

That's the truth, and now you can realise why I've had to sit down and weep to you about it before I can go to bed.."

The next letter is from father to son from "City of Derby", 17th August 1934 because it encapsulates so succinctly what I have tried to say about our relationship and the expected length of a voyage:

"Port Louis, Mauritius

Dear Bernard,

I have written to Dorothy and Laura before and now it is your turn. It feels as if I have been away from home ever so long already, though it is only two months since we left London. Now we are at Mauritius, an island in the Indian Ocean: Dorothy will tell you all about Mauritius if you ask her. Next we are going to the Philippine Islands and Java and the Malay States to load cargo for America. So I expect I shall come home when the summer comes again. I hope so, for I love the garden and the flowers you know. And you know I like to wake up and hear the cuckoo too. And you and I would be able to sneak out early and quietly, so as not to disturb Mummy, on Sunday mornings and go for long walks before breakfast again. I used to enjoy those walks; didn't you?

I am glad they made you Saint George at school while I was at home. I was quite proud of it, because that is quite an honour and I don't suppose they would have done that if you had not deserved it, my son. I should like you always to remember that Saint George stands for England and Truth and Chivalry. That last word is rather a long one and means a lot of things that you will understand better as you grow up. But I expect if I tell you three things which it means, you will remember them. It means "Help whenever you can: Never kick a man when he is down: And never hurt a woman or anybody weaker than yourself if you can possibly avoid it".

I must not make a sermon of this letter, only you see I should like to help you to grow up a real English gentleman because, apart from other reasons you will be the man of the family bye and bye, and will be able to take the place, for your mother and sisters that I should like to take if only I could stay at home. So just be a good boy and do the best you can, at home and at school, my son.

You can write to me whenever you like, you know, and I will write to you again bye and bye. Give my love to Mummy and the girls. And please give my kind regards to Miss Shelmerdine and your teacher. God bless you. Goodbye, with love and kisses from

Daddy."

This was produced in immaculate block capitals, suitable for a seven-year-old.

Now for a very different letter indeed, which covers an eventuality common to both of us at different times and which never fades from the memory. I am referring to sudden death of a well- loved shipmate on board ship. In Dad's case this occurred on the same voyage, eight months after his letter to me. It came from Rangoon 9th April 1935:

"Dear Little Lady,

I'm going to start my next letter now, though my last one only leaves Rangoon today. You will know that I was a bit upset when I finished that letter off, but you needn't worry, Sweetheart, I'm quite O.K. again now. Of course, I haven't felt very cheerful these last two days; perhaps it sounds a bit childish in a grown man to admit that, on account of another man, he couldn't laugh and couldn't eat and couldn't bear anybody else to look at him or speak to him. And yet, when you've lived with a man, and eaten with him and laughed with him, for nearly twelve months, it does hurt like hell to be called on without a moment's warning to wash him and dress him and close his eyes and fold his hands, and follow him to the cemetery: and then to leave the place and sit opposite his empty chair, and think of him lying there alone, thousands of miles from his people. But I'm quite all right again now, Girl; and I think I'd like to tell you about his funeral: because I'd like you to know how, even in a tiny little foreign port we, who are neither Navy nor Army, say goodbye to our dead. He went without any warning. Got up from his deckchair and sent word along that he'd like to see the

61

Chief Steward. Cox went along, found him unconscious on his settee, and flew back for the Skipper, met me just after he had told the Old Man and I nipped along as well. I was only a few yards behind the Old Man, yet the Chief was already dead when I got to his room though I think old George actually saw the last of him. We sent ashore for the doctor, and although we really knew he was dead of course we worked on him till the doctor arrived and told us it had only been a matter of seconds and that no doctor could have done anything for him.

Of course the Old Man was just about knocked out; so were Cox and I for that matter. But still it was my job anyway, and incidentally it was only fitting that someone of his own rank should do the things for poor old Morgan that he couldn't do for himself. So I said to Cox, "Give me a hand Old Man". And we stripped him and washed him and dressed him in a clean white shirt and trousers: and I closed his eyes and took off his ring and folded his hands on his chest. The Old Man of course went ashore and notified the agents, and they ordered the coffin to be made and sent on board, and ordered a steam launch to take the coffin and funeral party to the jetty: and arranged for the wreath and a hearse and the English Padre and fixed the funeral for 5pm.

The coffin came on board at 3pm. No native hands touched him. His four engineers and Cox and I carried him out on deck and laid him in his coffin. The 3rd Mate and I put the slings round the coffin for lowering into the launch and then went down into the launch and landed it as it was lowered. And I covered the coffin with a new Red Ensign. And so we went ashore leaving only the 3rd Mate and the 3rd Engineer in charge of the ship. The officers of the "Cape Howe" enquired the reason when we half-masted the flags and sent a letter of regret on board and a request that they might attend the funeral. We had decided amongst ourselves that, for bearers, any question of precedence or seniority did not matter: the six of the nearest height to each other would be best. So the bearers were the 2nd, 4th and 5th Engineers, the 2nd Mate, Wireless Operator and Carpenter.

And they decided (although the temperature was 96° and the Chief weighed 12 stone) that they would carry the coffin on their shoulders and not by the handles.

When we got to the jetty we found the remainder of the party awaiting us. The Skipper, Officers and the Engineers from the "Cape Howe" in white trousers and black jackets (as a slight distinction from our own crowd who were all in white uniforms). The English Padre: the Agent's Manager and his wife: the Agent's Head Clerk and his wife: the two heads of the Stevedoring Company and their wives. They had all brought their own cars with an extra car or two so that the entire party could be accommodated for the 3½ mile journey to the cemetery. There were 13 wreaths: our own, one from the "Cape Howe" and the remainder from the Britishers ashore. We lifted the coffin, with the ensign draped over it, out of the launch and placed the wreaths on it; the bearers hoisted it on their shoulders: and we followed up the jetty and into the street where the hearse and cars were waiting. The Skipper rode with the Agent's Manager and the Padre, I with the Head Clerk and his wife and the remainder split up amongst the other cars.

When we reached the cemetery the coffin was shouldered again and we followed it on foot through the gates and into a little open-air chapel (just a sun-roof on pillars) where it was lowered on a trestle and the Padre held the funeral service. I don't really remember much of what he said: to tell you the truth Dear, I couldn't see him: and neither could the Old Man, I know. Of course, all of us were upset, but I suppose the Old Man and I felt it most because we were nearer Morgan's age and married men too.

Then we lifted him again and carried him to the grave where I bent down and lifted the Ensign from the coffin while the bearers lowered it in. And we stood round bare-headed while the Padre read the Burial Service, and waited till the grave was filled in. Then we came back to the jetty in the cars that had taken us to the cemetery. He had been with us in the morning and in the evening we left him close to the trees amongst a dozen other

English graves in a tiny little out-of-the-way patch of the British Empire. There were scores of Burmese and Indians at the cemetery gates and round the railings of course. They may not have sympathised much; they probably didn't understand it: but at least they saw how a Britisher and a Sailor goes to his last sleeping place.

Of course it knocked us all endways for a day or two, but I am glad to realise that there was no hitch, that we left nothing undone that we could have done for him, that we took him to his grave as one of our own cloth should go.

We left arrangements behind in Moulmein that a teak-wood cross should be put on the grave with a carved inscription:

In Loving Memory
of John Morgan
Chief Engineer
ss "City of Derby"
Born 1888
Died 6th April 1935
"Gone Home"

It was after the ship finally returned home that Dad transferred to his beloved "City of Khartoum", ex "Karroo", for the last time and that portentous Christmas came and went.

Once this event was over he returned to the ".. Derby" and as a final observation of the inter-war years let me introduce the "Derby Daily Digest".

Without private radios on board the crew were completely cut off from home and world news and Sparks, the radio man, took it on himself to produce a daily paper.

This frequently ran to eight pages and covered not only the news but included such items as Dad's "The training of watch dogs for home service" which commenced:

"In the first place your dog should be black in order that at night an intruder may fall over him.." This item was carefully printed and beautifully illustrated by the author and accompanied pages of quizzes, puzzles and editorial comment from Sparks. What more evidence is required of the length of these voyages?"

As a Charlton supporter I can't resist quoting this home sports news item from the edition of 19th September 1937:

"The riddle of the English F.A. League is Charlton Athletic, they are probably the least costly team in Div.1. yet are the only team not to have lost a match this season. They are top of the league having the low goal total of 8 for and 5 against. Portsmouth who are 21st have scored more goals. This is regarded as very extraordinary for a team who have come up from Div.3 in three seasons. Last year they were 2nd to Sunderland (who are in the lower half of the list). Manchester City are in the middle- on Saturday they drew with Portsmouth 1 -1 and Manchester United lost, though we forget the name of the team that beat them 1 - 0!"

CHAPTER FIVE
LULL BEFORE THE STORM

In the run-up to World War 2 my childhood developed along lines as stable as they were frugal; the youngest in the family and the only male in a female household, I suppose I ploughed a somewhat lonely but contented furrow, spending much time living in the imagination, reading widely and avidly in a way that doesn't appear to be done today.

Schooling was reasonably satisfactorily performed in its initial stages and I have to register my moment of fame in 1937 when as a member of a select few at Torridon Road School, I joined with a few thousand other school kids at Wembley country dancing in front of the King and Queen as part of the Coronation celebrations.

At that time I was giving a sort of lip service to my father's school record which goes like this, in the first instance at school-leaving and then eight years later from a letter to my mother, then his fiancée:

Brownhill Road School, Central Commercial Department, Lewisham 25.7.1911.

"I have much pleasure in testifying to the excellent character and ability of Arthur Ernest King, who has been one of my pupils for the last four years. He secured admission by means of competitive examination.

He was always punctual and regular in attendance; diligent, painstaking, and successful in his work; and his conduct was most satisfactory.

His masters without exception, speak in high terms of his industry and progress, and are confident he will do well in any work he may undertake.

In addition to the ordinary school subjects he has a very good knowledge of French, and speaks with ease and accuracy.

I can strongly recommend him, and feel sure he will give great satisfaction to his employers.

Colston Regan, Headmaster."

4.12.19

"My Dear Catherine,
I enclose a splendid letter I have received from Arthur. Please let me have it back when you and Mr. and Mrs. King and Elsie have read it.

I am very proud of Arthur in every way. Life has not been quite a failure when one has assisted in forming a character like his.

Yours sincerely,

Colston Regan."

Breath-taking, not to say utterly infuriating; what a recommendation, what an example, what a totally impossible act to follow.

Fortunately I wasn't aware of it at the time although the message had been well drilled into me. My initial report from primary to secondary education was more or less acceptable but from there onwards became something of a rake's progress. Luckily I had ill-health and a war to blame it on.

I squeezed into Grammar School by the skin of my teeth, having achieved a free place at Addey and Stanhope in New Cross, but after a couple of terms I was confined to bed and thereby rescued from a situation in which I was distinctly uncomfortable. The reality of my state of health was quite unfathomable, probably something psychosomatic, but what the doctor said, that my heart had moved out of position was quite meaningless. Anyway after prolonged absence, I returned to school for a term or so, to coincide with the outbreak of war. Evacuation on 1st September '39 was with my younger elder sister's school, the object being to avoid splitting families any more than absolutely necessary, so from then on I never darkened Addey's doors again.

After some nine months of phoney war I left Worthing High School where I'd been gloriously happy, to return home to the family. Laura's schooling had been completed in Worthing and I had then been isolated when she returned to work in London and it was therefore logical that I should return to the fold. After a farcical spell of part-time education in Lewisham, the blitz began and in response to an offer of haven in Knebworth the family took cover in the home of erstwhile neighbours who were being moved out by an evacuating branch of the civil service to North Wales. Brian, their son, who was born next door to us six weeks before I was, remained, and together we went by train to Letchworth Grammar School.

We house-sat until mid-1942 when Mum got itchy feet again, worrying about our unoccupied house in Catford. This meant returning home again to a slightly better organised but still highly unsatisfactory South East London Emergency College for my final term of school life.

Herewith my two reports to compare with Dad's:

"London County Council Report of Progress	Torridon Road J.M. Easter 1938
King Bernard. Number in Class 43	Class 1A Position in Class 7
Scripture	82/100
English	188/220
Arithmetic	83/100
History	46/50
Geography	27/50
Science	21/50
Art	27/50

Craft	40/50
Algebra	21/25
Geometry	22/25
Conduct / Attendance	Excellent

Class Master: L. Gascoyne
Head Mistress: E. Scoble."

Followed by the final accolade:

"London County Council   S.E. London
Emergency Secondary School for Boys
Report for term ending July 1942.

King B.A.   Form VB
No. in form 25
General School Certificate Examination:

English	55	He is capable of very good work – more application is necessary.
Mathematics	50	He is capable of much greater effort.
History	32	He could have achieved a better result.
French	60	Not sufficiently serious. Is inclined to waste time.
Chemistry		
Physics	C	Does not take his work seriously enough.

Conduct – Very good.

Additional Remarks: Light-heartedness can become a serious handicap if he does not keep it in check when he should be working.

L.S. Obee Form Master

I'm afraid this is a record of what might have been achieved.
C.H. Rees Head Master."

This final period in London was enlivened by membership of the Sea Cadets which taught me to semaphore and the rudiments of square-bashing. We attended fund-raising affairs like Warship Weeks and I suffered one agonising fortnight at camp in Dorset which taught me once and for all the enormity of the gulf existing in the comparative mentalities of the Royal Navy and us who served under the Red Duster.

My formal education was completed at Sir John Cass Nautical College in Jewry St., London EC3 while I marked time waiting for the ship on which I would start my sea-faring career. I was without academic qualification, a matter of little significance when there was a war to be won. I shared lectures with time-expired Cadets who were studying for their 2nd Mate's Tickets. Whilst I picked up something of the U.K. buoyage system I learned rather more about my fellow officers to be.

Coincidence decreed that I should be called to a vessel that I was already familiar with thanks to visits on board when the ship docked at Tilbury and Dad was serving as Mate and subsequently in Manchester when his promotion finally came through shortly after the outbreak of war.

His first command, the "City of Keelung", was appropriately my first ship and as ever, thereby hangs a tale to be recounted in due course.

CHAPTER SIX

WAR AGAIN

Dad was back on the "...Derby" at the outbreak of war and on return to the Bristol Channel in October '39 the great day finally dawned and was duly recorded as follows:

"H.M.T. "City of Keelung"
20th October 1939 to 3rd November 1939
First Voyage.

20th October:
Docked Newport in H.M.T. "City of Derby" at 2.00am. After breakfast Tom Labey from "...Keelung" burst into my room highly excited – "Congratulations, old man! Hurry up and pack and come up to the shipping office and get paid off. Your command's across the dock and you're sailing tomorrow." All blind rush after that. Paid off "...Derby", took over "City of Keelung" from Labey, flew up-town and bought new cap and cuff-bands, visited Naval Office and chased round generally till 8.00pm. Didn't realise how much "...Derby" crowd thought of me till it came to leaving her. All hands hung about until 8.00pm to make sure of shaking hands with me. Quartermasters carried my gear to "City of Keelung" – would have carried me if I'd let them. Stannard (Q.M.) said "if you ever want quartermasters, Sir, just say the word and we'll all come over flying". Poor old Pierce nearly in tears – didn't feel too sweet myself.

Telephone conversation with Macdonald in afternoon, "Well King, I suppose you're very excited at getting it at last after all these years?" "Yes Sir and I'd like to say thank you very much". "Well, well. See you make a job of it." "I'll do my best." "Sorry I can't come down and see you before you sail but I'll pop down some other time. Cheerio, King. Good luck"

In the evening received notice from S.N.O. to embark Commodore and Signal Ratings in Barry Roads am 22nd. Telephoned S.N.O. that would have been delighted to have commodore but unfortunately had no accommodation to offer him. Received reply that in that case would probably get word next morning to cancel instructions re commodore in favour of some other ship.

21st October:

Busy all day with sailing arrangements. Told by S.N.O. over telephone that in view of lack of accommodation could safely reckon that some other ship would be appointed commodore. Privately disappointed about it, but couldn't see any way of helping matters. Went to Naval Office for sailing orders. Captains of all the other ships there, all asking each other "who is commodore ship?"

Told them "I was officially supposed to be but I've been unofficially informed that I'm not: so at present I'm damned if I know quite who I am or what I am or anything about myself at all." Sailed at 11.30 pm still wondering.

22nd October:

Anchored in Cardiff Roads at 2.17am. Hove up at 6.30am and arrived in Barry Roads at 7.04am, just breaking daylight. Signalled examination boat; signal answered: signalled again "Have you any instructions for me?": signal ignored. Tried shore station with same result – second signal ignored. My pilot very anxious to be finished with the job and off home and tried all sorts of hints to persuade me to let him go. Eventually "You know, Captain, my job's finished when I've brought you into the roads." I said "I know that, pilot - but I haven't signed your pilotage note yet, have I?" – rather a dirty dog method of holding him but the only means I had.

It wasn't at all a comfortable position for me. All the other ships of the convoy were anchored round us and according to the sailing list in each ship I was commodore ship – with no commodore on board and not knowing if he were on board one of the others instead. According to the Route Instructions I was supposed to be already moving out to sea with the rest of the ships following in their proper order. I hadn't got time to go inshore and anchor and I couldn't keep steaming about in a crowded anchorage for long. Then the pilot had a lovely brainwave "Captain, my boat's here waiting to take me off. I'd advise you to remain under way and dodge slowly out to the Breaksea Lightship." Marvellous idea!!! I said "Like hell I will, pilot. How do I know the commodore is on board any ship yet? The moment I move out to the Breaksea every other ship will up anchor and follow me: and wouldn't I look damn fine towing fifteen ships out to sea and leaving the commodore sitting ashore hollering his head off for us? Do you want to get me hung?"

"Well, Captain, what will you do?" I said "Five minutes more, and if somebody can't tell us something about ourselves by then we'll go close inshore and anchor till they can." A few minutes and I was just on the point of moving in to anchor when we spotted the Admiralty launch tearing out to us. Picked up the commodore and four signalmen; shepherded the pilot into the launch with many thanks and profuse apologies for having to keep him waiting: hoisted signal "Convoy weigh anchor" and shoved off to sea. Met destroyer escorts off Breaksea Lightship at 8.00 am, dead on time. And the most relieved man in the whole Bristol Channel was myself when the commodore and his crowd came over the gangway.

The commodore, Rear Admiral Watson D.S.O., a great old boy, and must have a good memory for faces. Met him once before in the wardroom of the destroyer "Montrose" during assembling of previous convoy. When I met him at our gangway, he took one look at me and said "God bless my soul, Captain, I didn't expect to find you here. Its only a week since we were all having a whisky-and-soda together on board the destroyer and you were chief in the "City of Derby" then" I said "Yes sir. My first voyage in command and I'm commodore ship with the added pleasure of having you here." He said "Well, my boy, I think you might take that as a good omen." Told him my little difficulty about berths for him and his men and informed him that my cabin was entirely at his disposal. "That's quite all right, Captain. You've got a settee I can lie on and what more does any man want?" Flatly refused to take my bed and leave me the settee. "No. I never turned any captain off his own bed yet and I'm not going to start."

Convoy got to sea with a good flying start, sharp to time and everything satisfactory. Ships:-

City of Keelung (commodore)
Treverbyn (vice-commodore)
Clan Munroe
Margalau
Kerma
Baron Nairn
Fabian
Ciscar
Baltrader
Ronan
Pacific Coast

Joined later off Swansea by:
Anglian Coast
Pizarro
Yewmount
Devon Coast

Escorts:

H.M.S. Express, H.M.S. Encounter, H.M.S. Exmouth & 2 seaplanes.

With reference to the mix-up concerning the commodore's arrival, Admiral Watson explained that he'd been ordered to board us off Barry at 7.30am. He had originally been appointed to the "Treverbyn" but "Have you seen the "Treverbyn" Captain? I took one look at her and said "Nothing doing. Give me the City boat instead. So here I am." So here he is and here I am with a lot of extra hands spread about the ship. In addition to the Commodore and his four signalmen I've got Lieutenant Barnes and six men of the Queen's Royal Regt., and M.Le Cam, a Lieut-Commander in the French navy placed on board as emergency pilot for the French coastal ports.

The Commodore shares my room, our French friend sleeps in the Chart Room, Lieutenant Barnes has pigged in with the Chief Engineer and the signalmen and soldiers are spread about in various odd corners. But they're all quite comfortable with a general atmosphere of "Who cares in war-time anyway?"

The Frenchman is absolutely delighted. Admiral Watson speaks French fairly, though not so well as I do and Le Cam seems to think he has found a home from home. Yarns away at the table and everywhere else to the two of us, but can't speak a word of English, so when necessary at table I do the translating. Apparently in his last ship Le Cam was parked for ten days with a crowd who couldn't speak a solitary word of French, so its no wonder he's as happy as a skylark here. He is a typical Breton and vehemently insists that he is Breton, not French. Told Admiral Watson and me that we are from "la Grande Bretagne" and he is from "la petite Bretagne" – "alors M. le Capitaine, nous sommes cousins!"

Passed Lundy Island 3.00pm.

23rd October:

Cleared Land's End at 2.50am.Some of the ships making poor show of keeping station at times during the day. Have had to reduce speed of convoy a little already and even at that "Anglian Coast" seems to be having a struggle to keep up. (Something wrong, I should think, as all that company's ships should be good for 3 knots more than we are steaming). Have signalled her to proceed at full speed and keep touch as long as possible. Sorry for her if she has to drop out of convoy but can't risk fifteen ships for the sake of one. Have kept the signalmen busy at intervals strafing the whole crowd about what the commodore calls their "lousy station keeping". Captain Jones of the "Clan" and Moore of the "Margalau" will be after my blood when we get in!

However, general station-keeping considerably improved during afternoon. Its always laughable in convoy to see how the ships pack nice and solid towards sunset and daybreak. Noticed the same thing in the last war. At sunset the stragglers come scurrying into proper station with a pathetic "don't lose me in the dark" sort of air and at dawn those that have been rambling a bit during the night come packing in and you can see "let's get into station before that damn commodore starts to shout" sticking out all over them.

"Anglian Coast" still dropping astern gradually. Afraid she will be in a convoy all by herself before the morning. Position 1.10pm.(Apparent Noon) Lat. 49 20 N. Long. 5.25. W. Rounded Ar Men Rock Light at 4.40pm and are now on the direct track for destination. Have had marvellous weather and shall have to reduce speed even more during night to avoid arriving off the mined entrance before daylight.

"Anglian Coast" definitely dropping out now , just visible on skyline. However, he knows the course we're steering so will have to do the best he can for himself. General station-keeping much better at dusk this evening. Glad to see it as one final large alteration of course to make before daylight and wouldn't like to see a mix-up in the dark. Thank God for fine weather anyway.

24th October:

Reduced speed to 6½ knots at midnight. Should have picked up Belle Ile Light at 2.15am according to reckoning, so was out at 2.00 am looking for it. Never saw it and can't even tell if it is still lighted or not as so many lights extinguished or altered nowadays. However, got a fair idea of actual speed over ground by casting lead every half hour and at 6.00am made final alteration of course in dark. At 7.15am, just nicely daylight, sighted French destroyer escort about 3 miles on port beam; so hauled right up to meet them, increased to full speed and hoisted signal "form single line ahead". It really was a sight worth seeing. The commodore and I stood and watched those fourteen come into single line astern of us, and it was a sight to make anybody proud to belong to the Merchant Service. They came in at full speed in one grand sweep without losing a second; every ship hard on the tail of her next ahead, every man using his own wits and slipping into the nearest convenient gap. No fleet of destroyers could have done it better. We led them into the swept channel at full speed, all packed close and not a ship out of place, with a French destroyer steaming ahead of us. Fifteen of us in single line and as the last ship came into the turn, Admiral Watson turned round to me and said, "We've strafed those blighters a dozen times in the last two days, Captain, but by God that was lovely! Lovely! We'll put up a signal "Well done"" which we accordingly did.

Stopped engines in St. Nazaire anchorage at 9.30am and commodore transferred to H.M.S."Express" to return to Quiberon Bay for homeward convoy. While coming in I told him "I've only one regret about this convoy, Sir, and that's your make-shift accommodation". Reply: "Don't you worry about that my boy. I'm as snug as a bug in a blanket here and it's a damn fine convoy all round". Then he suggested that if accommodating his men was causing any undue inconvenience I might talk to Jones of the "Clan" or Moore of the "Margalau" after we tie up and see if either of them could take the signalmen off my hands. I certainly shan't do that, as if I transfer them, the ship that takes them must automatically become commodore ship for the run home. So I just hedged and said "Oh, I don't think I'll bother, Sir. As far as I can hear your lads are settled in quite comfortably here now and there's no point in mucking them about". The Admiral grinned quietly at me and said "I see,

Captain, you've come out as commodore ship of this convoy and you're determined to go home again as commodore, eh?". No sense in hedging about that so I replied emphatically "Exactly, Sir. I am. And of every other damn convoy I'm in if I can possibly wangle it". He threw his head back and laughed in a proper bull roar, banged me on the back and shouted "Good boy! Good boy!"

I was sorry to see him leave us, though I hear that the commodore who will take us back is also a very good chap. Watson's last words were "Cheerio, Captain, and thanks ever so much. Hope we have the pleasure of sailing together again very shortly." That sounds hopeful for future voyages.

Local pilot boarded us at 9.40am. Anchored off St. Nazaire at 10.06am to await tide.

Hove up at 12.13pm, entered river at 12.17 pm and moored on wharf in Nantes 5.42pm 25th October: Commenced discharge at 6.00am. At 10.00am. car collected all captains of convoy and took us to S.N.O.'s office for usual arrival conference. Captain Ratsey R.N. (S.N.O.) Very human and affable nowadays (!!!) As soon as I entered his office one of the other captains there jumped up and said "Ha! "City of Keelung" eh? Come here Captain, I'm waiting to cut your throat!" Turned out to be the skipper of the "Anglian Coast". I said "Sorry to have to leave you behind, old man, but if you couldn't keep up, that's your pidgin."Told him I was glad to see him in all right and asked what was the trouble with his speed as I was sure all those ships were good for at least 10 knots. He only shrugged and said, "Oh, I couldn't keep up with the rest of you" so I fancy he had engine trouble of some sort that he's not talking about.

When the usual conference and discussion was over I threw a bomb in the works. The S.N.O. enquired if any of us had any suggestions to make. Just what I was waiting for. Jumped up and said "Yes, Captain Ratsey. I've a suggestion concerning the sailing of ships from the wharf here. I want to leave here at such time as I can be definitely sure of making the run through to Quiberon Bay in one bite in daylight, or otherwise to be allowed to remain alongside this wharf till daybreak the next day. This business of chasing us off to Quiberon as soon as we finish discharging is no good to any of us, and sooner or later some unfortunate ship is going to get into serious trouble." Ratsey looked almost horrified and said, "Do you really mean to tell me, Captain, that you don't go straight through to Quiberon Bay in one run, whatever time of day you leave here?" I said "I do, Sir. The French pilots absolutely refuse to go beyond St.Nazaire anchorage if they can't get through the mine-barrage at Quiberon before dark. Consequently we have to lie off St.Nazaire all night, and I think I am voicing the opinion of every master here in saying that it is a totally unsafe place to lie for any length of time. Personally I consider St.Nazaire a handy spot to lie for an hour waiting for the tide. Otherwise under the best of conditions its not a good anchorage, and in a breeze of wind or under winter conditions its utterly impossible. To put it very bluntly, if you order me off this wharf at such time as I consider unsuitable for getting right through to Quiberon, then as a matter of absolute compulsion, I'll go, but only under very strong protest."

At that the skipper of the "Pacific Coast" jumped up and said "I wish to say that I entirely agree with every word this Captain has said": and immediately all the rest came to their feet with a chorus of "absolutely correct", "quite right" etc.

The S.N.O. looked at us for a moment and said "Well, Gentlemen, I can only say that neither I nor the Naval Authorities at St.Nazaire had the faintest idea that such a thing was going on, and I give you my word that this question shall be thoroughly investigated. Meanwhile I think you may safely take it that – except when the berths are urgently needed – this convoy and all future convoys will be allowed to remain at the wharves till the final sailing day and will then leave to go direct to Quiberon."

If that comes off I shall certainly have done some good for all ships coming in here in future, especially in the winter. And for that matter, for the naval authorities as well: for its perfectly obvious that if any ship did get into trouble in St.Nazaire anchorage, however light damage she might get off with she would still be a dead loss to the Admiralty till she was ready for sea again.

The thing about it all that I can't quite make out is why none of the others have raised the question before. They have all been here in command before, some of them two or three times: it has obviously been in their minds all the time, from the immediate and unanimous support I received. The only answer I can see – knowing Captain Ratsey's previous reputation amongst the merchant captains – is that it has been just another case of the fool stepping in where angels feared to tread.

Whatever the explanation one result is obvious. Ratsey thinks I'm no fool and the other masters think I'm a damn fine fellow. So, anyway I'm achieving some sort of reputation to start with. Shall finish cargo tonight so we'll see what tomorrow brings forth.

26th October:

No question today of whether I started things buzzing yesterday or not. Lieutenant Soper from Naval Office on board just after breakfast said, "By gosh, Captain, you did a damn fine spot of work for yourself and all the rest of us here yesterday. Your argument is the talk of all the port today. In the ordinary way we would have sent you off the wharf today, but you won't shift now before Sunday morning." Very good news indeed, but the real climax came at 11.00am Quarter master came up and said, "Commander of the port just coming on board, Sir." Nipped down to the gangway and sure enough it was Captain Ratsey R.N. and on a purely social visit!! "Good morning Captain. Thought I'd trot along for a yarn and see how you were getting along." Took him up to my cabin and sat him in my armchair, gave him a cigarette and enquired if he would care for a small spot. He said "I'll tell you what I would like Captain. I'll split a bottle of beer with you." So we parked there with cigarettes and a Worthington apiece and yarned like bosom pals for an hour and a half. (Must tell Grove if we meet the "Derby". He'll have a blue fit.) Thought I would test reaction a bit so jokingly suggested that if I dug up any more snags the Navy would begin to think me a bit of a Bolshie. "Not at all, Captain, not at all! We've all got to pull together in this man's war, and any suggestions you can advance for our mutual benefit will always be welcome.

Personally I shall always be glad of any constructive criticism you can offer." So that's that, and, taken all round I'm decidedly pleased with life at present.

Ratsey's parting remark "Drop into my office any time you like, Captain, the more I see of you gentlemen the more I like you." Ye Gods!! Some change in a few short weeks.

29th October (Sunday):

Left wharf at 6.22am for Quiberon. So have definitely accomplished something. Three days alongside after finishing discharge and should have been there yet if berths had not been needed. Straight through to Quiberon and anchored in the Bay 1.13pm. Afraid we shan't sail before Wednesday, though, which means tight fit for Newport weekend.

1st November:

Noon, all convoy ready for sea, only waiting arrival of commodore. At 2.10pm commenced heaving anchor as destroyer escort arriving fast. At 2.20pm Commodore, Rear Admiral H.C. Rawlings D.S.O., boarded from H.M.S. "Express". Hove anchor right up and proceeded to sea immediately. Cleared Teigneuse Channel at 4.36pm. By 5.05pm all convoy outside and closed up in station, so hauled round and started off for Ushant. Wind freshening from S.E. and barometer falling. Shall have a S'ly blow before we get across to Lizard. Fair sea running and rolling quite a bit, but don't mind so long as it stays behind us.

Admiral Rawlings a fine chap, not quite so bluff and hearty as Watson, but every bit as nice. After many protests have managed to insist that he has the bed and leaves me the settee. Quite contented with his temporary accommodation. Not much chance of sleep tonight. Too many course alterations to make. Should be round Ushant and away for Lizard before daylight.

2nd November:

Bit of excitement last night at 11.30. Third Officer called me out and said he could see several ships ahead of us in the dark. Turned out to be French convoy making in for Brest, steaming directly across head of our convoy. All cleared except rear French ship who carried on across my bows with no hope of clearing. Had to reduce speed in a hurry, swung over to starboard a bit, switched on side-lights and gave one blast on whistle. Frenchman promptly retaliated by hauling round on parallel course to us and stopping his engines altogether and I had to slam on full speed again to clear him and prevent our next astern from falling over us. Last I saw of Frenchman he was drifting through our lines with his engines stopped. Good job my 3rd Officer has got sharp eyes.

Managed just two hours sleep last night. Passed Ushant 6.15am. Blowing hard from S.S.E. all day. Passed Wolf Rock at 4.22pm. Very satisfactory: when we picked up Wolf discovered I was only ½ mile out of my estimated position.

Half mile adrift in 10 hours run, right across strong Channel tides and with empty ship and half a gale blowing is pretty good, so I am quite pleased with myself again. Have come along at 9 knots so far, convoy keeping well together. Shall manage tomorrow afternoon tide yet with a bit of luck (certainly shall if I can wangle a bit more speed out of them all in the morning.) Tomorrow (Friday) afternoon in Newport means Saturday with Cath to me.

3rd November:

A perfect end to a very satisfactory trip, thanks to good tides throughout the night plus some judicious wangling of the speed, we saved the midday tide in Newport with three hours to spare.

At midnight last night I was satisfied that in spite of darkness and the awkward weather the convoy was well closed up and keeping perfect station, so quietly touched up the speed a bit: at 2.00am I came out for the rest of the night when we sighted Lundy Island Lights, made the necessary course alteration and as general stations were still perfect, bumped the speed up a bit more. Passed Lundy at 3.45am and from then on the "8 knot convoy" was making, with the help of the tide as well, a steady 12 knots over the ground, Stopped engines off Breaksea at 8.28 am, an easy 5 hours ahead of our brightest hopes. Landed Commodore and party in Barry Roads.

On arrival at Breaksea Admiral Rawlings signalled senior destroyer, "Many thanks for your escort from Quiberon. Consider this arrival constitutes a record over the course." Destroyer replied "We fully agree." When leaving us the Admiral shook hands and said,"I want to congratulate you and your officers, Captain, on very excellent navigation under awkward conditions. I've thoroughly enjoyed the run and I wish you all the luck in the world." I said "I thank you, Sir, and I hope we sail together again very soon." Reply,"I think we shall, Captain".

Moored in Newport Dock at 1.30pm, having licked the Slow Convoy record for the run by an easy four hours.

Everybody's happy: to the merchant ships it meant comfortable docking in daylight instead of in the middle of the night: to the Admiral it meant an extra day with his wife in Cardiff: to the destroyer escorts – hard worked enough at any time, poor devils, God knows – it meant an extra day in harbour. And to me personally, it means without any conceit, a good job well done; and more than anything else, a telephone talk with Cath tonight and Her here beside me in comfort tomorrow.

I think its very likely that when the Admirals' official reports go in, this voyage will have done me quite a nice quiet spot of good with the company. Well I told Captain MacDonald I'd do my best. I've done it and I'm damned pleased with the result."

The enthusiasm and sheer joie-de-vivre showing through this log indicate relief after so many years of waiting and the satisfaction of being able to make a really worth-while contribution to the war; a war that had, at all costs, to be won to enable us to put the Germans in their place once and for all. Like so many of his generation Dad put the blame for the mindless slaughter of the trenches squarely on the shoulders of the enemy. As far as he was concerned the only good German was a dead one.

With this example before us, my generation very quickly found the prospective death of any member of the Axis powers a matter for celebration for which any sacrifice was justified. We learnt to live with death at our elbows with very little in the way of sensitivity in our reactions, more a feeling of bitterness and hatred. Our pleasure in times of emergency was in the killing of our opponents. This became our philosophy, our way of life and is something which no amount of description or explanation can possibly convey to any who have not lived such experience for themselves.

The indiscriminate butchery of the Blitz did much to consolidate our attitude and it may help when reading the history of our war experiences, trying to comprehend our motivation and readiness to face the unfaceable, to bear the sheer savagery of our attitude in mind.

At the end of Dad's first trip in command his time was probably too fully occupied to maintain the practice of detailed log-keeping, certainly in the early part of the war when ships were being loaded with war materials, waiting for convoy, sailing to and discharging their cargoes at convenient French ports before the inevitable delay for the accumulation of enough ships for the return convoy. Only very fast ships were allowed to proceed independently.

The disadvantages of the convoy system are obvious enough but they were out-weighed by the protection given by the attendant naval escort and the sense of safety in numbers. Merchant ships were armed for their own protection, usually with a four inch, anti-submarine gun aft and such anti-aircraft devices as were available and practicable at different stages of the war. Throughout the war merchantmen remained non-combatant civilians and were considered either too much occupied or simply not competent to fire their own guns, for which purpose service personnel (Dems gunners, the dems being short for "Defensively equipped merchant ships") were carried. As time passed these men became integral members of the ships' crews and numbered some twelve or fourteen on the average 5,000 to 7,000 ton ship. They could be Army or Navy or a mixture of both in the charge of a sergeant and/or a leading hand or petty officer and lived in their own accommodation built into erstwhile cargo space.

At all events a convoy under air attack could produce a remarkably daunting defensive barrage from probably eight oerlikon guns per ship with the odd bofors and if practically possible and necessary, a four inch shell or two.

After the fall of France and Norway ships were convoyed from the UK northward to Russia or Iceland, westward right across the Atlantic and southward to Gibraltar and to North African ports. Once a comparatively safe area was reached, ships with destinations other than those of the convoys were allowed to break away and proceed independently.

There is no detailed record of Dad's voyages after October '39 for the best part of a year, but he remained on the "...Keelung" and I think it was in this period that the King paid a visit on board in Liverpool and I know the ship was selected as commodore on other occasions, once possibly on one of the quieter Russian convoys.

The next written record came when Dad coincided in Suez (Port Tewfik) with an old school chum, now Captain Collister of s.s."Beaconstreet." This was a nine ship convoy to Bombay 5th to 19th September 1940 formed by three columns of two ships and one of three, the "...Keelung" once again commodore, leading the column one quarter of the way in from the starboard flank, the only one in this instance with two ships astern of her.

The commodore seems to have occupied this particular position irrespective of the number of ships or columns in a convoy, presumably so that escort vessels making rendez-vous with any convoy would know where to find their liaison vessel at any time of day or night. Or was it just a stupid habit? It's certain that the enemy also knew where to find the commodore, but more of this later.

Routine reports and correspondence such as the following show that in this early stage of the war encounters with the enemy were common-place.

Thus the reports on one particular Atlantic convoy:

"s.s. "City of Keelung"
15th March 1941
Report of Submarine Attack on Convoy O.B.C. 290

On 26th February 1941 at 00.00 B.S.T., vessel was in convoy O.B.C. 290, distinguishing signal 54. Estimated Position Lat. 55.54 N. Long. 13.45 W. Course 234 degrees. Approximate speed 8½ knots. Wind West force 4, no moon, dark and clear.

At about 00.05 flares were fired from one of the escorting vessels on port wing at rear of convoy, and at about 00.25 two distant explosions were heard and slight concussion felt, consistent with dropping of depth charges at a distance. Emergency turn of 40 degrees to starboard was made by signal from commodore and occasional gun-fire heard from port rear of convoy. At about 00.40 a vessel on port wing at rear of convoy sounded two groups of six short blasts and fired two rockets, and escorts in various positions round convoy fired flares.

Nothing further occurred until about 01.00 when more flares were fired and shortly afterwards a vessel on starboard wing rear of convoy sounded one group of six short blasts. Gun-fire occurred at intervals thereafter with the use of flares until about 01.22 when s.s. "Diala"(No.44) abeam of s.s. "City of Keelung" in next column to port suddenly fired two white rockets.

Simultaneously with the firing of the second rocket an explosion was heard and a flame observed to shoot up from the "Diala" on port side just forward of her bridge. Immediately thereafter "Diala" hoisted a red light signifying that she had been torpedoed. Sending out a wireless message at the same time she gradually dropped astern of the convoy. For about ten minutes after this occasional flares were fired and gun-fire took place at intervals from the port side of the convoy, after which nothing further occurred.

Throughout the attack s.s. "City of Keelung" maintained a restricted zig-zag, consistent with the maintenance of correct station in convoy, engines were at full speed throughout the greater part of the time, with occasional sudden reductions and increases as necessary to avoid too close proximity to other ships.

The entire crew was mustered at Action and Emergency Stations until the attack had completely subsided. At no time during the attack was any trace of submarines seen from s.s. "City of Keelung".

The behaviour of all Officers and entire crew throughout the attack was all that could be desired and the response from Engine Room Staff to all orders from Bridge immediate and complete.

Signed, Master, "City of Keelung"."

"s.s. "City of Keelung"
5th March 1941
Report of Aircraft Attack on Convoy O.B.C. 290

On 26th February 1941. Vessel in Convoy O.B.C.290, distinguishing signal 54

At 09.40 B.S.T. Estimated Position Lat. 55.30.N. Long. 16.00.W. Course 213 degrees, approximate speed 8½ knots. Wind South force 5. Sky overcast with low cloud at estimated height not exceeding 1,000 feet.

At about 09.45 a single aircraft (low-wing monoplane bomber) suddenly appeared out of cloud over port wing of convoy, dived and dropped bombs. Anti-aircraft fire was opened from escorts and from ships in port section of convoy and aircraft flew off astern shortly afterward. No action was taken nor fire opened by "City of Keelung" as range was considerably too great for Hotchkiss guns.

After attack s.s. "Melmore Head" fell out of convoy burning fiercely amidships; fire appeared to spread rapidly fore and aft and when last seen astern "Melmore Head" was apparently burning out. A Greek steamer (name unknown) also fell out of convoy, was abandoned and apparently settling by the head, presumably from a near miss.

At 18.45 B.S.T. Estimated Position Lat.54.00 N. Long. 17.00W. Course 213 degrees, approximate speed 8½ knots. Wind NW force 5. Sky overcast with low cloud at estimated height not exceeding 1,000 feet.

A formation of aircraft suddenly appeared astern in low level flight appearing to be as follows:- Three twin-engined low wing monoplanes in arrowhead formation followed closely by a single four engined Condor bomber. On overtaking convoy formation broke up and attacked, two monoplanes working along port wing of convoy, one towards centre and Condor attacking starboard columns. At 19.00 B.S.T. Condor at a height of about 150 feet, opened fire with a machine gun on a Dutch steamer (name unknown) on starboard quarter of "City of Keelung" and distant about three cables. Simultaneously "City of Keelung" opened fire with Hotchkiss guns at a range of about 600 yards. Machine gun fire from aircraft suddenly ceased and aircraft proceeded ahead along starboard columns, releasing bombs. It then circled out to starboard until abeam of "City of Keelung" and then turned and attacked head on and down wind. Fire was held until aircraft was in a range of about 800 yards and rapid fire was then opened with both Hotchkiss guns (Bridge and Boat deck). Aircraft again sheered suddenly to starboard and released its two remaining bombs which appeared to fall into the water in close vicinity of ships in next column to starboard. I am definitely of the opinion that this particular attack was originally directed specifically against the "City of Keelung" and was turned only by close-range rapid fire from the Hotchkiss guns. Fire from both guns appeared to be absolutely accurate, the tracer bullets apparently striking directly into aircraft. Aircraft continued its turn to starboard until clear of port columns and eventually flew away astern on a course of about 033 degrees. At 19.08 B.S.T. orders were received by signal from Commodore, to disperse and proceed independently. Vessel was manoeuvred as necessary to comply with this order and by 20.03 "City of Keelung" was proceeding on independent route at Full Speed.

Ammunition used by "City of Keelung" during attack was 147 rounds .303 Hotchkiss Ammunition.

During the attack a steamer in starboard section of convoy (identity unknown but believed to be the Dutch steamer "Beursplein") was observed to be on fire aft. An explosion was suddenly heard and ship was seen to sheer vertically in the water stem uppermost, and sink rapidly stern first. s.s."Llanwern" and s.s."Sovac"were observed to be on fire and burning fiercely; they fell out of convoy and when last seen astern both appeared to be burning completely out.

Hotchkiss guns in s.s."City of Keelung" were manned as follows during the attack:

Bridge gun:	Third Officer R. Simkin and Apprentice J.P.M. Price.
Boat-deck gun:	Colour Sergeant F.C.J. Watham R.M. and Fourth Engineer W. Drybrough

Throughout the attack the coolness of all officers and members of the crew was exemplary, and Engine room staff worked throughout in the fullest possible cooperation with the Bridge.

The nearest miss observed from s.s."City of Keelung" was on an approximate bearing of 168 degrees and at a distance of about 500 yards. Signed Master "City of Keelung"."

These reports were followed up in due course (14th May 1941) by a letter from the company (signed E. Aubrey Lloyd?) addressed to Dad:

"Dear Sir,
The Director of the Trade Division, Admiralty, has written us in regard to the encounter between your vessel and enemy aircraft on 26th February 1941. Captain B.B. Schofield, the Director of the Trade Division, requests us to offer his congratulations to yourself and the members of the crew of "City of Keelung" on the result of this encounter. He points out that the defensive equipment was used with such effect that the enemy was driven off and that the good timing and accuracy of the ship's fire undoubtedly deterred the aircraft from making any further attack.

We would like to add our own congratulations as your owners to those of the Admiralty.

Yours faithfully,"

This letter indicates a protocol whereby the ships appear to have communicated with the Admiralty via the shipping companies and this prompts me to make a point or two on the very complicated structure of shipping administration in war-time.

Whereas finance, insurance, freight income, chartering and so on remained a closed book to the seafarer, he was aware of continuing to work for his particular shipping line irrespective of the fact that all the ships were now requisitioned by the Ministry of War Transport and he was working for at least two bosses.

The shipping company though no longer required to seek cargo or determine its destination, continued to work as normal with its own agencies abroad, manning its own ships, training its own staff as hitherto.

Port control remained much as normal but with additional bodies like the Sea Transport Office to organise convoys and liaise between Navy and Merchant Service, hence a minimum of three different interests were involved, each having a say in the ordering of the ship.

There were so many strands, crossed lines and no doubt tangles in the new system, it was an object lesson in banging heads together and teaching disparate bodies to work in harmony. Needs must when the devil drives.

Before the war seamen were so poorly paid that when the realisation struck that this was a more than slightly hazardous profession in war-time, the Ministry very quickly slapped a £12.00 per man per month "danger money" bonus on the pay (£6.00 for beginners!) This became a bone of contention when they came into contact with conscripted soldiery who were not in a position to opt out and look for other work! Perhaps they didn't realise that an Essential Works Order prevented seamen from opting out either, but they did see an apparently unjustifiable pay differential.

For the most part they weren't there when the ships were being sunk or they might have been a little more sympathetic!

As the losses increased, so the tempo of ship building went up and the losses were replenished with, outside British yards, the American Liberty ships, the Canadian Forts and in the course of time, the "Oceans", the "Empires" and the "Sams". Whilst these remained Ministry property until the end of the war, they were allocated as replacements to the shipping companies.

As survivors of sinkings were repatriated, in particular the ordinary crew members as opposed to officers, with no ship to employ them they reported to the Shipping Federation Pool of seafarers to whom ships applied to fill vacancies however caused. No doubt the Pool also provided the crews that were flown or shipped to the States or Canada to pick up new buildings.

It's time to pick up on Dad's last voyage on the beloved "...Keelung".

As usual his log speaks eloquently for itself, but it omits to give the pretext under which he was asked to go to Newfoundland to take over command of a Fleet Supply Ship (thereby placing himself directly under the Navy's orders!). Someone was needed urgently to relieve the incumbent master whose health had broken down and Dad was the man in the right place at the right time.

Whatever the truth – here goes:

""City of Keelung"
Voyage 14
11ᵗʰ July 1941

Arrived Hull from Methil 11ᵗʰ July 1941 (Friday) to discharge full cargo; docked in King George Dock at 10pm. Arranged everything on Saturday morning for paying off on Wednesday 16ᵗʰ July and then caught 1.50pm train for Kings Cross. Grand week-end. Arrived home Saturday night and left again Monday night. On return found everything fixed up for a hurry-up job with only the chance of another week-end. Paid crowd off and signed again on Wednesday and pushed off home again on Thursday night, found Laura at home as well. Splendid! One of the loveliest week-ends I ever had: just the entire family and nobody else.

Left London again Sunday night and found everything being rushed to sail on Tuesday. Mitchell arrived on Monday to go across with me to relieve Doidge as Chief Officer of the "City of Dieppe". Informed by Wilsons that instead of coming back home from USA am to load in Montreal for India. Long voyage, damn it.

Tuesday 22nd July 1941:
Everything finished by 6.00pm. 928 tons general cargo and 1909 tons bunker coal on board. Degaussing gear [anti-magnetic mine cabling] has been overhauled so must adjust compasses again before attempting to go down river. Pilot Bury and Compass Adjuster on board at 5.00pm. Ordered to sea as soon as cargo should be finished, when two things happened at

once; heavy rain and thick mist set in, killing any hope of adjusting compasses in river: and Wilsons sent a car down in a hurry to take me up town for fresh route orders as Methil run was cancelled and I was to go into the Tyne for some special Admiralty cargo.

Went up-town to Naval Control and got new route orders, then proceeded to deliver a shock. Convoy sailing from Grimsby Roads at 5.00am tomorrow and in view of weather and impossibility of doing anything with compasses pointed out that I could not possibly leave the dock tonight. Must have clear weather to correct compasses before going down river. Rang Wilsons from Control Office and told them the same. Then things started to hum. Wilsons' hands went up in horror "But if you don't get out of the dock tonight what about all the overtime we'll have worked for nothing? And you're urgently wanted in the Tyne". I said "Sorry but I'm not going to put the ship aground just to justify the overtime and the Admiralty's hurry up order." Spoke to Mr Bayly (Managing Director) on the phone and he of course agreed that the responsibility and the final decision were both up to me alone.

Next came the Senior Naval Officer (speaking on the phone from his home, by the way). Wilsons said "You're supposed to go", Senior Naval Officer said "He ought to go" I said "I won't go". And all the Naval Control staff (all ex-shipmasters with Reserve commissions) agreed privately that I was quite right. I know damned well I'm right so that's that. Sent the pilot and the Adjuster home again and we leave the dock at 5.00am tomorrow – weather permitting.

Wednesday 23rd July 1941:

Left dock at 6.01am. Weather much clearer. Three runs over Degaussing Range then proceeded to adjust compasses. Received private pencil note from Naval Control by pilot, "If you get adjusting finished in time and see convoy at sea ahead of you, never mind official instructions: go ahead and catch them up."

But unfortunately weather sold us a pup again. Finished adjusting and licking down river at full speed when suddenly ran into dense fog again; visibility absolutely nil. Managed to crawl to Killingholm Buoy and anchored at 7.40am. Fog cleared and we got under way again at 9.23am but too late. No sign of Convoy at Grimsby Roads and gate closed. Convoy must have got away in a break between fog banks, so that's that. Next Convoy for us. A pity but anyway she's still afloat which she wouldn't have been if I had tried to get down river last night.

Thank God the fairies must have put a philosophic streak in me when I was born. For when I have bucked against all the Powers that be and then in the finish a patch of bad luck has let me down, it just doesn't worry me. I sleep just as easily. So long as I know that I have done my best and I was right anyway, the final result doesn't worry me one little tin damn.

Left Grimsby Roads with north-bound convoy on Friday, 25th July 1941 at 3.20am.

Arrived off Tyne entrance at 11.32pm. and anchored outside Breakwaters until 7.47am on the 26th.

Saturday 26th July 1941:

Docked at Elswick Jetty (Vickers-Armstrong) to load Admiralty cargo. Cargo consists of new fittings for Cruiser "Naiad" refitting in New York (what an answer to the fools who curse America for being neutral!!) One piece alone weighs 80 tons and consists of guns, mounting and turret all complete. I should imagine the "Naiad" must have been mixed up in the "Bismarck" affair as she is one of the new cruisers and shouldn't need replacements like that in the ordinary way.

And the Admiralty certainly intends that this particular cargo shall get across all right. They insist that I shall be fitted with heavy anti-aircraft gun and all my European crew put through a fresh gunnery course before leaving here, that my degaussing gear shall be re-tested and compasses re-adjusted: and that I shall be kept to wait for a special convoy and special protection. And that's all going to take time; but apparently time is no object

94

so long as the "...Keelung" gets her cargo across all right.

Dems Authorities have decided that mounting of our new gun (a 12 pounder A.A.) will be done at present berth alongside Elswick Jetty so that's very nice.

Monday 28th July 1941:

Finished loading Admiralty cargo at 4.00pm. No work on new gun started yet so phoned Cath after tea and asked if she would like to come up for a day or two. Answer was a foregone conclusion of course. She will be here tomorrow. Thank God. We ought to get a few days of heaven out of it after all. Cath told me on the phone that Bucknalls want me to leave this ship in New York and go to St. Johns, Newfoundland to take over the "City of Dieppe" from Tibbets. Couldn't ask questions and afraid for her to say too much on phone, so don't know any details but will get them tomorrow anyway.

Tuesday 29th July 1941:

Word from Agents this morning to phone London this afternoon, so rang at 2.30pm and got official instructions to be ready on arrival in New York to hand this ship over to Mitchell and go to St. Johns to take over the "...Dieppe". Agreed without any hesitation, of course. Couldn't do anything else: refusal would be out of the question in any case. But I shall hate leaving this ship.

Met Cath at 3.40pm.

Back to office from station and fell into hot argument over phone at once. Vickers- Armstrong have fallen down on job of fitting my gun and Dems want me to shift to Tyne Dock on tomorrow morning tide (6.30am) and it just can't be done. On the strength of their assurance that ship would remain at Elswick I have given Chief Engineer permission to start a small but necessary engine repair. And they haven't given me sufficient warning for shifting now, so we can't have steam ready for the morning. Tomorrow afternoon, but not tomorrow morning. Arguing the toss backward and forward on the phone till

6.15pm. Dems can't understand why I shouldn't attempt this river without main steam. Sheer madness and I told them so. Anyway the result remains the same. I won't shift until my engines are ready and everything is arranged now for tomorrow evening.

Kept poor Cath in the office, dying for her tea, until 6.15pm.

Tuesday 29th July till Monday 4th August:

Heaven with Cath. It has made up for the two tiny little weekends which we thought were all we were going to get. And I'm glad she was able to live on board for she loves living on board so much. And this is her ship as much as mine. And I'm very glad she was able to live here with me for the last time before I leave this ship. There is a God in Heaven.

Tuesday 5th August 1941:

Saw Cath away on the 10.45pm for Kings Cross. Couldn't get into Newcastle in time for naval conference this morning if I had gone back to Shields last night so Cusworth (my coast pilot) and I put up at the Douglas Hotel. Conference at 10.00am.

2.36pm.

Cleared breakwaters and found my own special escort, H.M.S."Valorous", waiting outside for me and two fighter planes circling. Pushed off through swept channel, "Valorous" following close astern and planes making a continuous sweep. Joined main north-bound convoy off Buoy 20R at 4.20pm. Filthy night tonight. Rain, rain, rain. "Valorous" sitting tight alongside of me and our fighters singing in the cloud above us all the time. What a grand job the Admiralty has found for my little "Keelung" this trip, for our last run together. I may be sentimental, but it seems so entirely right. I've done my damnedest to make a lasting name for her, and now that we're making our last voyage together the Admiralty has given her a special cargo and a special escort of her own. They couldn't have arranged it better if they had known I was leaving her.

Wednesday 6th August 1941:

Better today. Weather has cleared quite a lot. Rain gone, but strong WNW wind and fairly heavy swell. However, we'd better get that now and have it over before we reach Pentland Firth tonight.

Noon position 57 06 N 1 50 W. Average speed 7.2 knots. Cusworth is a godsend as far as I am concerned. If he hadn't been here I shouldn't have had many minutes off the bridge: that's all right on a short run with a break at Methil, but not so good on an unbroken run to Loch Ewe.

Thursday 7th August 1941:

2.49am. Passed Duncansby Head and entered Pentland Firth. 3.09am. Passed Swilkie Point. Weather smooth through the Firth, for which thank God. This place can be hell in a gale of wind. 10.45am. Passed Cape Wrath. 6.00pm. Arrived at Ewe Buoy. Thought we were going to get an early finish and a long night in bed, but found a coastal convoy coming out of the Loch so had to steam round and wait for them all to get clear. Time going on and ships still coming out, when suddenly in the dusk saw a ship I couldn't mistake. Called her "Is that "Derby"?" and got the answer "Yes". Had a yarn and a laugh with Grove and White. Damned glad to see her, for I haven't heard of her for months and hadn't the faintest idea where she might be. Its great to fall across your best pals unexpectedly and find them still afloat and cheerful. 34 ships came out altogether and it was 11.40pm before we finally entered Loch Ewe.

Anchored in Loch Ewe at 12.38am 8th August 1941 and got a shock. Sub-lieutenant from Naval Control Office boarded with all my Secret Instructions and informed me "You're sailing at 6.15am Captain. Convoy conference was held today and here's all your papers. We didn't need you at the Conference anyway – you know the game all right." Just as well I do know the game. A new master would have been in a hell of a hole.

Sidney came on board just after the Control Officer left, at 1.00am. He and Cusworth and I sat and yarned till 1.45am and

97

I got three new kites [anti-aircraft devices] from Sidney (nothing like having an old pal in the right department).

Know how tight things are ashore here so made Sidney take a bottle of gin and 300 cigarettes ashore with him. He wanted to pay for them but nothing doing. The kites were more than worth it anyway. Sidney and Cusworth left at 2.00am, Cusworth taking my mail with him. Left orders to be called at 6.00am and turned in.

Friday 8th August 1941:
Convoy commenced getting under way at 6.15am. I was 16th ship to move so didn't get a start till 8.01am. Passed through the gate at 8.43am. Pushed up into station at 10.26am then dodged along dead slow, waiting for main convoy which was coming up on our port beam to overtake us. Joined main convoy at 12.30pm. As usual didn't waste any time: watched for a convenient gap in the columns and soon spotted one, so ignored routine instructions and dived through the hole into my proper station. First ship of the Loch Ewe crowd to get settled in station in the main convoy. Have got my special place all right. I am No. 62 in the centre of the convoy and next astern of the commodore. H.M.S. "Keppel" sticks pretty close to me all the time and our fighter escort, after circling the convoy for a while, makes a periodical run diagonally over us. I like the sound of those engines roaring over me every now and then. Of course its pure sentiment but it strikes me as a sort of official salute to my old "...Keelung" for our last run together.

My position also means that when we meet the ocean escort, the cruiser will be parked alongside of me all the time.

Have told the watch officers that I want to be hard on the Commodore's tail all the time, not a yard out of station day or night: also that nothing else in the convoy has got to come anywhere near us at signals. Having told them that, I know I shall get it. I've got a good crowd and I have only to say what I want. This old ship has put up some damn good shows in convoy. She has got to do the best she ever did this trip.

Saturday 9th August 1941:

Heading up towards Eskimo land again and the weather is not by any means warm. Steering N 76 W. Noon position 59.34 N. 11.04 W. Average speed 8.2 knots. Wind SEly. Plenty of low cloud and continuous rain. Ideal weather actually: just what we want for the first four or five days.

For any jerry bomber that wants us has got to come right down under the cloud to hunt for us – and God help the jerry who rakes up enough guts to come low over this little bunch. All my guns are manned day and night and anything that gets inside our range will have a very thin chance of ever getting away again. And that pretty well applies to every merchant ship in the crowd, without ever considering the escort. 60 ships and 13 escorts here so we're a pretty healthy little crowd.

Sunday 10th August 1941:

Rain still holding on. Moderate Wly breeze and swell pitching a bit at times. But, pitching or smooth running, my officers are making a grand show of it this time. I don't think we've been a yard out of station at any time since we left. The Commodore keeps a very steady speed, which helps a lot.

Noon position 60.16 N. 17.23W. Average speed 7.84 knots. Course N 88 W. I fancy we shall be meeting the heavy ocean escort shortly, from the way the speed is being held down: evidently to make a rendez–vous at some definite time shortly.

Monday 11th August 1941:

As I expected, our heavy escort has arrived. Thought she couldn't be far away; she is either the "Wolfe" or the "Montcalm": I suspect the "Montcalm" though there is no actual way of telling, for the two ships are absolutely identical in appearance. As I knew she would be from the position they gave me in the convoy, she is planted close alongside on my port beam all the time. Its good to see a hefty cruiser like that sitting tight alongside all the time, because its good to know that out of all the ships in the crowd, I have got the cargo the Admiralty is most anxious to protect. "Keppel" and local escort left this afternoon. They will pick up a homeward convoy and go back with them.

Noon position 60.19 N. 23.51 W. Getting along. NW winds and still showery.

Tuesday 12th August 1941:

Wind all over the place today, very unsteady. And still continuous rain. Going south at last. Steering S 47 W. Noon position 59.04 N 48.21 W. Still sitting tight on Commodore's tail and cruiser hanging on tight alongside all the time. If I move up a yard, so does she. I've a feeling this cargo of mine is going to get to New York intact if we have to bust through the whole Jerry fleet to get it there. And we shan't have to do that, jerry being jerry.

Wednesday 13th August 1941:

A really fine day at last. Light NEly winds, slight sea and no rain. Steering S 45 W. Noon position 56.42 N 33.01 W. Average speed 8.12 knots.

Getting well to the westward now and I shouldn't be surprised to get the "disperse and proceed" signal any time now. We are further west now than they have ever taken us in an outward convoy before. Well, the sooner we break up, the sooner we'll be in New York and the sooner I'll have the job to myself. Convoys are grand things, no question about that: but its great to be away at full speed and using only your own brains against any damn thing that may happen to be in your way.

Thursday 14th August 1941:

Noon position 54.08 N. 36.55 W. A mucky sort of day. Light SE winds and banks of thick fog at intervals till 5.00pm. Towing fog buoys all day. Cleared after 5pm. and thin rain set in instead. And suddenly at 7.03pm., without any previous warning, came the "disperse and proceed". We split up in the rain, full speed and get on with it.

Steering S 52 W to my first position. And so we're off and the rest is up to me. And this cargo is going to get into New York whatever happens.

Friday 15th August 1941:

Weather clearing up again after a mouldy night. Thick fog banks at intervals all night. Set in about 9.00pm. Third Officer sent down to tell me it was getting very thick and it certainly was. But nothing to be done about it of course. Can't use lights or whistle or anything now. Told the third Officer "Sorry Mr Robinson, but there's nothing we can do about it. You'll just have to keep looking at it. Its hell for leather into it and hope for the best." But I can sympathise with a junior officer's feelings on the bridge banging full speed into fog. Had plenty of that myself in 1917.

Fog cleared about 9.00am today and I started the zig-zag. Keeping it up day and night of course. I never do take any chances, but I certainly wouldn't this trip.

Noon position 51.12 N. 42.12.W. Average speed 9.74 knots."

The log ends here a week before arrival in New York whence Dad was flown to Gander, to take over the "City of Dieppe" in St. Johns, leaving the "...Keelung" and its cargo behind. The "..Dieppe" had the unenviable task of sitting in port going absolutely nowhere for month after weary month and the tragedy of this was that the ship, owned and officered by a native crew company, had been re-organised to be manned by a European crew.

European crews in those days were extremely variable; the white crew companies had their regular men which left the outside companies to use whoever was available to them via the Pool; this invariably included at least an element of the kind of individual that Dad had to live with in his sailing ship days. Add to this the impossible situation of more or less permanent residence in one of the bleakest places on earth and it takes little imagination to appreciate the disciplinary problems that arose.

I've always believed that Dad was selected for this job because of his enthusiasm, his comparative juniority (the seniors would

101

have turned it down flat) and the fact that with his background he was probably one of very few masters who could have made a success of it at that time.

He was under the impression that because the "...Dieppe" was about the biggest ship in Bucknalls at the time and the job was prestigious, he was being honoured, in effect promoted, by being offered the job.

The fact is that it was a year of sheer purgatory and it ended with nine of the crew being sent to gaol when the ship was finally reprieved and brought back to the UK.

It was also a prime element in Dad's rapid aging process. In retrospect it's clear he paid an unacceptably high price for this "promotion".

Because he had succeeded where others had failed he was now lumbered with the questionable honour of commanding Fleet Supply ships for the rest of the war.

After a spot of leave he returned to the "...Dieppe" in Liverpool and commenced a voyage over a particularly significant period of family history; stationed in Freetown, he arrived some five to six weeks before his son and heir travelled overnight Kings Cross to Glasgow to join his beloved "City of Keelung" as one of two brand new junior cadets!

For the next twelve months he remained in the vicinity of West Africa and Western North Africa while I was on the opposite coast working gradually ever nearer so that on 1st July 1943 I visited Malta for the first time from the eastward and went on to Tripoli for the second time. At this stage he was travelling from Sousse to Malta, overlapping the "...Keelung" and arriving 19th July (his log records "...Dieppe" in Bizerta at the time of the Sicily landings; "...Keelung" was discharged and killing time in Tripoli). So near and yet so far, our paths had crossed but we didn't meet.

But I have anticipated his final complete log of the war which says:

"His Majesty's Fleet Supply Ship "City of Dieppe"
Second Commission August 1942 – August 1943

Sunday 30th August 1942:

Left Liverpool for Freetown, Sierra Leone, in 9 knot convoy. Passage entirely uneventful, except for four days bad weather (speed down to four knots) west of Ireland.

Friday 18th September 1942

Arrived Freetown to relieve F.S.S."City of Tokio".

"City of Tokio" going south for refit.

Freetown: One of earth's dog-holes. Principal attractions – Malaria, black-water fever, coast fever, vile oppressive heat, all kinds of filthy flying and crawling insects, stink and an occasional tornado thrown in for luck. Remained there until 12th March 1943: six of the most awful months I ever spent And to crown it all, of course, that most damnable of all jobs – waiting. Watching other fellows go to sea and wishing to God we were with them. And worse still, seeing the other fellows come in as survivors. Anything from ten to fifty a day, in all kinds of craft and all kinds of clothing (?) and all kinds of physical condition. The hospitals were kept darn busy with Merchant Navy survivors, for weeks and weeks on end. The Hun must have reaped a wicked harvest, far worse than our official news ever mentioned. And mails!!! The word ceased to exist. It was simply "if and when". We got letters if they got through and when they arrived. And we knew that at least half the letters we wrote never got home. Damnable!

Anybody who ever says a word against Hospital Nurses will hear something from any of us who were ever on the Freetown Station. The Military Hospitals (51st and 34th) handled all the Army, Navy and Merchant Navy cases – and God knows there were plenty. The Q.A.s (Queen Alexandra's Imperial Military Nursing Sisters) were splendid. They worked their soul-cases out under conditions of climate and surroundings and shortage of ordinary comforts that no woman ever ought to be asked to endure. No man ever born would have stood up to it as they did. He'd have growled his head off and then gone sick. Yet those women served their 18 months in Freetown and worked their heads off and worried themselves stiff if they lost a case that was hopeless from the start.

On one occasion a boat-load of five survivors arrived – 49 days in an open boat – and were rushed to Mount Oriel Hospital (51st General). Among them was a first-voyage apprentice, a kid of 16, in the last stage of exhaustion. The only hope of saving his life was glucose. No such thing to be had in Freetown. After the Military and Naval Authorities had spent hours in finding out that there wasn't any, somebody had a brain-wave and suggested that perhaps the "City of Dieppe" as a store ship, might have some. As it happened we had, purely by accident: one solitary tin among the Steward's stores, picked up in Canada on the previous commission. As soon as I got the enquiry I rushed the tin up to Mount Oriel Hospital and it arrived – one hour too late. Later the hospital rang to thank me for the effort and tell me they were returning the tin and the Sister who spoke was almost crying into the telephone when she said the kiddie had died an hour or so earlier.

We often hear the Q.A.s referred to as "hard-bitten Army Nurses". From what we see they will work their heads off 24 hours a day for anybody needing help and break their hearts when the luck goes against them. Hard-bitten or not , so far as we have seen, the Q.A.s on foreign station are absolutely magnificent, every one of them a Florence Nightingale.

Our main diversion was pictures at the R.A.F. mess (Wing Commander Dixon, Sq.Ls Harris, Tilley, Barnett and a whole crowd of darn nice fellows) or the R.E. mess (Major Wynward, later promoted Lieut-Colonel) on Sundays. Sq.Ls Tilley and Barnett were subsequently shifted up-river to Fourah Bay mess, and thanks to this we managed to obtain our liquid refreshment for Christmas. No such thing as beer available in Freetown. Tilley rang me up a couple of days before Christmas and said the Fourah Bay mess had surplus beer but no butter, bacon or anything to make a Christmas pudding with and "what about it?" So I took the cutter to Fourah Bay with some butter and bacon and the makings for a pudding and returned with two cases of beer . Also returned with Tilley and Barnett who spent the rest of the day on board and helped to christen the first case.

My souvenirs of Freetown – five scars of Tumbu-fly bites and a dose of Coast-fever which returned at intervals for a couple of months after we left the place.

12th March 1943:

Left Freetown for Gibraltar with a convoy bound for the UK, the only ship for Gibraltar. Joined off Dakar by three French ships recently released – "Dunkerque", "Hoggar" and "Chelma", with escorts U.S.S. "Auk", two Free French corvettes and one American mosquito craft. "Dunkerque" and "Chelma" for Casablanca, "Hoggar" for Gibraltar. In the evening of 22nd March received signal from commodore "You will be detached at about 07.00 hours to proceed in company with "Hoggar", "Chelma" and "Dunkerque" to destination".Detached at 7.00am on the 23rd March. Fell astern with "Hoggar" and "Dunkerque" – "Chelma" a lame duck struggling along on the horizon astern, steaming a hell of a long way in a hell of a long time.

American mosquito craft called me up "Has commodore been appointed?" Answered "No" and got by return "Request you will act as commodore and navigate convoy to Casablanca. Do you agree?" Naturally I answered "Agreed". He then sent "Please arrange speed to arrive Casablanca Swept Channel in daylight as early as possible, remembering speed of "Chelma". Asked him "Do you wish me to adjust speed to allow ship astern to catch up?" and got the answer "Yes please". That properly tore it. "Chelma" over the horizon astern, with no hope of catching up for hours. Reduced speed to 5½ knots. No chance of making Casablanca before dark. Only 96 miles to go and practically 24 hours to kill for daylight next morning. What a picnic! Blowing hard from SSW with thin rain, no hope of sights, only dead reckoning to work on. Ship so foul after six months in Freetown that I couldn't estimate her speed to a knot, speed so low that patent log couldn't register correctly, echo-sounder so choked with weed that it wouldn't register at all.

All the ships were dead light and blowing sideways like crabs, and God only knew what the leeway might be. Absolutely nothing to work on but just blind guess. About the lousiest job I've ever struck yet. "Chelma" caught up about 4.00pm. Took a wide sweep to seaward and increased to 7 knots to try to counteract the effect of wind and current.

"Chelma" immediately began to fall back and I had to reduce to 6½ knots to hold her. And I spent the rest of the day and all night cursing the "Chelma" and every other crock that ever floated, and everybody that ever pushed on and left the dirty end of the job to some other poor devil. A British commodore of a French convoy (and colonial France only just newly decided to side with us!) with a mixed American and French escort! Whatever happened, I must get them safely to Casablanca. And every scrap of weather and luck dead against me. I did more strenuous calculating and re-calculating and hard blind guessing and weighing up of odds than I had ever done in my life or ever want to do again: and prayed in the intervals that no stray Hun might turn up to queer my pitch in the end. Just before sunset I sent the escort a signal "Expect to detach Casablanca ships off swept channel at about 0700hours tomorrow. Will make usual dispersal signal". Did my best during the night to wangle speed and courses to hoist the dispersal signal at 7.00am sharp and gave orders for that. Suddenly at 6.30am the Escort signalled "You may detach Casablanca ships at any time now if you wish".

I didn't need a second invitation. Laughed and told the Chief Officer "For God's sake hoist the "disperse and proceed" before he has time to change his mind".So the "Dunkerque" and "Chelma", with the U.S. mosquito craft and one French corvette, pushed off. And was I glad to see them go!!

I pushed on with the "Hoggar", the U.S.S. "Auk" and the other French corvette for Gibraltar. Had lost so much time waiting for daylight off Casablanca that I had to kill more time to make the Gibraltar swept channel at daybreak next day, as I had no information as to which lights, if any, would be showing in the Strait, nor whether or not I would be allowed to enter during the dark hours. But I wasn't going to crawl around in that vicinity at 6½ knots so increased to 9 knots and adjusted the courses instead. 50 to 60 degree alterations every few hours, piling on distance and killing time. At least it was good evasive steering! No stray Hun could have made up his mind whether we were bound for New York or China!!

Entered the Straits Swept Channel at 4.30am 25th March and with a roaring current under her tail, ran the last stretch at about 14 knots. Anchored in Gibraltar Bay at 9.30am 25th March 1943.

At Gibraltar from 25th March until 16th June 1943. Met Law (ex"City of Christchurch") and Blewett (ex "City of Perth") while they were awaiting passage home. Both of them fairly lucky: got all their men away before their ships sank, although one saloon boy from the "…Perth" was left in hospital in Gib. Also saw Grove several times in the Civil Hospital. He wasn't so lucky: when his ship got it he was the only one injured – broken pelvis. Eventually they flew him home, all strapped up in plaster, in a Sunderland. Met another old friend my first day in Gib. Was walking along Main Street when I heard some shouting behind me but took no notice till I suddenly got a smack in the back that nearly knocked me over. It was Squadron Leader Tilley, ex Freetown and Fourah Bay.

Asked what the dickens he was doing in Gib. and he told me he had arrived by plane the previous night and was flying a Sunderland home the next day. Invalided home with T.B.!! He made the 4th person we had known in Freetown to be sent home with T.B. I hadn't realised the confounded place was such a breeding ground for that disease. He was quite cheerful about it; said he'd been warned that he would be at least six months in hospital when he got home, but that he intended to have a few days "bust" in his own home before reporting to hospital.

Met the Governor of Gibraltar, Lieut-General H.N. Mason-Macfarlane, several times and had lunch with him at Government House shortly before we left Gib. He and his entire staff quite a good crowd and full of laughs. One laugh against me at the opening of the Merchant Navy Officers Club, opened officially by the Governor. After the ceremony I was yarning with the Gov. and some of his staff, all standing in the corridor and each with a pint mug of beer in his hand (me too, of course), when two Spanish women passed along on their way to apply to the Secretary for jobs as cooks. The first was fairly old and very dumpy, but the second was very young, very slim and very Spanish. The Governor turned round to see where they were going and a few seconds later his A.D.C., Major Capurro who was standing a few yards away, also turned round to watch. So I slid over and said quietly "Now, Major, keep your eyes off that! The Governor saw her first!!" Capurro laughed with a bull bellow and the Governor – his ears must be sharp – strolled over to us and said "Now Major, do you mind telling me what the Captain said about me just now?" And the silly ass told him. Anyway the Old Boy laughed like the devil and said "Thank you Captain. Thank God I've got one friend in Gibraltar".

Definite signs of activity in Gib. Busy storing Force H. All the big fellows "King George V" "Nelson" "Rodney" "Howe" "Formidable" etc. and literally scores of lesser fellows, destroyers, corvettes, sloops and so on. And from the stores they want it obviously isn't for any Sunday-school picnic. Something brewing in the Medi before long, that's certain.

Left Gibraltar for Algiers 16th June 1943. Gradually moving nearer to life I think.

Arrived Algiers in coastal convoy from Gibraltar 18th June 1943. Passage entirely uneventful, saw and heard nothing at all. Told on arrival we should probably be here a couple of months. Something is certainly working up. Algiers is packed solid with ships and troops. Big troopers, British and American, simply crawling with troops; landing-craft of all descriptions: and H.M. ships buzzing in and out like bees round a hive doorway.

Wonder how much of it we shall see when it breaks! One air raid alert in Algiers, the first we have heard since God knows when. But it came to nothing. May have been a bloke on reconnaissance or even an unidentified plane.

The prophesied two months got a sad shock. Ordered at short notice for Bizerta. Things are moving all right: wonder what, where and when. Whatever it is its certainly coming soon.

2nd July 1943:

Left Algiers for Bizerta with nine other ships. Joined up outside with large convoy from UK Don't know who the other ships are nor where they are bound: it's a big crowd.

In the early evening of 3rd July the Commodore pushed on with the main bunch, leaving about 25 of us with H.M.S."Abercrombie" as Commodore. At 8.00am on 4th July "Abercrombie" called me up and said "I am leaving you shortly. Request you will take over as commodore on my departure". At 9.30am he signalled "Take over now" and pushed off: probably for Malta I think. Didn't know which ships were bound where so made a signal "Indicate your ports of destination". Got answers from ten ships: the other lazy fools were so straggled out that they couldn't read my signals anyhow. Why the devil after four years of war, we still get a certain number of ships in every convoy who can't and won't keep proper station I can never understand. It isn't that they haven't got the speed, in the case of a slow convoy, because you always find that the bird who cannot keep up at 6 knots can suddenly find a comfortable 10 knots if there's a submarine flap or if he wants to pinch a comfortable anchorage berth. Anyway, I didn't intend to be worried by fools, so I carried the crowd on at convoy speed (8 knots) and left the stragglers to sweat over their own worries. Noticed that in answer to my destination signal, H.M.S. "Jaunty" had hoisted "Malta" so when getting on towards Bizerta Channel approach signalled "Jaunty" – "I am proceeding shortly with Bizerta ships. Request you take over as Commodore for ships bound further east". What the Yanks call "passing the buck" but anyway I had to appoint somebody.

Entered Bizerta Swept Channel about 2.00pm and anchored off the port about 3.30pm. It turned out eventually there were 15 ships for Bizerta; ten of us went in together, the other tired blighters rolled up an hour or so later. French naval pilot boarded to take us in. Spoke a certain amount of ship English rather hesitatingly and as the inner channel is very twisting and tricky and needs quick action from the helmsman we very soon struck a compromise: the pilot gave me his instructions in French which I translated for the benefit of the 3rd Officer at the Engine Telegraph and the quartermaster at the wheel. The pilot, a Breton, turned out to be a special pal of my old friend Louis le Cam of St.Nazaire days.

Anchored in Bizerta Lake about 5.30pm 4th July 1943.

Bizerta – City of the Dead. Rubble and wreckage and empty shells of houses. The Americans certainly made a job of bombing the Hun out of Bizerta. Craters everywhere, palm trees torn to blazes, not one completely intact building in the whole city. No civil population, only the few necessary Naval and Military personnel.

Something big working up all right and looks like coming soon. Naval Store Staff (especially Victualling Store) working overtime now all right, really discovering they are alive.

Demand after demand from H.M. ships of all sizes. I'd like to know just when and where the jump is going to be – and incidentally just how it will affect this ship. Almost sure to be a change of programme, temporarily anyway.

6th July 1943:

Red Letter Day. At 3.50am the air attack alarms went off and the fun started immediately. Really hot and heavy while it lasted. Searchlights everywhere, and the devil's own barrage from shore batteries and every ship in the port including us. Then they caught a plane in the searchlight crossing astern of us from starboard to port. We opened up on him with all four oerlikons and the 12-pounder. First two rounds from the 12-pounder burst slightly ahead of him then the gun-layer yelled "I've got him in my sights" and fired again. A few seconds later there was an explosion right on the plane and he flopped over and nose-dived like a streak. As soon as we saw he'd got it we followed, or rather anticipated, him right down. Played all the oerlikons directly underneath him all the way to the ground. If any swine bailed out , which I rather doubt, he was chopped to ribbons before he ever landed. He nose-dived into the sand, went up in a beautiful burst of flame and burned till daylight. I've heard since that five planes were brought down and no survivors from any of them. We made damn good and sure there were none from our bird anyway. And that's score No.1 chalked off for Sandhurst Road School and the kiddies.

The show finished at 4.15am. Less than an hour but pretty hectic while it lasted. Very little damage done, none whatever to the ships although the Lake was packed with them. Later on heard that H.M.S. "Liddesdale" and a Yankee trooper both want to claim the bird we got. Makes no odds: we know who got him. The 12-pounder crew have chalked up a swastika and "Bizerta 6.7.43" in the gun-pit and I've painted my tin hat with skull and cross-bones surmounted by the Arms of the City of London. The decks were a mass of shell splinters at daylight. Five minor casualties (one quartermaster and four natives) all shrapnel wounds and all doing nicely. The Doctor is quite happy with a professional job to do.

10th July 1943:

So this is it. Sicily after all. We've all tried to guess where the jump would be, but I don't think any of us quite expected Sicily – probably because its so obvious. Well there's one thing, Churchill and staff must have good enough reason for making it Sicily and must feel pretty sure of results: otherwise the jump wouldn't have been made. Something the crowd in this ship now will be able to tell themselves in the future: big ships, small ships, landing craft and everything, WE stored the fellows who pounced on Sicily.

After the initial landing kept busy in Bizerta re-storing the fellows who have come back empty from Sicily, principally destroyers and landing craft. Re-stored and off back again, all of them. Ordered to Malta via Sousse on the night of 13th July, urgently wanted according to signal. All wondering if we shall see Sicily before long. At last we are living after all the months of waiting.

14th July 1943:

Sailed for Sousse as Commodore, with four other ships: "Zena", "Meta", "Hildur I" and "Empire Moon", at 7.00pm. Escorts one corvette (H.M.S. "Gloxinia") and one armed trawler. Supposed to be 6½ knot convoy, but I managed to sweat a little extra speed out of them and made Sousse very comfortably before dark the next day. Anchored off the port at 7.00pm on 15th July 1943.

Storing landing craft all the while in Sousse. All back clean empty from Sicily, all re-stored and away back there again. Picked up four passengers for Malta, Lieutenant Jackson, an Engineer Sub-Lieutenant and two naval ratings.

Left Sousse for Malta at 1.00am 18th July 1943, with nine landing craft and armed trawler escort. Commodore in L.S.T.421. Passage uneventful. Detached off entrance to Malta, North-West Channel at 11.30pm18th July, where met by armed trawler. Landing craft and original trawler all went on to Sicily. Anchored south of Valetta Channel at 2.00am 19th July and proceeded into Malta Harbour at 10.30am 19th July 1943.

Malta. Some Island. No wonder it sports the George Cross. The Hun and the I-ti certainly gave it a pasting, though Malta is getting her own back at last. Wreckage and destruction ashore quite as bad as anything I have seen anywhere, but life goes on just the same. Malta had had a quiet time for two months before our arrival, but made up for it on the first night. The heaviest raid since December, apparently in revenge for the Rome pasting. Started at 3.15am on 20th July. Beautiful moonlit night, but what a racket! The Bizerta barrage was heavy, but it was a fool compared with this show. Everything in the harbour opened up: the "Nelson" "Rodney" "Howe" "Formidable" "Indomitable" "Penelope" and every cruiser and destroyer in the port. So did we of course though we didn't get a chance to use much. No use wasting ammunition by firing blind. Only expended 150 rounds. Flares and bombs were dropped but the guns were kicking up so much hell that we couldn't hear the bomb explosions. One stick of five dropped right across, three to port and two to starboard, which put us neatly in between the third and fourth eggs. We didn't hear the stuff that dropped on board either, though it was obviously raining down all round us.

In the morning the gun-pits and upper bridge and decks were simply covered with splinters and chunks of shell, some pieces $3\frac{1}{2}$ inches and an inch and a half wide. Why the gunners and we on the bridge weren't wiped up I'm damned if I know, but we never even heard the stuff come down. And not a man scratched!! It only lasted about three quarters of an hour, but it was some show while it lasted. Results – slight property damage and a few casualties ashore: and in the ships, nothing at all. But of course Rome Radio has since put that right by announcing heavy loss of life and damage to property and three ships sunk in the fairway!!! Well, we are living at last. Bizerta and a Hun of our own: and now we have shared in a real Malta raid.

27th July 1943.

Our second Malta raid. Started just before 3.00am and we didn't get the "all clear" till 5.00am. It was pretty hot and heavy for the first hour, but very spasmodic after 4.00am. And we came in for the usual plastering of shell splinters and shrapnel – still with our usual luck – not a single casualty! How it happens I'm damned if I know: shrapnel and chunks of shell all over the bridge and the decks afterwards and still not a man scratched. I probably got the nearest to it this time. I was on the bridge with the signalman getting the aiming instructions broadcast from the "Indomitable" and passing them on to the oerlikon gunners. We could hear the stuff clattering down all round us at intervals but of course couldn't see it. I heard one nice heavy piece land somewhere close and ricochet into the wheelhouse – I was in the wheelhouse doorway: and after the show was over and I came down below again I discovered that the same chunk of shell had torn up a splinter of teak deck-plank and pinned it through the seat of my trousers – a neat splinter of teak about 3 inches long. Either I was too damned busy or my pants are too damned baggy, for I didn't know the darned thing was there: it was pinned through very nicely, yet I never felt it and it hadn't even scratched me. Just as well – a wound in the backside might be so awkward to account for satisfactorily.

As usual the barrage was hellish. I haven't the faintest idea whether any bombs were dropped near us or not. The noise of our own was so great and their flashes blinding us so much that we could neither have heard nor seen any bomb explosions. And we didn't get a hun to aim at ourselves: all the ammunition we expended was used in shooting out the hun flares. He was certainly after the entrance-boom, for we are only just inside the boom – first ship in – and his flares were dropping all round us.

Incidentally, I'm inclined to believe that at times my voice carries better than I sometimes think it does. Westlake was standing by on the lower deck with his fire-fighting squad: he told me afterward that he heard me above the noise of the barrage shouting at the oerlikon gunners "Shoot those – flares down! Aim for the parachutes". Have since heard that two of the swine were accounted for – one in the entrance to Sliema Creek, just on the other side of the Point from us, so he wasn't so many hundred yards from us when they got him. Damage as usual practically negligible, nothing at all in the harbour. The swine appears to be finding Malta expensive at last. And close to Smith's (our Agents') office seven unexploded dud bombs were picked up and carted away in the morning. Smells like a spot of sabotage on the other side to me.

And Pot-belly, the Ice-cream King has gone at last!!! Wonder what happens next and how long it will be before somebody decides to assassinate him? Little Big Bad Wulf Hitler's turn next

I hope. And assassination might be the best solution for them all in the end. It would at least make sure of the lousy tykes before our People could change their minds about hanging them.

29th July 1943:

Another attempted raid – very much merely "attempted". Warning went at 10.40pm, barrage started immediately after but didn't last more than five minutes and the "all clear" sounded soon after 11.30pm. Quiet night, no wind and a heavy smoke-screen. Don't like the Malta smoke-screen. It is certainly effective, but I'd almost rather have the planes. Just a dense black fog that blots out everything at two or three yards and makes you wonder who your lungs really belong to. The only possible way to breathe is through a wet handkerchief. And if you do get a whiff or two it keeps you coughing and choking for hours afterward. At least it does me.

31st July 1943:

Orders again at last. Have completely de-stored, and now we're to go back to Gibraltar for convoy home. Thank God. None of us is at all sorry. Personally I'd like six months holiday – there are times when I find myself feeling very, very tired. But holidays that aren't given without asking can't be asked for in war-time – at least, not in this kind of war. And I don't know whether I want to come back on this kind of a job or not. There's as much to be said against as for it, from my own point of view. Its not a young man's job: a man 15 years older than I could do it just as well and fret about it much less. I hate rotting in port for months on end when I ought to be taking a ship to sea. And at times I get so infernally sick of having to live in the same ship as young squirts whose only watch-words are "status" and "dignity": especially knowing that that is the penalty for the privilege of operating a damned combined "Woolworth and Sainsbury". I don't suppose I shall ask to come out unless the Owners choose to take me out. They put me here and even when I am most fed up I certainly don't intend squealing. But oftener and oftener I'd give my soul to be out of this and back in a ship that goes to sea.

Sunday 1st August 1943:

Shifted out to the anchorage at 3.30pm. Left at 7.00pm for Gibraltar, in company with five ships for Bizerta and also a crowd of ships from the anchorage who were going to sea for the night to return to the anchorage next morning. Hitler's gang from the other side of what was once "Bomb alley" are getting so windy now about the stuff that Malta is pushing across to Sicily that they are trying lately to concentrate on Malta anchorage at night in the hope of getting rid of ships and supplies in the anchorage before they can start across. So the ships leave the anchorage and go to sea at night, to return at daybreak. Spent the night steaming through the swept channel. Doubled on our track at 1.00am and steamed back toward Malta. At 6.00am, south of Marsa Scirocco Light, the Bizerta ships and I left the others and doubled back to seaward and I took over as Commodore to rendez-vous at 10.15am with main convoy from Alexandria to Gibraltar. There was a bit of fun going on over the south end of Malta Island at 1.00am, gunfire and a few bombs, so the hun had evidently been to the anchorage and found the birds flown. No activity over the convoy. Met the main Gibraltar convoy nicely on time. Commodore (naval) in one of Brocklebank's ships – "Marwarri". Got planted in as No.71 – starboard wing column leader. Always seem to get a leading job somewhere – much better than being parked down the column.

3rd August 1943:

Convoy into three columns at 8.30am approaching North African Swept Channel. Previously, at 1.00am about 30 miles south of Pantellaria, heard a fair amount of gunfire from the island. The hun is evidently going frantic to hold up the Sicilian show as long as possible. No activity over the convoy. Passed Cape Bon just before noon. Soon afterward Commodore shifted me over from starboard side to lead port wing column and run my paravanes, so he is evidently suspicious of mines. The Medi looks almost pre-war again, except that the crowds of ships we have passed all day have been all British supply convoys, stiff with troops and supplies. Scores of ships all on the way to give the hun more headaches. As for the other bloke, we haven't seen a sign of him at sea since we left Gibraltar. And this is Micky Mussolini's "Mare Nostrum". Ha! Ha!! Ha!!!

4th August 1943:

Ran paravanes all day yesterday and through the night until 6.00am, sweeping ahead of port wing column. Hoisted them in at 6.00am, convoy back in normal formation: we are leading starboard wing column again. Six more ships joined up from Bone.

6th August 1943:

At 7.00pm anchored in Oran Bay with remainder of convoy to await further routeing instructions; one unexpected night's sleep

7th August1943:

7.00am. Left Oran for Gibraltar with American convoy under U.S. Commodore. 58 ships and how in hell any of us ever got anywhere intact I still don't know. Harry Tate could have learnt much from this bunch. No proper organisation, not the faintest semblance of convoy procedure. "By guess and by God and by damned good luck". Never in the history of human endeavour did more people know less about nothing at all. A thorough rag-time outfit! A permanent 24-hours-a-day worry so long as we were in it, and a glorious relief to push into Gibraltar and leave the crowd to work out its own damnation.

Anchored in Gibraltar Bay 2.50pm Sunday 8th August 1943 and at 4.30pm shifted into inner harbour and moored at Detached Mole.

Awaiting convoy home.

Saturday 14th August 1943:

3.00pm. Left berth at Gibraltar Mole and proceeded direct to sea with UK convoy ($7\frac{1}{2}$ knots). Commodore (Vice-Admiral Goldsmith) in "Marwarri", for Glasgow. Our orders Liverpool. H.M. Destroyer "Highlander" in charge of fairly heavy escort, destroyers and corvettes.

Quiet passage, moderate weather; uneventful so far as the convoy itself was concerned though there was one incident quite interesting to watch, which fortunately turned out better than it might have done. We had air-cover all the way from Gibraltar Strait, sometimes two Liberators, sometimes only one, but always one anyhow. They worked in reliefs, each relief remaining with the convoy submarine-hunting for about 4 hours being then relieved by another one or two Liberators. Caused many a stand-by for air attack, of course, as we all stood by to give everyone that appeared a bellyache until he was satisfactorily identified. Got quite used to turning out half a dozen times a day to train the guns on a machine that eventually proved to be a Liberator.

Anyway, at about 5.30pm on the afternoon after we passed Lisbon, when we had one Liberator (L) with us, two other heavy bombers suddenly appeared on the horizon to starboard. We didn't have long to wait that time. In a very few minutes the commodore hoisted the signal "Aircraft bearing 136 degrees are hostile". The two of them – F.W. Kondors – passed up the starboard side of the convoy fairly low but a long way off – hun airmen aren't too keen on closing a convoy nowadays: they prefer to sort out a good angle for attack and then drop their eggs from as great a height as possible, as they have no love for our anti-aircraft armament now. They circled round ahead of us about four miles away, obviously sorting out a good position for attack, when our Liberator (in touch with the commodore by R.T. of course) suddenly appeared and pitched into the pair of them. It was some little dog-fight: a very unusual sight, as a fight between heavy bombers is not a common occurrence. I think the huns got a surprise at first, as the Liberator was plastering both of them with his guns before they appeared to realise he was there. After a few minutes of heavy scrapping – we could hear the roar of their guns and see the tracers passing among them four or five miles away – one Kondor broke away and seemed contented to leave the rest to his mate. The Liberator then turned and gave the second Kondor all his attention. They were scrapping fairly close down to the water when the Kondor suddenly exploded and crashed into the sea. The Liberator turned and attempted to make for the other Kondor but before he'd gone very far he suddenly jettisoned his bombs and a few seconds afterwards went into the drink himself.

Our senior escort, the "Highlander", tore off to where the Liberator had crashed and the original Kondor made a half-hearted attempt to go and make sure of what had happened to his mate, but the "Highlander" immediately swung round towards him and planted four bursts of heavy anti-aircraft shell very close to him and he decided to call it a day and go home. I rather think he was very badly damaged too for he was "hedge-hopping" badly and obviously couldn't rise: he wasn't very far above the water when we lost sight of him. I think the whole convoy was disappointed that he didn't find enough guts at the last to make one final attempt at us: we were all out for blood after the Liberator crashed and if that hun had only got within range there's no doubt of the result. Every damn gun in the convoy would have made mince-meat of him in one grand burst.

The "Highlander" circled the spot where the Liberator had flopped and a few minutes after came tearing back and flashed the Commodore "Entire crew of Liberator, "L" for love, recovered". Very satisfactory, only our plane lost, all its crew saved; one bedraggled Kondor flopping off home with a darned good chance of not getting there, and the other and its crew a heap of cinders. The spot where it crashed was marked by a dense cloud of black smoke for half an hour afterward. The probability that the other fellow never got home and couldn't communicate by wireless is very much increased by the fact that there was no subsequent attack of any kind on the convoy. If he had got back or communicated, it's an absolute certainty that there would have been an attack, certainly by submarine and probably by aircraft as well, within the following 24 hours. We all more or less expected it all that night and all next day, but nothing happened.

On the morning of 24th August the Commodore called me up and sent "Commodore to Master: your station keeping has been exceptionally good".

At 7.00am 25th August Commodore went off with the Loch Ewe ships, leaving the rest of us with H.M.S. "Seapool" as Commodore. Before he left us I signalled him, "Master to Commodore: Many thanks for safe passage and for signal re station-keeping. We have been glad to do what we could to assist generally. We wish you the very best of luck with all your convoys".

At 7.00pm 25th August the "Seapool" hoisted the general signal, "Disperse and proceed to your destinations". Off Rathlin Island at the time. I opened out to full speed hoping to make the morning tide for Liverpool. We arrived at the Bar Light, first of all the Liverpool ships, at noon 26th August, but missed the tide by two hours. Anchored in the river and docked at Queen's Dock, Liverpool at 9.31am 26th August 1943.

Voyage Ended."

And a colourful voyage it had been by anyone's standards.

A word about Sandhurst Road School is called for, in view of Dad's reactions. I think I am right in saying that both he and Mum had attended there in their early school years, and in any case he had lived in Ardgowan Road (in which the school stands) in the house in which his parents still lived. Grandpa was in the street during the notorious raid when the school was bombed and the children machine-gunned. Strange how fast bad news could travel, even in wartime; I read about it in a news magazine in the Officers' Club in Alexandria within a month or two of the event and Dad clearly knew about it at much the same time.

As a matter of interest, all three of my children started their education at the very same school which has been rebuilt and considerably extended since those days.

On his return home and after a hectic spell of leave, Dad wrote me the following letter which I include to indicate the vital importance of leave in the retention of one's sanity after too long away under too great a pressure; you can feel the lifting of tension as the magic of home life took effect:

"My Dear Bernard,

I don't know that I've anything in particular to write about, but your mother is writing and Dorothy is tying knots round two needles with a bit of wool – a sock, night-cap or jumper, I'm not sure which (and neither is she) – and I'm sitting here wondering if it will be tea-time before tomorrow's breakfast-time, so I might as well write. I may have to shove off at any time now – as a matter of fact I'm waiting for a phone call now. I'm not going back to the Old Wagon after all: Captain Chapman has already taken her over from me. At present its not certain whether I'm going away for keeps very shortly or remaining ashore for a while to do some relieving. I'm going down to relieve Captain Mitchell at any time now and if he wants to stay ashore and take all his back-leave I shall take the ship away. I've had over three weeks at home now, much shopping, much washing-up, and much visiting. We've been to Brixham, Otford, Deptford, Catford (often), West Wickham (twice), Farnborough, Cudham, Downe and Verdant Lane (two visits to 226 and several to Northover Abbey). We've also seen one or two shows and eaten several dinners in London with incidental calls at Mr Hennekey's baronial hall – Dorothy loves getting merry on gin-and-lime in working hours. Your mother prefers vintage port, either free at Mr Taylor's or two-and-a-tanner a time at the ancestral home of the Northover family. I have to drink common or garden beer at tenpence. On one occasion I took your mother and Dorothy to dinner at the "Curb" and then mistakenly introduced your ma to the Merchant Navy Club for afternoon tea. She saw the evening dinner menu and promptly decided that I wasn't in a hurry to get home. Result- two dinners in one day and a permanent shock to my constitution to say nothing of my pants-pocket. I doubt if I shall see you this time and anyway you won't be back in time for your birthday, so many happy returns of the 28th. Packing up now, take care of yourself, keep grinning and all the best. Cheerio from Dad."

Whereas the letter was dated 26th September there is a stamp on the back "Ellerman Lines Ships Mails Dept. 12th November 1943"!!! What a nightmare mails were for all involved. I think I finally received my letter on my return to London though it may have caught me up in Gibraltar, but in any case after the historic date of 8th November, of which more later.

CHAPTER SEVEN
BAPTISM BY FIRE

In view of the importance of the "City of Keelung" in our lives I think its time to introduce her in greater detail.

She was one of the series of average sized five hold ships that plied the seas at that time; they ranged upwards from somewhere over 4,000 tons nett registered tonnage, 7,000 tons-plus gross. This sizing has nothing to do with weight or, if you prefer, displacement tonnage.

Tonnage was important for assessment of port or harbour dues and those were based on the earning capacity of a ship. It makes a sort of sense that the cargo spaces were measured and the cubic capacity expressed in tons at 100 cubic feet per ton, a generous average space to contain one ton of cargo; this measurement gave the nett tonnage. The average five hold ship should have been able to carry a minimum of 4,000 tons of cargo when full.

This gives no indication of the full size of the ship when taking the superstructure into account and when considering the size of accommodation, deck storage, bridge and engine room spaces etc., the more sumptuously appointed, the higher the gross tonnage, the figure normally referred to as the ship's overall tonnage.

This all comes about because of the impracticability of passing ships over weigh-bridges!!

The "City of Keelung" was instantly recognisable by virtue of being a well-deck ship. That is to say that No.1 hatch was situated abaft the break of the fo'cs'l head and because the hold consisted of two decks only- the lower hold and the 'tween deck-it extended in a "well" to the forward end of No.2 which had a third deck (the upper 'tween or shelter deck) and was reached by steps from No.1 The same applied aft where No.5 was between a break at No.4 and the raised poop deck accommodation and storage block.

The unbroken deck from the forward end of No.2 to the after end of No.4 carried the bulk of the superstructure with the foremast and No.2 hold winches right forward before No.2 hatch coamings (the vertical box forming the hatchway); No.2 was the largest cargo space, the hatch opening reaching little over half the length of the three decks previously referred to, the shelter deck extending underneath the saloon/bridge housing to the forward bulkhead of No.3, the smallest hold which sat between the saloon housing and the engineers' block.

During the war No.3 was used exclusively as a bunker hold, all three decks being completely filled with coal before the ship could start a voyage of any length. At the after end of the hatch a vertical ladder led down to the stoke-hold which was fed directly from No.3 with some 20 tons of the best Welsh nuts every day at sea to feed ever hungry boilers. A somewhat smaller quantity was consumed in port, but steam was still required to keep never silent winches chattering and to fulfil domestic needs.

Abaft No.3 hatch was the galley standing in front of the funnel; the Engineers' accommodation stretched aft on either side underneath the boat deck which carried a single cabin forward (this ultimately became a Cadets' cabin) and a small accommodation block aft for the Goanese catering staff. The centre of the boat deck was occupied by the engine room skylight separating the two central lifeboats and the Oerlikon gun-pits.

At the after end of the Engineers' block on the port corner was the domestic fresh water tank which was kept under lock and key and was made available to the crew twice a day only , this rationing being essential to keep the ship independent of the shore as long as possible.

Next came No.4 hatch with the Gunners' accommodation cut into the shelter deck on the port side and with the mainmast at the after end together with those inescapable winches.

I cannot place the mast exactly; it had to be between No.s 4 and 5 holds in order to support the steel lattice derricks, two per hold, but whether it came before or after the break into the well deck I can't say.

What I can say is that at the after end of the well deck were insulated store-rooms which were loaded at the last minute in the home port with vast ingots of ice delivered by a "North Pole Ice Co." van. Frozen meat followed and this stock lasted for about six weeks whereafter ritual slaughter, by our Mohammedan crew, of the sheep that were housed on the poop, started. We carried chickens as well which served the dual purpose of egg-layers and Sunday lunch.

The native crew (approximately forty men, twenty deck-men and twenty engine room) had its own galley right aft reached by a vertical iron ladder down to the bowels of the ship while overhead were the last two of our six lifeboats at the for'd end of the poop deck.

Right aft was the four inch anti-submarine gun, which, with the Oerlikons on the boat deck and the machine guns on the bridge and, if I remember rightly, a Bofors or 12-pounder situated forward, completed our armament.

In port, catwalks situated at the forward and after ends of the central deck were raised vertically to be lowered on completion of cargo work to connect No.2 to the fo'c's'l head and No.4 to the poop giving the option to avoid use of the well decks, a useful adjunct in rough weather at sea.

The saloon housing consisted of the dining saloon itself, forward central at main deck level with, on the starboard side, the Chief Officer's cabin in front of the 2nd Sparks' and Chief Steward's cabins which were across the alleyway from the centrally situated pantry-cum-serving point. Abaft the pantry was the Chief Sparks' cabin.

On the port side were the 2nd and 3rd Officers' with what was previously a dirty linen store room. On the after end Chippy, the Carpenter, was housed.

Beside the pantry a stairway led up to the Master's cabin on the next deck; this led directly into the Chart Room which was also reached by a ladder on the starboard side down one deck from the Bridge.

The Old Man's cabin with chart room and wireless room attached occupied what was known as the Captain's or Lower Bridge, an area out of bounds to all except the Master and those who had business in the forward lifeboats on either side.

The Bridge proper consisted of an enclosed wheelhouse also equipped with engine room telegraph, voice pipes to master's cabin and engine room (operated by blowing to activate a whistle at the other end, it worked both ways) and surprisingly (to me) a pigeon-holed cabinet of International Code flags. Outside the wheelhouse was a walkway to either wing where Hotchkiss machine guns were emplaced.

A vertical ladder on the side of the wheelhouse gave access to Monkey Island (in effect the wheelhouse roof) which housed the Standard Compass in free space so as to reduce variable magnetic effects of any extraneous materials around. This was where the ship's compass error was checked every watch, mainly by celestial observation and the ship's magnetic course was applied to this compass. Constant comparison had to be made between this and the helmsman's compass on the bridge so that when all the necessary amendments were made, the man at the wheel could steer so as to achieve the required true course shown on the chart!

At various positions near the wheelhouse doors, halliards from the triatic stay overhead and from the yardarms were made fast, these fixtures and fittings being amongst those things, some at least of which had to be removed in port to give clear access to the hatchways.

Towards the end of 1942 it had become clear to the concerned that it was advantageous to have a cadet on duty throughout the 24 hours and it followed that ships carrying one cadet required to be adapted to the accommodation and carriage of, for preference, three.

When I was awaiting the call in October of that year several options suddenly became open to me.

I was invited to choose between three ships, the "City"s of "..Hong Kong", "..Bedford" and "..Pretoria" with a strong recommendation to take the last named of them. While waiting an approximate period of six weeks for the "..Pretoria", the dirty linen store on the "..Keelung" was converted to a two-berth cabin for cadets and I was duly informed that I could join her in only a couple of weeks. No contest! I accepted with alacrity.

A brilliant choice, of course, as, for the record, the "..Hong Kong" was in collision with loss of life, the "..Bedford" struck a mine, also with loss of life and in due course, the "..Pretoria", returning from the US with a cargo of munitions was lost with all hands off the south coast of Ireland having been torpedoed or mined, I'm not sure which.

On such arbitrary trifles did survival depend.

Late in the evening of Sunday, 25th October, three days before my sixteenth birthday, a lad named Veale and I met at Kings Cross station and travelled together by sleeper train to Glasgow where we reported on board the "..Keelung" early the next morning.

From there I wrote home every day and I might as well quote the first letter verbatim:

"Dear Mum,
We arrived at about 8 o'clock this morning after a fair amount of sleep on the train. We had a bit of bother finding the ship which is in the Southern Basin.

Then after a jolly good breakfast we went with Captain L.E. Smith to the Ellerman Lines here and then to some office or other where we signed on. All the time he chatted to us and we like him very much. That goes for all the other officers and the ship as well. She is smaller than more original impression of her led me to believe. I'm temporarily in Sparks' cabin next to the mate's but will share a cabin with Veale when arrangements have been made for the Senior Apprentice, David Sapp to move out. Sapp is a jolly nice chap too and altogether I'm enjoying life.

This afternoon (after a jolly good dinner) I did a bit of work for Captain Smith, just looking at some books and calling out necessary particulars which he requested and then looking for blokes and getting a few more particulars. The whole business only took about half an hour and we've had the rest of the afternoon off, roaming about the old bus. This evening we walked out and watched them manoeuvring wacking great girders (ssh) into the holds.

During the course of conversation with Capt. Smith I learnt that in all probability we will not call at Freetown.

That's about all for now, Love to all, etc.

PS We'll probably be shoving off on Friday."

The signing on referred to was done at the shipping office, the dotted line being on the ship's Articles, a document committing us to serve on the ship for up to two years or the voyage end, whichever was the sooner.

The "roaming about the old bus" included climbing the foremast, a feat for which we were reprimanded later – well, how were we to know it wasn't the thing done?

On completion of loading, which had been continuous since our arrival, we started our epic voyage on Thursday, 29th October.

Fifty-nine years later my most vivid recollections are firstly the raucous song of riveting hammers that seemed to be sustained day and night all along the Clyde which memory paints as one vast shipyard. Whether building or repairing I have no idea now, but I can still hear them.

We stopped and waited at anchor in the Gare Loch for compass adjustment and probably convoy, although we may have proceeded independently to Loch Ewe to await formation of the ocean convoy. By contrast to the hum and bustle of the Clyde, the Gare Loch returns to me in its majestic midnight silence with a black velvet background emphasising the brilliance of thousands of stars arranged in the well ordered constellations of the northern hemisphere.

Having drawn the short straw and been placed with the 2nd

mate on 12 to 4 watch, I immediately started to reap the benefits which go with the quietest of the watches. That very first night watch I was introduced to stars whose names and positions in the sky I have never forgotten.

Loch Ewe was every bit as awe-inspiring, a northern wilderness of sheep-spotted low green hillsides surrounding an extensive bay where ships were slowly accumulating. In temperatures close to freezing we could marvel at the clear view of the mountains of Harris with their tops already snow-covered. Who could blame us for wishing ourselves away southward to the sun in spite of the glory of this cold northern panorama?

Our cargo destinations were Durban, Aden, Port Sudan, Suez and Port Said, but first we had to plod in an 8½ knot convoy north around Ireland and a substantial distance across the Atlantic in company with America-bound ships, awaiting the day when we would be ordered to break away.

Before this came two very significant events occurred; firstly we encountered a succession of severe gales which confirmed me in the rightness of my choice of careers.

I was able to sneak unseen onto the holy of holies, the Captain's Bridge, and from there drink in the sights and blend into the wild movement of the ship as she struck or was struck by mountains of water which broke apart over the bows and thundered down on the decks while throwing spray over the masthead. The ship shuddered, flung herself down, leaped up, rolling and lurching the while yet always somehow retaining sufficient control of herself to keep moving forward into the teeth of the gale. It was then that I became vividly aware of the enormity of the power of the naked elements and I found a brand new God to worship, a God far removed from the one made in Man's image that we worship in church.

I think this weather was responsible for loosening the incipient epilepsy in Veale, for while I was on watch he was found unconscious in our cabin, but the suspicion as to cause was not confirmed until months later when he was attacked again in a moment of excitement. This time there was no room for doubt and he was repatriated for treatment at home leaving David Sapp and myself to share an unrelieved period of eight months during which we worked effectively twelve hours a day every day and with additional action stations thrown in whether on or off watch.

When the day of dismissal arrived we did a sharp left turn and sped rapidly into higher and higher temperatures. This was all very well but for the unbelievable fact that neither the company in its dress instructions nor my mother with all her experience of Dad's requirements, had thought to equip me with a solitary pair of shorts. Eventually the 2nd mate took pity on me and gave me a pair of his, but by this time it was so late that while working in full exposure to the sun in the lifeboats, the skin on my legs, hitherto protected by trousers, succeeded in frying under the Vaseline that I had thought to improve matters with. Well, we live and learn.

The southern journey took us through enchanted waters which flashed will-o-the wisp phosphorescence at night and opened up in the day time to spit out shoals (or is it flights?) of flying fish with, from time to time, dolphins leaping in separate groups all the way to the horizon.

The sea frothed and bubbled with life more prolific than I have seen it since. Or was this merely the intensity of impression on a young boy's mind when introduced to the wonders of the deep for the very first time?

Somewhere about the equator the Old Man and the Chief Engineer could be seen in earnest conversation, becoming more and more concerned until the inevitable was accepted and wireless silence was broken. The simple fact was that our diversionary route combined with the strain on coal consumption in all that bad weather had left us with insufficient fuel to get us to Durban.

Such exotic names as Pernambuco were bandied about in whispers, necessarily as this was such an unconventional not to mention risky procedure that we felt that if we spoke too loudly the enemy might hear and take advantage of our predicament.

After an exchange of coded messages we finally learnt that arrangements were to be made for us to call in and bunker at Rio.

My boyhood's cup ran over copiously. Rio de Janeiro was one of those intoxicating places that I had read about and dreamt of and the thought of smallpox or yellow fever simply didn't cross my mind, it was enough to be on our way there.

It all became reality when we made landfall one morning and were greeted by land birds – hawks from the looks of them – and small sailing fishermen. We closed the approach in the afternoon seeing on our port bow the incomparable Sugar Loaf Mountain guarding the entrance to our totally unintentional destination.

We were piloted in to an anchorage in sight of the sea-level airfield surrounded by a huge ring of mountains including Mount Corcovado with the celebrated statue of Christ at its summit.

It didn't take long for the bum-boats to find us to barter bananas for cigarettes. Bananas! I ask you! We hadn't seen one for several years and now in a matter of a few hours I was to scoff thirty and all without ill-effect.

The most shattering effect came that night as the sun set and the whole of the city became a blaze of light. It took our breath away after three years of black-out, to be illuminated in such a profligate manner as though a raging world war was not known about.

A never to be forgotten bonus, my very first foreign port.

We bunkered next day from lighters, keeping a low profile and leaving the port discreetly on completion, thereafter to plough the South Atlantic until the approach to the Cape.

In the days before landfall the wind increased and the white horses ran across a greyish base under scudding overcast and in these conditions came the permanently haunting presence of the albatross. This bird appeared on the horizon astern as a small speck, growing initially very slowly and then faster and faster until it passed overhead, all the time gliding motionless and silent as though drawn on an invisible wire.

In spite of the paradoxically motionless movement, the albatross was very much a sensate, living creature, majestic and, to me, awe-inspiring. The sight was yet one more of those events so early in my seafaring that will never leave me.

Finally the day arrived when we approached our first official port of call, our first discharging port. The Bluff is a finger of land on Durban's southern flank and was in those times both a penal colony and a bunkering station combined; of course, our first need was for coal and we duly went alongside.

Next day heavy planks were stretched over the ship's side amidships to enable convicts to run aboard laden with baskets of coal and down again in a continuous circulation; they had an additional burden to carry, the chains and shackles around their ankles. Unpleasant though they were they appear to have been effective.

On completion of bunkering we shifted ship to a discharge berth within the dock complex. From there we could walk via Point Road into town and as events which followed were to have such unforeseen consequences, a contemporary letter home will set the scene adequately enough.

The letter was undated presumably because, due to events described, we were shifted out and shore leave was stopped; the letter was then written in a hurry to catch a fast ship home but must have gone on or about New Years Day:

"Dear Mum,

I have written to you once from here, Durban, and I sent it airmail but I doubt if it will go airmail. We've got a chance to send letters by a fast method this time, so I'll take the opportunity.

I have spent a lot of money here, but I don't regret it. We got alongside and ashore on the first night and I got an idea of the lay-out of the place. The town itself is not very big but it is beautiful and it is clean. When all things are considered there's not much to do here except go to the pictures and there is a good chance of that. There's not even much opportunity to go out on the booze because they shut before we can get ashore, nevertheless the gunners managed it all right and there has been some trouble.

I took the opportunity to see "Mrs Miniver" on the second night ashore and I really enjoyed myself. The third night I had to stay on board, so I got the afternoon of the next day ashore and did some shopping. It was then that I got an invitation for a Christmas dinner. I made enquiries and found I was able to get ashore on Christmas Day. I accepted the invitation and after having a bit of fun with Chippy on Christmas morning I got ashore and took the bus to Durban North.

I arrived about 12 o'clock and after getting used to the people in whose midst I now found myself I began to enjoy myself. Mr and Mrs Wilson have four daughters, two older and two younger than myself. They had a few relations in before a very late but very enjoyable dinner. When we got up from the table we felt we couldn't eat another mouthful. There was an army fellow from Manchester who had taken part in the Madagascar operation there too.

I cannot speak too highly of their hospitality. Mrs Wilson had seen me in a Forces' Canteen where she is a voluntary helper and she had, after speaking to me, asked me to her house. There I, an utter stranger except for about ten minutes conversation in the Victoria League and a telephone conversation, was treated like a relative or near friend, having the best of everything and being treated as one of them. Mr and Mrs and Grandma seemed to take to me right away and I to them. They are as Mrs Wilson said, "living in the lap of luxury and anything we can do to help we will do willingly".

The afternoon came and went in a flash and no-one could eat any tea. The evening was spent like this: first of all the girls, Jack the soldier, Squibs the dog and myself went for a walk. Then we came back, the girls wanted to go to the pictures but had left it too late, so they asked Jack what he usually did on Christmas

Day. He told them he always went to a football match in the afternoon, come what may. They asked me what I did and I told them as best I could. I then introduced them to some of our Christmas games; they had never heard of "Murder" or "Earth, air or water" or anything like that. They played a couple of South African games like "My mother had a rooster" (I presume it's South African) and then we finished up the evening screaming ourselves hoarse with "Earth, air or water". Jack and I had to catch a bus back then and it was with great reluctance that we left them. I felt that my miserable box of chocolates had in no way repaid them for their hospitality and I only had time for a few muttered words of thanks at the door. So I rang up from the Post Office and spoke to Mrs Wilson. She sounded very grateful for the call and I hope it helped to repay what I owe them. The next time I set foot in Durban I will immediately ring them up and see how they are getting on.

When I got aboard there was trouble waiting. Two gunners, one of whom had spent a night in jail two days previously, and the other of whom came aboard drunk on my duty night and tried to chuck me overboard, had come aboard with naval pickets. They had been chucked out of the pictures where they had drunk a bottle of brandy between them and this was their method of returning to the ship. That was mild compared with the rest of their behaviour. The gunners had put them to bed but they got loose again, one running around naked. They kicked up hell. One of them managed to fall overboard. Thanks to the 2nd mate who immediately dived in after him, he wasn't drowned. In fact he came aboard again much the same as he had left. Mayler, a young gunner who had left the pair of them in the pictures to get drunk had appeared with two mugs. Hawke, the one that had been jailed and who fell overboard, caught sight of him and feeling some grudge against him, gave him a mighty swipe. One of the mugs was driven right into his jaw and it is lucky that it didn't cut his throat. He was rushed to hospital ship where he had four stitches without anaesthetic. His dickey was saturated with blood and he is probably disfigured for life. The china cut

134

well into his gums and it's a wonder his teeth weren't damaged.

When I got on board the fun was over; the drunks were in bed but Mayler was terrified of going below to turn in, in the same room. He was babbling like a lunatic and kept on saying, "What have I done to deserve this?" I'm sure it didn't do his jaw any good. The drunks were taken ashore separately in the morning and they'll be on Foreign Service draft or something. God help them now if they try to get drunk. They probably won't see home again for a long time. Mayler went ashore too, he won't be fit for sea service for a long time yet. Blimey! We do have fun, don't we?

Well I'd better end here and wish you again a happy new year. I hope you got my cable and I have written to Auntie Jessie.

Give everybody at home my love and don't worry about me, I'm enjoying life. I don't think I could have had a happier Christmas at home than I had out here. We'll soon be on our way, so until the next letter, goodbye and love to all.

From your loving son,

Bernard"

I didn't see Durban again until shortly after the end of the war and at that time something inhibited me from attempting to make contact again with the Wilsons; I can't explain it, but it still worries me from time to time, even today.

At this stage of the war the waters between Madagascar and the African coast were deemed to be sufficiently dangerous to warrant travel by convoy. We were appointed commodore ship of a small group of ships destined for Aden. This convoy included the first American merchantman that we had encountered and this chap's inexperience showed in a trigger-happy response to the imagined sighting of some threatening object in the water. The first shots that we had yet seen fired in anger!

We spent a sufficient period in Aden to become reasonably accustomed to the place; the children who greeted us with outstretched hands the moment we stepped off the gangway; the ever present goats snuffing through whatever rubbish hinted at something edible within; the little shops offering cigarette lighters, trinkets, fezzes or similar embroidered white hats; the cinema completely open to the heavens inviting the odd glance at genuine stars while the film was running. The overall impression was pleasurable and the entertainment of a somewhat higher calibre than we found in Port Sudan.

There the first thing to impress was the high development of the dock facilities and then when the stevedoring gangs boarded, the incredible pompadour style hair-dos affected by the men, complete with long spear-like wooden hair pins that they manipulated to shift whatever live-stock may have been moving about in all that fuzz. It was initially very difficult to approach closely by reason of the pungent, sour, stale smell of their clothing or bodies or preparations that they used on themselves. Whatever the cause, the effect was literally breath-taking and there was no pleasure in working in an enclosed, airless tween deck in the high temperatures prevailing when in close proximity with these gentry.

Ashore there was little or nothing for the European except to mingle and observe. I still remember the small but growing crowd attracted by a story-teller or sooth-sayer (shades of Hyde Park Corner), for, not knowing the language allowed the imagination to fly away, he might very well have been advertising a patent medicine or such-like.

The harbour waters were clear and there were known to be three very large but unidentified fish that were the target of every fisherman for miles around. Despite biting occasionally they had evaded capture for a very long time. I suppose they died of old age in the end.

Our next stop was Port Tewfik (Suez) where I fell in for the first time with one Bernard Davies, Chief Sparks of the "Tarantia", one of several ships with which we had frequent contact over the next few months. We coincided again in Port Said where we completed discharge of the last of our outward cargo.

We arrived in Port Said in February 1943 nearly four months after the El Alamein barrage and the routing of the Afrika Korps.

It was then that Veale came across his brother unexpectedly and in preparing to go ashore to meet him for a meal he suffered a second seizure. With qualified medical help available his condition was confirmed and he was obliged to leave to seek proper treatment at home.

Now we were reduced to two cadets it was decided that I should share David's boat deck cabin as the one that Veale and I had lived in had long since been found to harbour bugs, a legacy of the dirty linen store days.

Let me refresh the memory of those times to set the background for what follows:

The system (?) that obtained prior to Alamein was a push-me pull-you style warfare where our armies pressed westward from Egypt across the Libyan desert while Rommel's forces pressed eastward from Tunisia and Tripolitania, one side gaining an advantage, forcing the other back and in so doing shortening the losing side's supply lines while increasing the victor's. After a while the losers developed reinforcement fast enough to be able to snatch the initiative and start advancing in the opposite direction. Eventually Rommel pushed our forces some eighty miles into Egypt at which time Montgomery was appointed. Benefiting from the unfortunate experience of his predecessors he refused to move until he knew his superiority to be overwhelming and in three days of bombardment he all but destroyed Rommel's Afrika Korps.

What followed was a complete rout, initially a mopping-up operation and wild chase combined, but it was essential to keep the initiative to prevent the enemy from making a stand.

This demanded permanent air superiority which in turn required inexhaustible stocks of high octane as close to the front line as it was possible to establish.

By the time of our arrival on the scene the old bogey of over-long supply routes was raising its head again and the Sea

Transport Offices in Port Said and Alexandria were tearing their hair out as they searched in vain for tankers to carry their supplies of aviation fuel.

The solution was to ship the precious liquid in ordinary ships in extraordinary containers. Forty gallon oil drums materialised from somewhere in every condition and degree imaginable, the bulk having arrived at the umpteenth time of re-use. There was a limit to the number of such drums to be found and they were supplemented by ten gallon drums, five gallon drums, two gallon cans, billy cans and any and every suspect container in creation including what looked like biscuit tins and probably were just that.

It stands to reason that such motley packaging must include a few with leaks (??) It is also obvious that none could be loaded to an ordinary vessel without considerable precaution and preparation.

Thus it was that the Sea Transport Office singled out each and every cargo ship that employed a steam-smothering system for fire-fighting. The proven theory was that when hatches are battened down and the holds flooded with steam under high pressure, the steam spreads rapidly forcing the air out through the ventilators and smothering the cargo with a fine oxygen-free mist.

All that was necessary was to insert a valve through the main deck to connect with the steam line, to feed steam into the hold and draw it out through this new ejector valve, drawing with it any petrol vapour free in the air in the hold. If this operation was undertaken at regular intervals (a quarter of an hour every four hours) the theorists considered that the ship would be safe enough provided that no-one wore shoes with blakeys or hobnails or dropped lighted matches around carelessly or smoked in the wrong places.

Guess what the "..Keelung"'s fire-fighting system was, and indeed that of the "Tarantia" and the "Ocean Voyager".

Loading was farcical because it was operated in such deadly seriousness; the drums were placed on trays on the quay where a soldier with chalk in his hand inspected every one, marking any that was noted to be leaking and removing it if possible before it came on board. A second soldier stood at the receiving end making his own inspection and ensuring that every leaker was marked and returned ashore.

Where did the leakers go? How were they repaired? Did we get them all back? Repaired? You tell me.

The great moment came one afternoon when the last drum had been loaded (No.s 1 and 2 holds were completely filled with octane, No.s 4 and 5 had a miscellany of bombs, ammunition, foodstuffs etc.) the last packing case stowed and the hatches battened down and all low ventilators for'd removed and the airways plugged. High ventilators remained in operation but were turned off-wind.

The pilot boarded and we set off for Alexandria, an overnight run, to await convoy to Tripoli.

As we drew abreast of de Lessops' statue at the Mediterranean entrance to the port, the third mate ran along the deck and howled at the bridge, drawing attention to the smoke issuing from No. 3 hold ventilators. It appeared that our bunker coal was on fire.

The port authorities were within shouting distance and it quickly became apparent that they weren't going to allow us back alongside. We were ordered to proceed to Alexandria Roads, whether rejoicing, lamenting or panicking was entirely up to us, just so long as we ceased to darken Port Said's doorstep a moment longer than absolutely necessary. The pilot too was in something of a hurry to get off the ship. Why?

As we had no option but to go, we went on overnight with the mate and Chippy tackling the fire with hoses, guessing from the thickness of the smoke the likely direction of the seat of the fire.

They operated in smoke helmets, a somewhat antiquated apparatus requiring an airline feed worked by foot pump and requiring a reasonable sense of rhythm from the third party concerned.

Needless to say their best efforts were in vain, they only succeeded in making themselves ill and bleary eyed.

Oh to have been a fly on the wall in the office where life and death decisions were to be made and made in a hell of a hurry that day! To bring the ship alongside was to put the city at some degree of risk, certainly the port facilities could be very seriously damaged. To abandon her in the Roads until such time as the fire burnt out or the ship blew up was to negate the whole purpose of the emergency loading and to jeopardise the entire operation to some degree.

In addition to the urgency of need of the cargo there was a gratuitous factor in our favour in that a Clan boat (was it "Clan Mackay"?) had previously been in a similar situation with fire on board expected to spread to an explosive cargo. She had been left to her own devices which turned out to be nothing at all for over six months simply endangering approaching shipping. I didn't hear what happened to her in the end but the authorities did not want a repeat of that fiasco.

So it was that in the middle of the day we were summoned to an isolated berth equipped with a grab. Funny, but I've no memory of any other ships in the near vicinity. There the remaining coal in the square of the hatch was removed and dumped along the quay while the grab bit deeper into the hold and hoses were played on the forward bulkhead.

In the course of a couple of hours a large patch of burning coal came to light and as you will have guessed this was situated hard up against the bulkhead where it was separated from octane vapour by a stout sheet of red-hot steel. Vivid memory paints this red-hot area the full span of a man's reach, a minimum of six feet, but I'm quite prepared to be corrected in this to, say a modest four feet across but I know it was not an inch less.

All our coal was removed and replaced with fresh, cool stuff guaranteed to remain inert for as long as we were likely to be carrying octane, but the time lost caused us to miss the convoy in which our chummy ships made the first incursion into liberated Tripoli. They found a harbour littered with sunken wrecks, many with the markings of hospital ships. The entrance had been barred by a block ship which the navy had succeeded in moving sufficiently to allow our ships to squeeze through.

Once the convoy had settled in it received a hideous shock delivered by the celebrated lone wave hopping bomber which arrived from Lampedusa in the early evening by dodging under the primitive radar screen.

I have no record of the extent of the damage done, but I know the harbour was transformed into an inferno for an uncomfortable period before the plane made off inland.

As far as I am aware that was the only time the defences were caught napping; the harbour was ringed by 150 anti-aircraft guns and with a twelve ship convoy in the middle each armed with at least eight guns an umbrella of tracer fire of such proportions as to enable the reading of a book by its light was produced as to deny any aircraft any hope of penetration. And the noise! When our turn came I was unable to distinguish the sound of our own guns firing a few feet over my head and I found myself inadvertently hugging myself and jumping up and down in the heart of the action. An aircraft caught in the searchlights had such close attention paid to him that he lost no time racing away inshore to jettison his bombs.

My experience in Tripoli duplicates Dad's in Bizerta except that we had instructions to maintain fire in a fixed direction so as to keep the umbrella intact, so we cannot claim to have brought down an enemy plane, only to have contributed to the overall protection of the ships in port.

All this anticipates events following our bunker fire and replacement of the coal, the consequence of which was a tedious delay of another week before the next group of ships was ready to go.

When the day arrived the old man came back from convoy conference about midday looking ready to burst with pride; it was to be a twelve ship convoy, four columns of three ships, and every leading ship was a city boat, if we include the "Fort

Tadoussac", one of ours commanded by Captain Mitchell who had taken over the "..Keelung" from Dad in New York. He was to lead the first column and we the second, the third column leader and therefore commodore ship was to be "City of Guildford" while the "..Evansville" took the fourth column.

Events were moving rapidly at this time and no sooner was conference completed than orders came from somewhere for the R.N.R. commodore to be flown back from Tripoli immediately on arrival. This meant that a relief commodore would travel with the outward man in order to get the feel of the job for the return journey and of course each commodore had his own retinue of signalmen.

Late in the afternoon it was discovered that the "..Guildford" lacked sufficient accommodation for the other ranks to be carried as required by King's Regulations, the senior staff could be asked to "rough it" but not the lesser mortals. We were the obvious second choice and the Commodore's launch duly came alongside and it was soon established that, thanks to the hanky-panky in Durban, we had accommodation to spare and we were duly promoted commodore ship.

As ten of the ships were unaware of these developments, the Commodore pointed out that it would be more practical to leave the order of movement and the position of ships in convoy as they were rather than trying to exchange positions of "..Keelung" and "..Guildford", any confusion could quickly be sorted out in daylight (convoys at that stage invariably formed up and sailed by night).

In view of the arrival in Tripoli of the first convoy, even if the enemy had no information from Egypt it would be reasonable for him to expect ours and to prepare a welcome and so we maintained a very high standard of vigilance on our way along the coast.

A brief glimpse at an atlas will show that the first three or four days of our journey was unavoidably predictable, we would be close in to shore under cover of shore-based guns in closely patrolled waters; once into the Gulf of Sirte we could manoeuvre more freely. By the same token the obvious place for a lurking submarine would be somewhere near the break away point.

The "somewhere near" turned out to be a point close to the little port of Derna when at about half past three in the afternoon and by unhappy coincidence those on our bridge were studying their opposite numbers on the "..Guildford"'s bridge, the hatchboards of her No.2 hold suddenly flew skywards followed immediately by a great sheet of flame that leaped hundreds of feet in the air. The explosion came virtually simultaneously and this caused me, off duty in the boat deck cabin to finish polishing the shoes I was holding, look round to see what else had to be done before rushing off to action stations. It could only have taken me a matter of seconds but when I stepped outside I found we were already in process of making an emergency turn to enable the surviving eleven to confuse the submarine and also to evade driving into the stricken "City of Guildford" whose major crime was to occupy commodore position. She was on our port quarter when I emerged with her stern rising rapidly to something like 75 or 80 degrees at which stage she slid down and under the surface which was burning fiercely.

Like the rest of us she had on board some fifty army personnel returning from leave, bringing her full complement to some 120 souls of whom, in the course of time, sixteen men were rescued in varying states of injury, something of a miracle in itself considering that her momentum had carried her into her own flames and there couldn't have been much room for swimmers to survive in.

Astern of the "..Guildford" had been the first American to join us on equal footing, the "Sir Francis Drake" whose bosun had seen the wake of the fateful torpedo and had therefore been able to photograph the moment of impact. This was a strictly forbidden procedure but understandable when there's a camera handy.

The speed of organised reaction to the sinking proved to be enough to prevent further disaster that day; apart from the movement of the ships, the escort was everywhere depth-charging and searching, and we were able to enter the comparatively safe Gulf of Sirte and make reasonable distance during the night.

In the morning the Commodore was faced with an impossible situation; having lost one ship he now found that our one and only tanker was missing having dropped back with engine trouble. Could he leave her to her own devices? After a lot of discussion with the escort he made the incredibly courageous decision to turn the convoy round and steam back for six hours to pick up the straggler and tuck her under his wing. Who knows, that might have put the finishing touch to any hope of enemy pursuit, at all events we reached Tripoli without further mishap.

We squeezed through the harbour entrance and picked our way between wrecks to a suitable position to anchor and pass a head-line to a mooring buoy. Because there wasn't room to swing without fouling some obstruction, we were obliged to pass a line out aft as well and this we made fast to a metal bar protruding from the water.

The "Ocean Voyager" had been loaded with a full cargo of octane in that first convoy and she was one of the bomber's victims; the metal bar had been her stem-post, all that remained of her above the water-line.

Discharge was effected by use of ship's gear overside into lighter, Palestinian troops acting as stevedores and this implies a time consuming exercise. With ten other cargo ships and one tanker to deal with as well as having to land cargo ex lighter onto the shore, this all took a great deal of time. Our main diversion was swimming amongst the wrecks which sat in the shallow water of the harbour; when there was a group of us we would play "convoys" until the day when we discovered an unofficial escort, a shark probably minding its own business, but we all tried to estimate the likely last man to reach the gangway and to allocate his personal effects in the fairest share-out we could devise.

One brief spell ashore found Tripoli to be in much the same state as Dad's log described Bizerta; I found two or three shops selling white metal souvenir rings and pig leather wallets, otherwise a city of the dead , although a brothel was said to be in operation somewhere, but there were no signs of life, let alone the presence of members of the opposite sex.

At the time of our first arrival in Tripoli, Dad was still in Gibraltar, but when we came the second time via Malta, he was in Bizerta and before we cleared the port he had leap-frogged and gone on to Malta.

To recount my findings would be to duplicate his in respect of Malta and in general as to air raids or rumours thereof, but I would observe that on completion of discharge of our second cargo, we suddenly appeared to have become yesterday's men. There was no urgency in dealing with the empty ships which simply lay about watching the movement of landing craft which became increasingly busy until on 9th July they took off and on the following day the news broke of the landings in Sicily.

After a while the activity in Tripoli died down and we were allowed back to life again. The next thing we knew we were the subject of invasion as a human cargo came aboard – Italian prisoners of war, not in dozens or scores, but by the hundreds and we viewed them with some degree of apprehension in spite of the accompanying armed guard.

It took very little time for us to discover our fears to be groundless, indeed to become complacent enough to suggest passing them the rifles to relieve our own men of sentry duty. They were so clearly relieved to be out of the war, praying that their country would soon be overrun and left in peace. They seemed to swarm all over the ship looking for a bit more brass to polish to avoid having to crowd below deck in the Mediterranean summer heat.

We were sorry to see them go once we reached Alexandria.

After the Lord Mayor's Show our haloes were dropping right, left and centre – we were no longer desperately important people on a war-winning mission, some at least were considered as excess mouths to be fed. The "Fort Tadoussac" returned home to coincide with the "..Dieppe" and Dad returned the compliment to Captain Mitchell and took over his ship!

We in the meantime were privileged to maintain our status as indispensables by responding to the next crisis.

It has never been clear to me whether at any stage, then or since, the general public were aware of the tragic events in India where famine of catastrophic proportions struck and was kept, necessarily, under wraps. Millions died in that summer and after we had disembarked the last of our prisoners we were rushed off to Suez to load a full cargo of rice for Calcutta, although we had calls to make at Colombo and Madras on the way.

Colombo to me will always be synonymous with fireflies and the social statement made by the carriage of the black umbrella; another lasting memory was the extraordinary number of sufferers of elephantiasis.

Madras comes back as a pleasant place of shops well stocked with silks and sarees, a doorway to the orient.

Calcutta in mid-September was altogether a different kettle of fish; we worked continuously in high temperatures exacerbated by intolerable humidity. The temperature in our cabin in the middle of the night remained in three figures Fahrenheit and sleep on board was impossible at any time, considering the noise and the heat from steam piping surrounding the hatches and the accommodation.

We were accordingly permitted to decamp and repair to the Marine Club to seek unbelievably cool and quiet conditions compared with those on board.

The major impression of that visit remains the incredible mass of humanity everywhere, mostly impoverished, skeletal and ragged, but at least still alive, although quite a proportion lay huddled, sleeping sometimes in the most bizarre places.

Some time in October we were on the move again, this time homeward bound and, at last, directly through the Mediterranean.

No specific memories of the Indian Ocean passage remain or

of the journey through the Red Sea, but back at Port Said the boffins came aboard with experimental rocket propelled piano wire, carefully boxed, intended as anti-aircraft screens. We also received our own private barrage balloon.

Grand ideas in theory, but our balloons in particular were hardly designed to hide the presence of a convoy, and whilst we had been able to come independently from Calcutta to Port Said, it was now convoy again all the way home.

Everyone knows the Mediterranean for its sunshine and idle comfort, but the seaman knows it as a zone where the most unexpected, unseasonal and violent weather will erupt from time to time.

Admittedly October was well advanced when our convoy set out for Gibraltar, but there we were, minding our own business, happily floating our balloons when, in the middle of the night, a thunderstorm broke. I think most of the balloons were shot down in flames by lightning bolts, but to add insult to injury, immense seas were flung up at the ships and several including ourselves sustained damage that we had been able to avoid in the worst of the weather that the Atlantic could dish up. We found bridge housing set back and boarding on one of the lifeboats stove in.

Whether these events influenced the boffins or not I don't know, but they discreetly removed the piano wire and the balloon gear shortly after arrival in Gibraltar and we all heaved sighs of relief.

We arrived alongside early in the morning of 8th November and, once settled, I seem to have been occupied on some odd job on the bridge, when from the gangway the 2nd mate called up to me, "Its your Dad", and sure enough a moment or two later Dad stepped on board and went, as protocol demanded , straight up to see the old man.

Dumbfounded and not a little apprehensive, I responded to a summons to the master's cabin to meet my father and be told that I would be excused duty for the rest of the day.

I went to my cabin and changed into respectable clothing with my mind in a whirl, wondering what awful tales out of school might be in the process of unfolding in the old man's room.

At this stage I was still the little child under adult scrutiny, ready to resent my father and whatever he might have to lecture me about.

Twenty- four hours later a minor miracle had taken place and I had metamorphosed into a fully fledged, totally acceptable adult. More than that I came to understand fully and for the first time in my life, that I was also the object of my father's love.

There is no point in detailing the events of that day, whatever we did, wherever we went, such events were completely immaterial to the revelation I had witnessed and partaken in.

Herewith the joint air-letter home:

"My own Beloved,
I have waited to see what happened before writing to you- and now the thing I have prayed for has happened. The odd chance has turned up, and honestly Girl, I hardly know how to write. I can't let the Young Fellow see it – though even at that I suspect he has seen what I simply can't hide. I didn't think I was such a sentimental ass. Sweetheart, I'm proud of him. It happened entirely accidentally. Of course I've enquired for him here and got definite news that there was no chance of meeting him: and then without warning today I met young Sapp on the wharf and got the shock of my life. As you can guess, I raced off and collected him and tonight he is sleeping on my settee. That fills me up too full for words. I sent you that wire even before I saw him – I just couldn't wait – but I showed him just what I had sent, and he quite approves.

He has just arrived in time as I couldn't have seen him later. He can give you all the news when he sees you. I'm getting along fine, all the worries I expected but no more than I can handle.

I won't write more, as I want to leave room for him to add a few words. My love – our love, rather, — to the Girls and Mother and Dad and everybody. God bless you all. To you, all the love in the world and millions of kisses. I'll be writing again very shortly. Goodnight, Beloved,

Your Arthur

Dear Mum,

Can you imagine the surprise when the 2nd mate yelled from the gangway up to me on the bridge "Its your Dad!" Well as you can imagine I left the ship almost immediately and met Dad's friends ashore – jolly nice people. I slept in Dot's berth for what was left of the night.

I might say that Dad was like a dog with two tails and 100 lamp-posts – I've never seen him so pleased. It was a great day for both of us, Dad says the proudest day of the war for him.

I certainly approved of the wire – he was very pleased with it.

Cramped for space, It's Goodbye, love, Bernard"

On the face of it, our meeting was just a serendipitous occurrence calculated to boost the morale of us both but in fact its repercussions were such as to establish it as the single most influential event in all my formative years.

I determined there and then that there would never be a recurrence of the estrangement that had existed between father and son in our generation; when my son or sons would reach my age I would want them to have known and understood me from childhood. To achieve this aim I knew that I had no option but to give up seafaring as a career at the earliest possible moment and this knowledge coloured my activities for the best part of the next twenty years.

Right then I had simply to wave Dad off on his way back to West Africa while kicking my heels in Gibraltar, waiting while eighty ships were gathering to form a formidable homeward convoy.

Midway through November we left Gib. complete with commodore, vice and rear commodores too. We were leading ship in the 2nd column a long way from the commodore. Even so we continued our endeavours to race him at signal hoisting. This requires a little explanation and reverts to my comment regarding the pigeon-holed flag cabinet which we had long ago dispensed with in favour of a line of hooks outside the wheelhouse and beside the halliards.

The system was simple; the Commodore hoisted a coded signal, whereupon the ships nearest read and deciphered it. Immediately the significance of the signal was understood each ship hoisted the same signal until every ship was flying it. When the Commodore took it down it was immediately complied with, if in fact it required action.

There was a limited number of likely flag hoists, particularly at set times of day and we soon had no need of the code book to decipher a message that we could well anticipate. It followed that whenever possible we read signals as each flag appeared, immediately clipping the same flag onto our halliards, and, assuming correct identification of the message, we would then complete hoisting our signal, not to the yardarm as the Commodore was obliged to do, but to the overhead triatic stay, a very much shorter haul. It pleased our tiny minds to complete hoisting the Commodore's signal while he was still struggling to raise his.

It was soon apparent that, perhaps because of the size of the convoy, we were giving the land a very wide berth, partly to avoid discovery (some hope!), partly to reduce the likelihood of heavy air attack by staying at extreme range.

We had a light air escort, a Hudson of the Fleet Air Arm flying high clockwise with virtually no armament.

After three days we turned northwards parallel to the coast and found ourselves with a second escort, this time a Dornier. This bomber flew round us anti-clockwise low down and out of our range, clearly reconnoitring. He had the good sense to go home for a night's sleep and return refreshed the following morning, biding his time for us to reach the preferred point for the enemy to launch an attack. Apart from his menace he was a great nuisance in keeping us at Action Stations for hour after unnecessary hour, but I suppose he kept us on our toes.

Inevitably the day arrived when early in the afternoon instead of the Dornier, four Heinkels arrived, this time well ahead of the convoy, high and completely out of range. Having made their preparations they released what looked for all the world like the round black bombs that are attributed in caricatures to all self-respecting anarchists.

These bombs seemed to float about in the air until, one after another, all bar one or two dropped down into the sea at an angle. Older and wiser heads than mine announced - "glider bombs; the navy's got their wavelength", and obviously enough these were remotely controlled weapons, probably still in the experimental stage – fore-runners of doodle-bugs perhaps?

One bomb evaded the escort and came down to our level and passed down the port flank of the convoy before turning and passing between, I think, the fourth and fifth columns.

Because of our position our view of the bomb was obscured by intervening vessels but at one point what I took to be a patch of smoke appeared, but as no bomb emerged and nothing seemed to have happened I persuaded myself I'd actually seen a waterspout as the bomb plunged down.

It wasn't until we reached home that we learnt that the bomb had destroyed the bridge of the "Delius", command of which was immediately assumed by her 2nd mate who was stationed aft.

Her engines were not affected and emergency steering was put into operation so that she didn't lose station but continued as if nothing had happened.

A couple of years after the end of hostilities I met and worked with Ron Hills who had served in Coastal Command. In discussion he recognised the "Delius" convoy and informed me that a full squadron of 24 planes had taken off from airfields near Brest and had subsequently been intercepted and sufficiently exhausted of the fuel required to get them out to us and back that only the four succeeded in making the double journey. That's what is known as doing good by stealth, we being blissfully ignorant of this background to the drama.

If we'd thought our troubles were ended with the departure of the Heinkels we were soon rudely disabused.

We were now well into the Bay of Biscay and the weather was beginning to deteriorate. Before nightfall the sky became overcast and when at its thickest we heard the drone of a heavy bomber close ahead of us. Suddenly it broke cover and at that instant every ship in the immediate vicinity opened up with a vicious fusillade of fire; we had a very good view and were almost certainly responsible for some penetrating shells. The plane, of course, picked up and shot straight back into the clouds. As it went it was agreed by all with any degree of aircraft recognition that we'd been firing on a Flying Fortress. This too was confirmed on our arrival in port when we heard that while a radio operator had been killed, the plane had survived and returned to base.

Our epic voyage was not to fizzle out on this rather sour note as, predictably, after the air attack a follow-up by submarines was inevitable.

This started about one o'clock in the morning as the wind was rising from force 6 to force 7 with choppy seas and an ever more violent swell. The whole convoy was illuminated by snowflakes, bright white flares floating slowly down, as the escort started racing along and between columns depth-charging relentlessly. The chase passed through the convoy and drifted away astern until it was lost to us completely and we reverted to normal routine.

At midday we received a signal relayed from the escort to the effect that one submarine had definitely been sunk, a second probably, while a third was damaged.

It's a little strange that, considering the bitterness we felt towards this most treacherous form of warfare, and even with old scores to settle, the news of this emphatic victory fell slightly flat when we looked over the side at that unforgiving sea churning and wallowing, quietly claiming its dead.

It may be that the deteriorating weather settled matters then as we were finally allowed to complete our voyages to our respective ports without further interference. The "City of Keelung" tied up in West India Dock, London E.14 on 1st December 1943, paying off the following day after 13 months and 7 days on articles.

CHAPTER EIGHT
THE PACIFIC CONTRIBUTION

I think it only fair that we were allowed sufficient home leave to take us over the Christmas period, by which time I had no doubt recovered from my initial strangeness. I remember well arriving back in my own home feeling like a complete stranger; I sat on the edge of chairs and found myself having to pick my words carefully in ordinary conversation, so used had I become to a vernacular not acceptable in respectable company ashore.

Strange at home I may have been, but not so cousin Bob from New Zealand. He and I were more or less contemporaries – our mothers being cousins. With a war going on involving the old country, like many of his compatriots, Bob could not wait to rally round the flag.

To get into things he joined a ship domiciled in the UK and therefore paid off there, whereafter he would be registered with the UK Pool.

He soon gravitated to our house and seemed to spend more of the war in my bed than ever I was able to do.

Laura had joined the WAAF and naturally brought friends and colleagues home from time to time, hence with three out of five in the family in uniform and visitors in and out, our house became something of a league of nations and it was sometimes difficult to keep a check on who was who or who else was where.

Dad was last seen south-bound from Gibraltar on the "Fort Tadoussac" which had only recently been converted to Fleet Supply and I have no record of how long she remained so or what theatre of war she was employed in after Dad left her. I only know that he wrote to me from home in June 1944, disappointed at not being involved in the landings across the Channel, while being transferred to "Fort Edmonton". He finished his war on her, spending the best part of two and a half years in the Pacific, right over the time that doodle bugs and V2 rockets were falling on London.

Dad was a natural born worrier and this last commission split him down the middle. He was by this time a war-seasoned master in a very responsible job of which he was rightly enormously proud. The idle periods gave him far too much time in which to use his imagination in regard to events at home and the length of time he was away effectively crucified him. At the start of the war he was a young man determined to give everything to the cause; at the end he was white-haired, weary and drained although it took several years of post war peace time to break through his guard.

The balance of his war story was covered, not in a log, but in a letter home written after the end of the war, covering the final period after some eight months in and around Sydney, N.S.W. as follows:

"Sunday, 25th November 1945

My own Darling Girl,
In two more days I shall be arriving in Colombo: and the weather's reasonably cooler now and much more like writing weather, so I must get on with this ready for posting on arrival. I don't think there's any necessity to confine my efforts to service cards any longer, so perhaps I'll be able to write something like a letter for the first time since God knows when.

Well, Sweetheart, I'm making my first voyage under peace conditions for six weary years: and it seems just unbelievable, but I suppose I'll get used to it. Anyway, with censorship completely lifted now I can write you a letter that may tell you more of the things you have wanted to know. Roughly, our service record comes to this: - We went up with full stores, days ahead of the fleet, in February, to Manus (Admiralty Islands) and as soon as we had got there stored them (they had overtaken us, naturally). As soon as they left to hand Japan her first punch (in the Okinawa affair) we went on up to extreme Forward Base

– Leyte, in the Philippines – to await their return and re-store them for the second operation. And Leyte will always be a source of pride to me. For there, we – and the Pacific fleet, of course – sat right in the jaws of the Jap and got on with the job. We sat for six weeks in a trap that might (and should) have been sprung at any time.

That was when I really knew that Japan was licked (you will remember that, as long ago as that, I told you that, though the job would take a bit of time, I was certain we'd got the Yellow Rat licked). The point was that at that time, in Leyte, we were actually completely surrounded. For the Japs were settled in very strongly in all the surrounding islands East, West, North and South of us. To my mind it was obvious that if he'd got the stuff to use, or the guts to risk it, he wouldn't have missed the opportunity. Yet we all sat and worked there, in Leyte Gulf, literally daring him to come in and snap us. Well I went back to Sydney in May and re-stored, and then up to Manus again for the next job, the second operation and the intention was that from Manus I would go on to the Bovin Islands (they're right on Japan's doorstep – you'll find them on the map) to re-store the Pacific Fleet for the final punch. But that didn't come off because Japan cracked before we could drive the last punch home. And, by the way, Girl, don't let anybody ever persuade you that the atomic bomb smashed Japan. We who have had the job to do knew months ago that the Pacific Fleets had settled the issue and put paid to the Japs. The atomic bomb hastened the end and saved thousands of lives: but it did not turn the balance between victory and defeat. The combined Pacific Fleets had settled that issue as long ago as last March.

Anyway, to get back to the "Edmonton". Japan cracked. The Pacific Fleet and Fleet Supply Train went up from Manus for the occupation of Japan, leaving the "Fort Edmonton" behind to act as duty store ship for the base and to store the ships bringing back repatriated prisoners of war to Australia, before returning to Sydney herself. What it really meant was that the "Edmonton" had done her job as a "fighting unit" of the Pacific

Fleet – and the Pacific Fleet itself, as a fighting force, no longer needed to exist; and as the "Edmonton" had been in the job and darned hard-worked right from the start she was being released first from the Fleet Train to return to Sydney while the others went on to carry on the work of the occupation.

One of the things I'm proud of; the "..Edmonton" was only one of ten supply ships in the Fleet Train, but in every operation, from start to finish, we were the first on the job – and the hardest worked. Our biggest boss, Rear Admiral Douglas Fisher, admitted that in a personal chat in his cabin the day before the Fleet and Fleet Train left Manus for the occupation. His actual words to me, when he shook hands and said cheerio, were "King, I know I've sweated the "..Edmonton" hard, but I had to. You know the size of the job we've had to do and I knew that whatever snags cropped up I could always rely on the "..Edmonton". You can go back on board, thank your lads from me for their farewell message and tell them I'm proud of them. You've done a grand job."

You will know by now from the newspapers the names of the commanders of the Pacific Fleet:-

Commander-in-chief Admiral Sir Bruce Frazer.

Commanding 1st Battle Squadron Admiral Rawlings.

Cruiser Squadron Rear Admiral Sir Philip Vian V.C. ("Cossack" – "the Navy's here" – You remember)

Commanding Pacific Fleet Train Rear Admiral Douglas Fisher (our own Big Boss)

Well, to get back to the yarn. When the Fleet and Fleet Train left Manus for the occupation on 30th August, I was left sitting there, as I have said. Felt somewhat like Cinderella, as you can guess, and accordingly a wee spot disappointed. "The old war-horse left out of the last job after all. Not needed any longer" sort of feeling. I think you'll understand what I mean. But Rear Admiral Fisher cured that before he left. In spite of the fact that in his own cabin on the previous day he had shaken hands and said "Cheerio and thanks" he sent me an official signal of farewell as

157

his flagship, H.M.S."Montclare", steamed out across my bows. I'm enclosing a copy of that signal and my reply to it – and I'm also sending copies to the Owners – I've an idea they'll be interested and anyway it'll do for their records.

So, I went back to Sydney in October: and now, I'm finished officially with the Pacific Fleet. I'm only going to Colombo to change my crew who are time-expired.

As soon as that job's done I'm off to Singapore to open up the Storing Base there.

Transferred officially to East Indies Fleet, which, as you probably know, is Lord Louis Mountbatten's command. So I can't possibly foretell what may or may not happen in the next few months. I'll go where I'm needed and do what I can, as I always have done. And when I'm not needed any longer I'll be damned glad to come Home and sit back for a little while.

We look more like a peace-time ship now for they disarmed us completely in Sydney. All guns and turrets and structures gone and its only the special build of her and the big storing barges on deck that give any indication that she's not a commercial cargo-carrier.

A week before we left Sydney I got a special invitation from the C-.in-C (Bruce Frazer) to a cocktail party on board the "King George V" at 11.00a.m. and it wasn't sent as an official signal in the usual way, but delivered verbally by a lieutenant as a personal invitation from the C-in-C! It was quite an affair. All the Pacific Commanders were there, Navy, Army, Air Force, and two Ladies from the Nursing Services. And only four Merchant Skippers including myself. (There were several Fleet Auxiliaries in Sydney at the time, but we were the only four invited: me, one hospital ship, one ammunition ship and one tanker!)

I was introduced to Frazer as soon as I got on board and it was very obvious that the "Edmonton" has made a name for herself. The opening conversation after he shook hands with me was "What ship is it, Cap'n?" "Fort Edmonton, Sir". And then an instantaneous very friendly grin and "Ah, yes! The fellows we couldn't do without! We couldn't have finished the show without you, you know." Well, anyway, I met them all and chatted with them all – Rawlings, Vian and all of them.

I won't write much more now, Sweetheart. The mail should be pretty rapid from Colombo, so you ought to get this pretty quickly.

God bless you all etcetera

Your own Arthur"

Dad was every bit as much time-expired as the crew he was obliged to change in Colombo, but as Master he was no doubt indispensable, so off he trundled for another eight months in Singapore before relief arrived.

The next, and as far as the war is concerned, the last letter was dated Sunday, 7th July 1946. it started with personal details and comments and gives clear indication of the need to leave the ship and its worries behind. Not until page 5 does he say:

"I'm enclosing something in this letter which I think you would like to keep. The "programme" of a special Church Service. There were three of Bucknall's V.S.I. "Fort" ships here: "..Edmonton", "..Providence" and "..Kilmar" (our old pal Georgie Law). The "..Kilmar" has suddenly been released by the Admiralty, as they no longer need so many Fleet Store Ships, and handed over to ordinary commercial service under the old Red Ensign. The Naval Chaplain here is a grand chap, moderately young and very human and as such has been a personal friend of all us "Merchant Service Toughs" who are temporarily attached to the Fleet. Well, Georgie Law said to the Padre, when he got his transfer orders (first of the Naval "Forts" to be handed over) "When I pull my Admiralty Ensign down for the last time, tomorrow, I'll give it to you for a souvenir if you like". The Padre jumped at the idea but said he would accept it on one condition only; that it should be representative not only of the "..Kilmar" but of all the V.S. ships who have worked with the Pacific Fleet; that it should hang in the Naval Church and be unfurled in a special Dedication Service.

Of course, we all agreed to that, so the Padre made all arrangements for the service for last Wednesday at 7.00p.m. Of course everybody on the Naval Base here was very keen on the idea, and the result was a very big congregation. Masters, Officers and crews of all the Supply ships, including the "White Ensign" Admiralty Oilers, and representatives of the Naval Shore Staff which of course includes the Vice-Admiral and the Commodore. It was a really grand and impressive service. A packed church, a very ceremonial Service, everybody in full-dress uniform, decorations, ribbons and all the rest of it. What I want you to know, eventually, is that I was picked by the Chaplain to help to officiate at the Service. Only an hour before it was due to start, he rushed down in his car, blew up to my room and announced, "Skipper, prepare yourself for a shock! I'm going to ask you to take over a curate's duties tonight and read the Lesson for us. Will you?" Sweetheart, you and I have never needed to discuss our individual beliefs and religious convictions, but I know you have always understood me and my ideas; so, I know you will understand what a lovely thing that request was to me: that after thinking for a quick second, I simply said "Certainly Padre, I'll do it".

Well, I read the lesson. And you know, Dearest, that for me there was only one way to read it. There was no stage-fright or vanity or quiet voice. The only way that I could possibly do such a solemn thing as that was to give it to them as I felt and understood and interpreted it myself. That, of course, is just all I did. I 'wrought better than I knew". After the Service was over the Chaplain beckoned me aside and clapped his hand on my shoulder and said "I knew I wasn't guessing wrong when I asked you to read the Lesson, old man. As you know, we parsons come out with the knowledge that it is up to us to give you fellows something. This evening, you gave us all something. I have never, in any church in the world, heard a Lesson read more beautifully and with such understanding."

Since then I have had many visits or phone calls from every senior officer who was present, the general motif being "thanks and surprise". Dearest, you know that it means more to me than I can put into words, to know that I was allowed to pass on, successfully, a reminder of the truths I have always believed in, to men equally old and hard-bitten as myself.

Law is sending a copy of the "programme" to the company and my V.S.O. is sending one to the Admiralty.

And so you still remember me as you saw me last at Euston. Yes, Sweetheart, I think that was the most awful evening I've ever had. Suddenly feeling so damnably lonely, knowing that that taxi was taking away all that was dearest to me: and everything in me shrieking "To hell with duty and belief and ideals. You've done enough. Chuck everything in and go back with them". But that's all past now, Girl, and I'm glad that, until we find, as we soon shall, our own peace and beauty in each others arms again, you remember me just as I was that evening.

With reference to the various O.B.E.s and so forth, of course I knew, as I said, just how mad you would be about it. But you don't really need to bother, for as you know it doesn't bother me in the least. Unfortunately, decorations have been, in my opinion, very much cheapened in the last few years. I certainly don't want anything "given away with a pound of tea". If they only knew it, I could sport three finer decorations than any of them could wear on their jackets. My own conscience and the knowledge of the good work I have done: the love and trust of a very lovely woman, my own dear wife: and a mention in despatches really earned in action in 1917. Don't let it get you furious for it doesn't bother me in the least. In fact, when I think about it, it really strikes me as a darned good joke. Somewhat in the nature of a distinction to be one who didn't have to be dished out with a decoration to tell him, in case he didn't know, that he had "been a good boy"."

This was the effective end to the letter and the reader is entitled to detect a note or two of sour grapes or not as he reads between the lines. But who could blame Dad for whatever disappointment he may have felt?

Complete disillusionment took longer to arrive, but for one who had given so much, the expectation that with the end of the war, all the participants would simply revert to what had been normal before the war, was rather too much to accept. It is hardly surprising that as time went on and the only goal left was ultimate retirement, reaction became inevitable.

The next several years saw Dad more and more as a little boy lost and at this juncture

I will leave the end of his tale till later and revert to my own adventures.

CHAPTER NINE
FINISHING MY TIME

The timing of the end of the first and the start of the second trip on the "City of Keelung" was immaculate.

I signed on for what proved to be a reward voyage for the hardships of the first on January 3rd 1944 together with only one remaining former shipmate, Johnny Mather the 2nd Sparks. All the rest had gone their separate ways and apart from David Sapp I never saw any of them again. This was a frequently recurring element of life at sea; we lived together as intimately as it is possible to do, exchanged handshakes at the end of the voyage and subsequently repeated the process with a completely new set of shipmates.

This second voyage lasted only two and a half months and felt like a holiday cruise as we were now back to three cadets, including one senior to me and one first tripper, hence four hour watches again followed by eight hours below: luxury! In addition there was a relaxation of tension with the Battle of the Atlantic swung firmly in our favour, and our itinerary we might have chosen for ourselves; outward cargo for Lisbon and a full cargo of oranges home from Valencia.

Lisbon was a light-hearted delight, and although as number two cadet I fell in for evening work so that the others tended to go ashore together and return with tales of great fun and games enjoyed in the bars with the ladies of the town, I was able to imbibe the atmosphere and save my pocket money at the same time. And what an atmosphere it was! The country seemed to be divided between the wealthy and the near destitute and on the hypothesis that he who is down need fear no fall, total lack of inhibition and great friendliness seemed to exude from all the needy, a friendliness which had a genuine ring to it in that part of the world.

Lisbon was unseasonably hot whereas in Valencia snow fell for the first time in thirty years. The people there were more reserved and we were warned to be on our guard in Franco's neutral but pro-German Spain.

In spite of the goldfish bowl feeling of being watched in neutral territory in wartime, the voyage went without a hitch and enabled me to clock up sufficient additional sea-time to become senior cadet on my next ship.

I signed on the "City of Windsor" 3rd April 1944 for the first of two voyages to India, on the first of which we returned home via New York, my first of several happy encounters with our American cousins.

I discovered Bombay and Karachi and the kaleidoscope of the crowded bazaars with their accompaniment of deformed and maimed beggars. I even went on a voyage of discovery down Grant Road in Bombay where girls for hire were retained in cages in front of the shops; finding myself a lone European in a somehow hostile environment I wasted no time there having verified the unpalatable facts for myself.

We arrived in New York early in May where I was directed by seniors to the British Apprentices' Club. I'd heard about it vaguely but only became truly aware of it on arrival there. To be in uniform in wartime opens all manner of doors and together with armed services personnel, we sailors were a pampered lot while hostilities lasted and we might have been forgiven for thinking of the club as just another option for a cheap night out or a useful source of information and advice.

Nothing could have been further from the truth; a senior diplomat rejoicing in the name Hollon C. Spaulding worked in the American Embassy in London during the first world war and subsequently expressed his gratitude to our nation by founding and funding the club. It was intended as a home from home for penurious apprentices on the loose in the big city, to entertain them and protect them from whatever pitfalls they might encounter.

I believe it started in exactly the same way that it was being operated when I first met it: run exclusively by the fair sex of whom there was an abundance at any time of the day, it was headed by Lillian, Mr Spaulding's widow. To describe her as extraordinary would almost be an insult; she was unique and a legend in her own lifetime.

The first time visitor, an automatic member if still a cadet or apprentice, would be interrogated gently and all the information elicited stored in Mrs Spaulding's filing cabinet of a mind and no matter what period of time might elapse before a second visit he would be recognised instantly and welcomed as a member of the family.

The hostesses were all very carefully vetted and no instance of hanky-panky passed unobserved or was ever allowed to recur. Complimentary tickets for the best Broadway shows were always available and a qualified dance teacher taught us the steps of all the popular dances and even persevered with the Tango and such-like. I have her to thank for the very mediocre showing that I was once able to produce – my fault, the mediocrity, not hers.

The club was on the second floor of the Hotel Chelsea, 222, West 23rd Street next door to the ground floor Oasis Bar and Mrs S was wise enough to insist that no member ever left the club without first consuming a pint of milk, ostensibly for the sake of its nourishment but coincidentally an excellent lining for the stomach in the event of the inevitable call next door on the way back to the ship.

I took in "Life with Father" which was a raging success on Broadway and Sonja Henni on ice at Madison Square Garden, and was enabled to meet and chat with the stars of "Pygmalion", having my programme endorsed with the signatures of Gertrude Lawrence and Raymond Massey. How did I manage to leave the damn thing on the subway less than half an hour later?

Apart from anything else, the club was a very convenient place to meet one's peers and make some very good if fleeting friendships.

Somewhere in the early 1950s Mrs Spaulding died and appropriately enough the club died with her; both are mourned to this day.

I took the opportunity to go out to the Arlington Hotel to meet cousin Bob; he had been shipped across with other crew members to pick up a "new building". While they waited for completion of construction at the shipyard they were housed uptown in what he described as a "doss house". Having seen it I had no reason to argue with him. What we did with ourselves then I can't for the life of me remember.

Times Square, Radio City, the Empire State Building, Greenwich Village, Jack Dempsey's Bar, the Brooklyn and Hoboken ferries were all grist to my mill on my initiation to the Big Apple and now I come to think of it, this was the first time that we had ever seen the revolutionary fork lift trucks that they used in our holds for cargo handling. An innovation like the walkie-talkie; progress speeded by the demands of war.

My second trip on the "..Windsor" started on my eighteenth birthday and brought me to the Bay of Bengal for Christmas 1944. By now the tide of war had turned in Burma and we were able to see the start of sweeping progress and a promise of an end to the misery. Imagine then the spirit abroad in Calcutta as the New Year approached.

With two shipmates I found myself drinking a beer in the Grand Hotel, Chowringhi, on New Years Eve. We were seated on wicker chairs facing wicker tables set on an extensive marble floor. How many tables were accommodated I can't begin to remember but what I do know is that as the room began to fill we started to tot up the number of different Allied nationalities present. We lost count at eighteen and remarked that with so many disparate bodies around it was extraordinary just how good humoured everyone was. At that point some fool in Merchant Navy uniform embarrassed us by starting a fight but it was soon quelled.

As midnight arrived , so hundreds of glasses were smashed and every stick of furniture was heaped up in a pile in the middle of the floor to be encircled by a snake of male humanity producing the longest Conga you are ever likely to see.

It wasn't long before the company splintered and we three piled out with an assortment of soldiers and fell on board the nearest unoccupied gharry.

I don't think the driver was given instructions, he just took off and delivered us to the red light district whether we wanted to be there or not. A few minutes sufficed to convince us that we really didn't want and somehow or other we wended our way back to the ship.

If there is such a thing as a defining moment, that was it. There was a very positive exultant knowledge that victory was ours – just around the corner.

At the end of that voyage spring was under way at home when I was despatched to Manchester to join the "City of Canberra" to start what turned out to be another epic voyage. No sooner had I joined than I was badgered by my newly met South African junior, Johnny Giddey, who was a little older than I and at least three times my size, to return to London over the week-end because he simply had to see a special girl friend there. Accordingly we both returned chez moi, one more uniform, one more fresh face for Mum to meet and feed.

Back on board we were soon joined by Bill Kershaw, our third member hailing from Bramhall in Cheshire. The second mate was David Sapp's elder brother Tom (?) but a few days before sailing the 3rd mate fell ill and had to be relieved and the only replacement available was David himself. Company regulations did not allow brothers to sail on the same ship so Sapp senior also had to be relieved in favour of Mr Rendall whose first name eludes me.

Apropos of Christian names and names in general, although I have produced some here, they were rarely if ever used at sea. Officers were referred to by rank and indeed I was severely reprimanded on my first trip for addressing the mate as Mr Wilson when I was called upon to rouse him for his 4.00am watch. The formula, I was told, was – knock, knock, "are you awake, Sir?". Fortunately, after many years of watch-keeping the officer concerned invariably responded satisfactorily.

Exceptions to the rule always created problems particularly if the culprit was senior to oneself.

We sailed with the elderly Captain Penberthy (Welsh) in command and Willy Kerr (Scottish) mate who, in the course of time, proved to be other than soul mates. I think the second mate acted as buffer from time to time.

If I remember rightly we were loaded for Calcutta via Port Said. Aden, Colombo, Trincomalee and Madras and we were three days out from Aden when Johnny, Bill and I were privileged to share one small bottle of beer between us as celebration of the date. It was May 8th 1945 – what a way to celebrate VE Day. At that moment we had no reason to foresee the complications that were to ensue.

About this time Johnny developed back trouble and in Colombo he was diagnosed as suffering from a slipped disc which immediately disqualified him from continuing on board. With his repatriation Bill and I were in the same position that David Sapp and I had been except that without perpetual need for Action Stations, we weren't required to keep watch, being regarded as more useful on day work.

When discharge was completed the complications started; the Ministry of War Transport was becoming more and more embarrassed at the number of ships under its control for which there was less and less work to be done.

Maybe it was panic on someone's part, maybe a stroke of genius, but the next thing we knew we were on our way to the Cocos Islands with stores for a garrison which had been withdrawn for quite some time when we arrived there. The Islands proved to be of the idyllic desert island variety with little other than palm trees and the Indian Ocean version of South Sea islanders sprinkled over the various atolls. The water was clear as the proverbial bell, the sea bottom being brightly visible with multi coloured fish swimming around the ship.

No sooner had we arrived than we were promoted to a bottle of port between four of us to celebrate VJ Day. We spent some happy time sailing a dinghy constructed by Chippy from a hulk that we discovered beached in Trincomalee.

Having discharged our unwanted cargo we were now sent off to Albany in South Western Australia at a time when the port appeared to be very young. There were strange licensing laws which required us to travel outside the perimeter of the town if we wanted an evening drink and the odd feature that comes to mind was the channelling at the roadsides acting in lieu of normal gutters indicating a very primitive drainage system.

With completion of work in Albany the grand new game started of "guess which port is next" whereafter on every arrival an agent's representative would come aboard with the wonderful announcement "You're going home!" and within a few days, usually when we were all still suffering the after effects of celebration, an alternative decision had been dreamt up.

Our next port of call proved to be Sydney and with the Australian man-power still to be repatriated from the various theatres of war, we actually weren't particularly interested to know what the next port would be, Sydney was good enough for us.

It was early in September and the weather was glorious, hot sunshine by day, blazing starlight by night and the pick of delightful Aussie womanhood to accompany us undeserving scruffy sailors. Memories!

We carried a couple of passengers to our next port which was to be Fremantle, one of whom was Nina Milkina's agent, a name which meant nothing to us at the time, but later became recognised internationally. We also carried on deck a small parcel of mangoes but not all of them reached their destination.

The stop at Fremantle was brief and we were soon on our way to Durban where we were quite definitely assured that we were homeward bound. The ensuing party broke many records, certainly as far as I was concerned, partly because the mate brought a bottle of whisky to the cadets' cabin. How much I consumed I cannot say, I only know that the combination of different beverages and the excitement had a most unfortunate effect upon my constitution, leaving me in a condition such as I had never previously achieved and have never repeated; embarrassment prevents me from saying more.

The home-going turned out to be another way of describing de-commissioning; we discharged, dry-docked, fumigated and meanwhile had our guns removed. Bill and I demolished the plastic armour surrounding the saloon housing using a cold set and a fourteen pound sledge hammer after which we had developed muscles to turn Superman green with envy.

We clocked up a total time of two and a half months in Durban during which time our social lives developed and expanded to the degree that it was probably just as well that the day came for us to leave when it did.

October, November and part of December in Durban was the equivalent of a prolonged summer holiday during which we were quick off the mark to start socialising with the local populace, in particular the eligible female element thereof.

Not long after arrival two young ladies appeared at the foot of our gangway and requested permission to come aboard and see over the ship. They proved to be on holiday from Johannesburg and it wasn't long before I started dating Freda on a regular basis whereas Ethel preferred the company of some of our naval rivals in port at the time.

During the war Del Monico in Cape Town and the Playhouse in Durban did a roaring trade with the Forces providing eating and drinking facilities, and in the case of the Playhouse, a cinema too, under a ceiling of artificial starlight similar to that provided by the London Planetarium today. I suppose Freda and I watched every current film in the south before wending our ways back, I to the ship, she to her hotel via the Snappy Snacks of fond memory where we supped before parting.

Meanwhile we all became embroiled with an extraordinary family living out in the sticks, the suburb of Jacobs.

A Scotsman named Murray arrived in Durban some time in the 19th century with his Maori wife, buying land cheaply and founding an extensive family. Eleven girls and a boy were produced and they in turn provided us, had they but known it, with their daughters for our company. Four cousins (including three girls) from the family took David, Bill and me (was Paddy the 3rd Sparks with us too?) on a day trip to Amanzimtoti, the Durban equivalent of Coney Island to New York or Bondi Beach and Manley to Sydney. By such means we became familiar with our new habitat and increased our social circle.

Mrs Edwards was the senior member of the dynasty and was rumoured to be fabulously wealthy as a result of ownership of all that family land; her daughter caught Bill's eye and they became very close, so that we were fortunate not to lose him when the ship finally sailed.

Before that day came, as I was at a loose end having waved my lady farewell at the end of her holiday, I fell into conversation with a local man who opened my eyes to other aspects of Durban of which I was previously unaware. We arranged to meet again to attend a performance given by the Munro-Inglis repertory company touring the country at the time and presenting Restoration Comedy. We saw "And so to bed" with Wensley Pithey in the leading part with Nan Munro, Virginia Pilkington, Rolf Lefebvre and Noel Hewitt to name but a few.

After the performance we went back stage and I was introduced to them all, finding in their company a tremendous gulp of fresh air after so long in the blinkers that until then I had been unaware that I was wearing. Social life on board was (and to me will always be) attractive and deeply satisfying, but this was the first time that I had seen it as somewhat limited.

It was with extreme reluctance that we finally broke away from Durban and its enormous influence on my formative period, to call first at East London and then Cape Town where I was able to turn the tables on Johnny Giddey; we called on him in his home to see how he was coping with life ashore.

Now we were loading, not for home, but for Boston, New York and Baltimore and they carefully kicked us out of port four days before Christmas. Once again the big holiday had to be observed at sea, but at least I had celebrated my 19th birthday in

Durban the day after my big sister, Dorothy, tied the knot in St. Andrew's Church, Catford. They could hardly have been expected to wait for us two, Dad and me, both in the southern hemisphere, after Dot's separation from Jack finally ended with his repatriation from Italy and release from the RAF.

In a matter of a few weeks our surroundings underwent a dramatic transformation as we arrived in Boston in the depth of winter with ice floating in the harbour.

At this point perusal of an atlas and the eastern seaboard of the States and Canada is of interest; Boston is tucked away in a corner of a long inset of land starting with the Bay of Fundy in the north and ending with the Cape Cod peninsular which sits above that treacherous area described by Hermann Melville in the 19th century and more recently by Sebastian Junger and Linda Greenlaw, the home of the whaling and fishing communities of the New England coast, recalling those romantic (?) names of Nantucket Sound, Martha's Vineyard and, for my purposes, the Cape Cod Canal. This waterway cuts the journey from Boston to New York appreciably and at the same time gives shelter from what can be a very rough stretch of water. Passage through the canal in January 1946 was like a prolonged visit to Santa's Grotto: the trees lining the edge were festooned with silver jewellery in the still, silent, frosty air. The journey lasted only a few hours but, as ever, the memory lasts a lifetime.

My only memory of New York is renewal of contact with the club and in particular with the Cappa sisters who were running affairs in the daytime. What mattered was the passage of time though I was as yet unaware that after leaving for Baltimore and then returning to New York for the second time, my cadetship was completed.

Having been given to understand that without recognised pre-sea training (a couple of years on the "Worcester" or the "Conway" or at Southampton Nautical College counted as a year's sea time) I would serve a full four years, it came as a complete surprise to be told in New York that a large proportion of my first voyage was acceptable as double time.

I was accordingly regarded as time expired and was transferred to the Ellerman and Wilson 3,000 tonner "Consuelo" on which I signed as supernumerary together with a character from Lockerbie, one Jardine, similarly time expired.

We shared a passenger cabin on this funny little cork of a ship in which we found we were provided with beds rather than bunks.

The ship was loaded with a full cargo of such weight, shape and size that she was as stiff as a poker. From New York to the north coast of Scotland she screwed her way across the ocean like a metronome, rolling some 90 degrees (i.e. 45 degrees either side of upright) in a period of about five seconds. Without bunkboards the only way to sleep, under these circumstances, is to lie on the deck jammed between at least two immovable objects.

We managed somehow, but pity the three poor passengers we were carrying whom we saw in New York and then for the second time about a fortnight later as we cleared Cape Wrath and entered the quieter waters north of Scotland. One had a completely green complexion and I'm sure had eaten nothing throughout the voyage.

A fitting way to round off nearly three and a half uniquely adventurous years.

We signed off in Hull in March 1946 and went our separate ways to attend nautical college prior to sitting our three part exams for 2nd Mate's Certificate.

And the ever-going-home "City of Canberra"? She left New York for Sydney NSW. via the Panama Canal and having thus circumnavigated the globe she went on to Japan before finally returning home after eighteen months away.

I never saw any of those shipmates again so I cannot vouch for their sanity at the end of their voyage. What price the "Flying Dutchman"?

CHAPTER TEN
HOW NOT TO SWALLOW
THE ANCHOR

The three month period required to stay ashore to take 2nd Mate's ticket was extended by leave due and the Easter break and we would certainly have stopped schooling over the period covering the Victory Parade.

As a captive member of Ellerman's in no position to deny my availability, I was one, perhaps the only one, to represent the company in the Merchant Navy contingent in the march-past. I see no way in which it could have been avoided, but the awful truth is that our group was fronted by a gaggle of elderly master mariners who had clearly never marched in unison in all their lives. Their broken steps posed an impossible problem for us following to decide whether to ignore them or to try to cover and hope they would readjust. The result was a sickening mess and as far as I am aware, we were the only ones to have passed the dais out of step.

In retrospect, I still feel proud of the privilege given me to be there and to march past the Royal family and all those famous warriors and politicians, too many to have taken in, in the limited time it took to pass by. Privileged too, to be amongst representatives not merely of our armed services, but our Commonwealth, Continental and American Allies together with numerous civilian services, all involved as we had been, in what was a titanic struggle, so difficult to reproduce realistically for those who have come along after the dust has settled.

After stuttering through my exams and much to my chagrin, I was appointed 19th August, not as 3rd mate but 4th on the new "City of Carlisle", her second voyage in fact. What a blow to a fellow's pride, a glorified overgrown cadet's job, still sharing a watch and not making proper use of an impressive new qualification.

The voyage was, nevertheless, compensation for the disappointment, a short trip that took us round Africa.

We called at Cape Town where the Chief Steward had a second wife and family – some people really ask for trouble; I think he had one or two dodgy contacts there too, as at the end of the voyage he was unable to produce my discharge book which had been put in his charge when we sailed and for which I don't doubt there was a black market at that time. As no receipt had been given the loss could not be put at his door and I was unable to complain that all my early record was gone. I simply had to start afresh.

Next stop was Durban where the second mate had an old flame working as a nurse up on the Beria, the hillside overlooking the sea.

The cadets and I were obliged to keep him and three others of the nurses company on evenings out on the town, all in the line of duty, you understand.

Next Lourenco Marques, Beira, Tanga and Mombasa, all fascinating new territory to me.

The "..Carlisle" was fitted with innovative hatch covers made of hollowed steel, the same hand manageable size as conventional wooden hatch boards, but intended to reduce the nuisance of wear and tear.

A shower in Mombasa required replacement of top deck hatch covers in a hurry to prevent cargo in the lower hold from getting wet. It was on removing these covers again that a hefty African stevedore slipped on a wet one and fell some forty feet onto an irregular heap of scrap iron. Unbelievably he was conscious when reached, but far too badly injured to survive. We were given to understand that his widow received five pounds in compensation for her loss.

It was here that we were told by the resident shipworker that Neville Heath, while serving in the RAF in Nairobi, had been involved in a murder that subsequently became his trade mark in the UK. On this occasion the native driver was hanged for the crime. If the story is true, there is no question that it would have been hushed up with all record probably untraceable.

The voyage ended on 3rd December and now, too late, came the happily expected promotion to 3rd mate. The world was now my oyster and I was unable to break into it due to a combination of two factors. As already explained I was impelled to start a new life ashore at the earliest opportunity and we now learnt that the Essential Works Order on the Merchant Service was to be lifted on January 1st 1947.

If today it seems extraordinary to walk away from a substantial, secure situation to enter into competition with the ever increasing flow of demobilised forces personnel, I have to point to the very powerful atmosphere of cooperation and camaraderie that continued from the war into the early post war period, to the feeling of renaissance, the need to rebuild our country from the ruins of the blitz. Indeed there was plenty of work available and the trick was to select the sort of work that was both suitable and with satisfactory prospects of permanence.

My problem was knowing what I didn't want to do without the foggiest idea of what I did want as a life long substitute for the vocation that I craved for yet proposed to abandon. I acknowledged a fascination for maps and it seemed reasonable to pursue a career with the Ordnance Survey. How theory and practice can diverge! I went like a lamb to the slaughter unaware of two essential requirements for such a career; firstly the job was in the hands of the Royal Engineers before the war and to progress one required an army background and preferably an R.E. tie! The second essential was a proficiency in draughtsmanship.

Having neither of these requirements my chances were doomed from the start, but I persevered in this new life style quite enjoying myself for about eighteen months, but at the end of that time the O.S. and I were mutually fed up and I succeeded in resigning a few days before they could sack me.

Now in October 1948 I had to face the fact that I was an unsuitable candidate for work ashore and I accordingly plied the

Shipping Company routes eating humble pie. Please can I have my old job back? But the answer was a firm negative.

I tried every office in Fenchurch Street, Leadenhall Street and all the associated side streets without success and was near despair until someone whispered in my ear "Blue Star Line".

This company operated, primarily, refrigerated cargo ships. They were fine, well appointed vessels trading with desirable ports in South America, Australia and New Zealand. It would have been expected to have a surplus of seafaring staff like all the other companies at that time but when I poked my head around their door in West Smithfield it was nearly grabbed from my body. I didn't enquire why that should be but simply took advantage of the situation.

They asked me what post I was looking for and naturally I told them I wanted nothing less than a 3rd mate's job. They regretted that they only had a vacancy for a 4th mate so I accepted this on condition that I would be first in line for the next 3rd mate vacancy.

The "Paraguay Star" was a seventy first class passenger frozen cargo ship of 6,330 tons nett (roughly speaking a 10,000 tonner) about to start her second voyage. She was one of four running from Victoria Dock, London to Rio (in nine days), Santos, Monte Video and Buenos Aires (in sixteen days). Discharge of outward general cargo and loading frozen meat, chilled oranges and bananas took a further three weeks and we called in at Tenerife to bunker both ways. From B.A. we called only at Rio homeward after a brief stop at Monte Video.

The great joy of these ships was that the mate was entertainments officer and did not keep a watch, hence a day or two after my call at the office I found myself in full charge of the 8.00p.m. to midnight watch on the bridge of an almost new few million pounds worth of ship and cargo with seventy V.I.P.s aboard capable of paying ten pounds a day for the privilege, belting down the English Channel faster than I had ever sailed before and frightened out of my wits at the responsibility.

It took a little while as I adapted to the new conditions, to start reading between the lines to find out why the company had such a turn over of sea staff.

Blue Star Line was (and presumably still is) owned by the Vestey family who appeared to have a somewhat hands-on, rolled up sleeves kind of attitude which affected not only the higher echelons of the company organisation, but had a knock-on effect throughout the entire personnel causing employees of whatever rank or seniority to spend far too much time looking over their shoulders.

Somehow an antagonism was engendered between deck and engine room at sea and this seemed to be orchestrated by certain eminences grises in the background seeking to divide and rule.

Obviously this sort of thing is impossible to trace to its source and conclusions arrived at are influenced by rumour and prejudice. All that can be said is that a disquiet existed which was alien to the character of the average seafarer and those free to do so usually left the company's employment as soon as it became convenient.

The first evidence of double dealing that I was aware of came to me at the end of my second trip on the "Paraguay Star" when I learnt through the grape-vine of a vacancy for 3rd mate on the "Norman Star" currently in the Mersey. My tentative enquiry with the London office received a blank denial whereupon I reminded them of their promise and informed them of the vacancy of which they professed to be unaware! By such strong-arm tactics I gained my promotion and duly joined "Norman Star" in Liverpool.

She was the biggest possible contrast to the "Plate boats" as it is possible to imagine; she was built in 1916 as one of the very earliest refrigerated ships and whereas she had all the 'fridge ship paraphernalia she had long ago been relegated to the carriage of general cargo.

She left the Mersey on a Harrison Line charter carrying mainly building materials to the Spanish speaking elements of the Caribbean; we even had a writer on board specifically to deal with the cargo administration, there being such a multiplicity of bills of lading, mate's receipts, etc. all in Spanish.

We called at Trinidad, Punta Cardon, Bachequero in the Gulf of Maracaibo and bunkered in Curacao before release and passage through the Panama Canal for a run in lovely weather northwestwards to San Francisco, the Puget Sound and then up the Alberni "canal" to Port Alberni to load pulp for Bremen. No seaman could possibly ask for pleasanter, more attractive runs than these that my new shipping company masters had presented me with and there was still South Africa, Australia and New Zealand to come!

Before proceeding with the next and most memorable voyage on "Napier Star", two incidents on the Plate run deserve report.

The fledgling National Health Service at this time was sending mobile units around to X-ray the general public in an attempt to reduce the incidence of tuberculosis and similar lung problems. In the process a suspicious shadow was discovered on my mother's plate and in the follow-up our family GP recommended complete rest in the sunshine.

Dad was currently serving on "City of Kimberley" on the South African service and the company was prevailed upon to send Mum on another of the South African ships to join him for a period in Durban. She went out on the "City of Paris" which delivered her to Dad in Durban on its way to other African ports. Having completed her outward schedule the "..Paris" returned to Durban homeward bound and picked her up again. The company at that time still could not allow any officer to be accompanied by his wife throughout a voyage and in any case the ostensible purpose for the trip was unarguably fulfilled.

Ellerman's, like Blue Star, bunkered their ships at Tenerife and the "..Paris" arrived there a day or two before the "Paraguay Star" was due outward on my second voyage.

Imagine my surprise and delight having picked up a ship dead ahead travelling towards us on our reverse course so that we both had to alter course to avoid collision, to discover that ship to be the "..Paris".

Messages were exchanged and much use was made of binoculars but the event occurred at breakfast time and we passed too rapidly to give Mum a chance of showing herself. Nevertheless it was good fun and we were left to wonder what the odds of such a thing happening might be.

I think it was on the same voyage outward bound that I went ashore in Monte Video to do some shopping in the late afternoon. While there I bumped into Sparks and we decided upon a cup of tea and a bite to eat before returning aboard and we accordingly entered a café-cum-restaurant.

A quick glance told us that we had chosen a bad moment, the place appeared crowded until we spotted a curtain with an ante room beyond apparently unoccupied. We enquired of a waiter if this room was in use and were assured that all was well, so while everyone else was supping cheek by jowl we found ourselves with plenty of elbow room to eat and drink in comfort. After a while two others appeared and occupied a table nearby, two ladies, one of whom attracted my attention for no obvious reason. In puzzling this out I must have kept glancing in the lady's direction in coming to the realisation that I was looking into a pair of eyes with no distinction between iris and pupil. It was the first time that I had seen genuinely black eyes.

My glances had not gone unnoticed and after a while the lady separated from her companion and moved to a table on her own. It was this action that told us we had elected to place ourselves in a place of assignation.

Clearly the system in Monte Video was for prostitutes to ply their trade with dignity in a respectable venue and in a completely respectable manner. What a contrast with the sleazy nonsense we have to put up with in the UK.

Normally on the homeward journey we would call into Monte for an hour or two to pick up a few bags of mail; only very rarely did we stay overnight but there was always that possibility. On the way back to the ship I mused aloud to Sparks that if by chance we called in for long enough homeward I had a very good mind to try finding the owner of that pair of eyes which had me completely hooked.

Predictably when the time came the ship was required to stay overnight in Monte. At the first opportunity I dashed ashore and found the café. Opening the door of the annexe I found the room empty. What to do next? I turned round and by some miracle saw the lady herself some ten feet away on the pavement. I rushed at her like a lunatic and frightened her half to death then realised I was confronting a girl who couldn't speak a word of English.

Making an apology in a foreign language of which one is abysmally ignorant is difficult enough, to discuss and negotiate terms of a particularly delicate nature can be extremely awkward. To be told that English currency is not acceptable is the last straw when one has nothing else to offer.

Fortunately Miss Black Eyes brought me back to sanity by pointing out the Cambio or exchange booth on the square to which we had moved and I was able to change my pound note for the required eight pesos. I suppose that if she had been obliged to make the transaction she would have received a less favourable rate of exchange.

At this point we linked arms and she conducted me to the back entrance of a highly presentable hotel. Here we joined a queue of some six or seven couples awaiting the availability of one or other of a series of small rooms each furnished with a bed, a chair, a bedside table and centrally situated, a bidet.

The bidet was fitted with a douche so that the girl was able to demonstrate absolute cleanliness before joining her partner on the freshly made bed.

Hotel staff changed the bed linen the moment each room was vacated and the keynote was cleanliness.

How the other half live, indeed. What an eye-opener this system was to me. I wonder if the penny will ever drop in this country of ours that prostitution always has been, always will be and can be conducted in a highly civilised manner if we can only work up sufficient honesty to acknowledge it as a part of everyday life.

Having discharged our woodpulp ("Norman Star" again!) in war ravaged Bremen, we proceeded to the Blackwater River in Essex via Aberdeen. Once anchored in the river we paid off on board and deserted the ship completely, allowing her to await her fate in the hands of unknown ship- breakers. It was not before time but nevertheless a sad way to treat an old servant. I had nothing but happy memories of her.

After a brief period of leave I was sent back to Liverpool and shortly joined the "Napier Star" a renamed wartime built Empire boat. In spite of my comments re strained relations on Blue Star ships, the "Napier Star" turned out to be the happiest ship that I served on, largely due to the no-nonsense character of the master, Charlie Horton, (not that he was ever addressed as such, but he was referred to in the company in that familiar way; he was a lovely man).

This voyage took me to the Cape, Port Elizabeth, East London, Durban, Melbourne, Auckland, Aden, Genoa, Plymouth, Le Havre and back home to London – a six month voyage, but what a voyage.

The first event of note was our coincidence in Port Elizabeth with the Norwegian ship "Breim". This was a wartime development pioneer of a ship which was one of the first to be built entirely without rivets. Every seam on the shell plating was welded and tests had proved the welds to be stronger than the metal that they joined. What was not appreciated was the existence of lines of weakness parallel to the welds. What was also not understood at the time was the fact that the plates joined by rivets actually move in relation to each other when the ship travels through water and the support pressures are permanently moving.

The "Breim" was taken over new in Baltimore and started eastwards across the Atlantic to meet a particularly violent storm in the western ocean. After some hours of being tossed about the crew discovered with horror that their ship was beginning to split on each side amidships, a process that could only end with her breaking in two.

All ships with respectable ports of registry must observe certain requirements to maintain a classification approved by underwriters and one result of this was the carriage of what was known as the "insurance wire". This was a coil of very thick wire set at one side of the poop and carefully manoeuvred round and otherwise ignored. It was never used being intended only for dire emergency.

Exceptional circumstances sometimes arise and "Breim" was suddenly very grateful for her wire. It was run from aft right forward and made fast to the bitts (a ship's version of bollards) at each end. The central part of the wire was no doubt subjected to a tightening system with blocks and tackle at suitable intervals so that the ends of the ship were effectively sewn together by the wire, countering the effect of the splitting.

After this experience a modification to the new welding method was introduced and ships were then built with some welding and a proportion of riveting.

As for the "Breim", her crew (all of them?) received gold watches to commemorate the event and reward the initiative that produced such a brilliant method of salvation.

All this was related to me by Albert Friiso, her second mate, when he came aboard to challenge us to a football match. I'm afraid we were not charitable enough to allow them to beat us, even though they provided all the equipment.

Our next stop of any significance was in Melbourne where, it seems to me now, it spent most of the time raining, certainly in the afternoons.

I found a wonderful second hand bookshop in one of the main streets and remember evening entertainment being organised mostly by a go-getting Missions to Seamen padre.

Our stay there was long enough to ensure that we spent Christmas in Auckland and it was there that Charlie Horton staggered me by suggesting that I should take two or three days leave and fly to South Island to reunite with cousin Bob who by this time had found employment in the building industry (why on earth did that never occur to me?).

I had not contemplated the remotest possibility of such an initiative and of course I took the opportunity with both hands. I had already spent Christmas Day in Auckland with another cousin Bob (New Zealand was liberally populated with my mother's relatives and I'd made myself known to the Auckland branch on arrival there), now to renew contact with Bob Wardrop in Nelson and meet his mother in Motueka.

Flying, on the other hand, was not so funny. I had not been up before and to do so meant being introduced to a Lockheed "Lodestar", an aircraft that was probably adapted from cargo to passenger carriage and which proceeded behind propellers operated, I'll swear, by a two-stroke engine. I was not particularly mechanically minded and this fearful experience fully justified my scepticism.

However, I still recall the candlewick effect of a deciduous forest passing below and the sight of Mount Cook in the distance during the couple of hours flight to Wellington and the confusion as we swung out over the sea and I tried to gain a sense of proportion; were those gentle wavelets close below or white horses considerably further down? It took some time for reality to assert itself as we approached the city coming in to land.

A change of plane, another hour in the air, and I was in Nelson to be met by Bob and ushered to the maternity wing of the local hospital to meet his wife Ruth and baby Vivienne who had just arrived. The little one could only be viewed through a glass barrier.

It wasn't long before I met the proud grandmother and spent an hour or two in Motueka, but wherever we were, I suppose Bob and I talked ourselves hoarse whether in his rowing boat or while playing tennis (?) - we could neither return the other's service – or just sitting in the summer sunshine.

Back in Auckland a second Scandinavian football challenge was received, this time from the Danish "Astoria", and some firm friendships were made. In this respect it helped that the Captain had on board his charming daughter from whom he had been separated together with the rest of his loved ones in occupied Denmark while he was making his contribution to the Allied cause, as indeed did so many other Continental seamen.

Such diversion alternating with visits to Auckland Bob's home helped to make this period a memorable one and to cap it all, on leaving we had on board no less than twelve passengers, all female and including several of the eligible nubile variety.

Perhaps I should add here that the Captain made it very clear that there should be no hanky-panky and you may be sure there was none.

This was the only voyage on which I participated in a crossing the line ceremony and although we made a good showing for our passengers, I don't remember certificates being produced, certainly not to compare with those provided by the "City of Derby"some twenty five years earlier.

Twenty-eight days without sight of land went all too fast for me, but Aden came and then Genoa now in mid-winter. Whilst the weather in port was comfortable enough, on leaving we managed to coincide with the Mistral churning the Gulf of Lyons into a savage roller-coaster due to an unbelievably short, high ground swell which created the effect of a full Atlantic storm.

To add insult to injury we discovered, too late, that we had a stowaway on board. At that time there were a great many questionable characters in circulation including fugitives from who knows what as well as genuinely stateless individuals without personal documents. They were usually separated from their homelands and without the means to return either because of the Iron Curtain or because they were not recognised by the authorities of the country they were currently trapped in. For the most part they wanted to cut their losses and emigrate to more prosperous zones where they would be obliged to enter illegally.

Once such characters succeeded in hitching a lift on a ship they produced the most enormous headaches as they were not acceptable anywhere that the ship went and were required to be returned whence they came, in theory at least. In practice this too was an impracticable proposition and I can't remember what happened to our lad, I presume he was dealt with by UK immigration authorities and it may well be that the company faced a hefty fine for its inadvertent sin.

We dropped our passengers in Plymouth before making a brief call at Le Havre on the way home to London.

By now I required a couple more months sea time in charge of a watch to be able to take my mate's ticket exam and I was accordingly transferred to the "Argentina Star" for a final Plate boat voyage. On completion of this I came ashore requiring a minimum two month study time at Sir John Cass nautical college before attempting to tackle the higher grade exam.

I had decided not to continue with Blue Star and still I was determined to stay ashore with no further idea of what to do with myself. The inevitable consequence when at last I became the proud possessor of a mate's certificate was a prolonged period in the doldrums – in a word – drift.

CHAPTER ELEVEN
DRIFT AND RECOVERY

Previous experience had knocked the confidence from me when it came to seeking shore employment and I suppose I just didn't try.

The exam for mate's ticket alone had taken the stuffing out of me due to the first two hour paper on which a 50% minimum mark was required to avoid automatic failure; after an hour I concluded a major exercise and saw that my findings were ridiculous. This discovery struck an unbelievable blow to my nervous system as panic and paralysis set in. Taking a grip, the only thing to do was to re-read the question and search for an explanation and it only took a moment for a stupid omission to come to light. Next a word of explanation to the examiner and a wild amendment to the working using all manner of short cuts. Then to tackle the rest of the paper in the time remaining at the end of which I was a limp rag.

This nightmare affected the whole of the exam which consisted of three days written work, an indeterminate period of eyeball to eyeball confrontation with a senior examiner trying to decide my competence and reliability in "seamanship", an ordeal going by the name of "orals" and a practical test of ability to read semaphore and morse.

When I was finally passed as competent my reaction was not one of elation as when passing for 2nd mate but rather of sheer relief. I found that the shock to my system would not allow me either to sit or lie comfortably, such was the intensity of the ache across the small of my back.

Knowing that I would not return to Blue Star I had no hesitation in awarding myself a holiday.

It was now late in August 1950 and somewhere about this time the family regained contact with a French friend the last survivor of her family with whom exchange visits had been made chiefly by my mother's sister, Auntie Dorry, before the war.

Germaine, a school teacher in her mid forties, came to see us and I took the opportunity to return with her to Bourges via Paris.

I found both the French capital and provincial France in the early post-war period fascinating and enchanting and I stayed for a long time refusing to speak my own language. This, I found, stretched such intellect as I possess and Germaine's patience in equal proportions and the resultant feeling at the end was of refreshment and renewal to an extraordinary degree. This was one of several two way visits with the Festival of Britain looming and attracting Germaine together with many other mobile Europeans and at some stage during the winter I was summoned to Bourges in order to take off southwards from there to go skiing in the Massif Centrale.

Meanwhile at home I renewed contact with friends from the Munro-Inglis repertory which had by now returned to Britain and become involved with Sadlers Wells and the BBC. I found myself watching a presentation of "Façade" choreographed by the unknown John Cranko who joined our circle of acquaintances thanks to the South African connection.

I was clearly living in cloud cuckoo land, putting off the evil day when I would finally have to take control of my life again. This moment arrived towards the end of 1951 when I became aware of a total self-disgust and a growing realisation that I was getting rather too close to Germaine who, after all, belonged to my parents' generation.

In fairness to us both I had to put a stop to my drifting, once again eat humble pie and present myself to the Shipping Federation pool which was still operating and request a ship, any ship, destined anywhere in the world and the sooner the better.

It was a few days before Christmas when I was sent to Runciman's office in Fenchurch Street to report for duty as 3rd mate on a ship which had just been bought from Hill's of Bristol. She was being gutted and refitted for the carriage of reels of paper for the Newsprint Supply Company. Her name was to be "Chepman".

On meeting Mr Jones of Runciman's who were operating the ships on the company's behalf (four ships in all), I was told not to hurry but stay home for Christmas and so I joined the ship in Avonmouth a few days into the New Year. I signed on 12th January 1952

At the outbreak of war, one immediate decision to be made was the manner of regulation to be adopted with regard to the newspaper industry. Entirely apart from the question of censorship and security there was the matter of paper shortage to be considered.

At exactly what stage the Newsprint Supply Company was set up I don't know but its function was to supply standardised presses with a maximum of four different reel sizes, all 36" diameter, a substantial reduction of the previous variety in existence.

When I joined them at the start of 1952 newsprint importation was still virtually exclusively through this wartime organisation although its days were numbered. Even so the ship I was to join was to replace an earlier "Baskerville" at considerable expense and a year later a brand new ship, the "Isaac Carter" was built.

What I was soon to learn was that newsprint is a somewhat delicate commodity which requires specialist handling. It has to be stowed on end to avoid crushing and must have a flat base on which to stand in homogeneous tiers (i.e. no mixed sizes) and in a combination of sizes to fill stowage spaces with the minimum waste of space.

Loading presented no labour problems as this was invariably done at the mill of manufacture, but discharge was always best carried out at specialist wharves like Convoy's at Deptford or more commonly at Purfleet. Elsewhere I have seen dockers using hand hooks, not recommended, as a very little damage on the edge of a reel will render the remaining continuous length of paper insufficient to be acceptable to the press by virtue of the increased frequency of reel changing and the consequential machine down-time involved.

189

Because the firm was small, and in its way, unique, a few ships visiting a few ports with a very specific purpose to fulfil, there was an intimate, family sort of feeling.

The ports, usually small, were close to coniferous forests where an abundance of clean fresh water was an essential requisite for the production of the paper and this had the unfortunate side effect of condemning the ships mainly to heavy weather or wintry conditions.

For a little under six months of the year we picked up our cargo from Newfoundland, the Gulf of St. Lawrence or with occasional trips to the Baltic, but in October ports like Botwood and Cornerbrook were denied us as the ice closed in and we were pushed southwards to Saint John, New Brunswick or back into the less solidly frozen Baltic ports.

Either way we quite fairly described our occupation as "eight months gales and four months fog", forgetting the balmier summer days (and nights) in the Baltic.

The diabolical aspect of this was the fact that the company was not interested, quite rightly, in alternative cargoes and in consequence we proceeded into the worst Atlantic weather in light ship condition i.e in ballast..

To describe the effect of this situation would make demands on the reader's imagination which I'm sure are beyond me but I would make one or two points which are not generally clearly understood:

Firstly, it pays to bear in mind that we sit on a globe of earth and water encased in a jacket of air; the globe rotates about its axis and moves through space at an angle to the revolutionary movement. This angle (the obliquity of the ecliptic) is responsible for our four seasons and ensures a daily variation, no matter how slight, in wind and weather conditions. As the earth turns the air jacket is heated locally by the sun and cooled again so that there is perpetual air movement as temperature, pressure and volume are in a constant state of change.

Secondly, when a high wind hits a large expanse of open water it not only lifts the surface making waves and spray, but it forces the entire mass of water to move in the direction it is blowing.

The only means the water has of resuming its level is for the leading edge to drop and turn back under itself creating what is effectively a succession of long cylinders of water which wheel across the ocean in front of the wind, travelling in an irregular and unpredictable rhythm. This we know as "swell".

To some extent air and water movement is self-contained within a storm, but not in the case of swell which is so difficult to pin down and define. Because water is incompressible it follows that when substantial pressure is put upon a large expanse of sea on the eastern coast of America, in pure mathematical theory there must be an instantaneous awareness of it on the French and Portuguese coasts. Unrealistic though this obviously is, the fact remains that when there is a storm brewing in the western Atlantic, the first real warning in mid Atlantic comes in the guise of steadily increasing swell from the direction of the storm's current location.

Some degree of swell is ever present regardless of wind strength, the gaps between the wheels of water lifting and dropping the ship's bows or stern to cause pitching and occasionally pounding and depending on the angle of the ship to wind direction, causes the ship to roll. Pounding is more or less the equivalent of a swimmer performing a belly-flop when attempting to dive.

When barometric pressure starts falling, the wind rises and the swell gets heavier and the ship starts rolling and pitching in a more determined manner, it is time to ensure that everything mobile is lashed down and to run out lifelines along the decks if necessary for anyone exposed on deck to grab in the event of need.

As the wind rises, so the surface of the sea is turned into racing, white-topped waves which, when struck by the ship's bow fling themselves upwards and break into bullets of spray. In combination with the ship's movement forced by increasing swell, whole seas rise up and thunder down onto the forward part of the ship, blinding those on lookout with spray that will lift to a hundred feet in the air with ease. Wind and swell together will try to jerk the bow to one side or the other as the helmsman struggles to maintain the course.

In these conditions it is imperative to keep a ship heading directly into the weather; any angling against the swell, any loss of steerage way must introduce a risk, no matter how small, of rolling too far over and doing untold damage if not actually capsizing.

Imagine standing braced and holding on for dear life against roller-coaster movement on the bridge of an empty ship being tossed around like a cork. At this point comes the crunch; as the bow falls into a pit in the maelstrom, so the stern lifts and the propeller is exposed, the engine races threatening to tear itself from its mountings and the engineer immediately cuts the speed to a bare minimum.

Too big a speed reduction risks loss of steerage way, hence the engineer is discouraged from over-reaction and responds by reducing the speed overall to avoid over much pressure fluctuation on the working parts, the ship becomes less manageable, rolls more heavily but possibly pitches a little less.

This general discomfort and sustained vigilance in the teeth of a screaming wind can persist for two or three days on end and I remember a famous occasion when we clocked up a day's run of precisely six miles. Well at least it was six miles forward. Throughout this weather the sky remains overcast and gloomy and heavy rainfall usually adds to the misery.

I think its fair to say that the seaman adapts to this kind of challenge from the ocean early in his career and in general derives pleasure at coming through more or less unscathed, but I've yet to meet anyone who enjoyed a single minute during days of constant fog, particularly in cold latitudes where the dampness in the air draws the heat from the body and one is effectively blind and regularly deafened by the ship's own siren announcing its presence to what is in all probability an empty sea.

All too often such fog materialises at the time of year when icebergs are drifting into one's course and the best indication of their presence is a sudden sucking away of what little heat the gods have left on an exposed bridge.

On these occasions the end of the watch cannot come quickly enough.

Given an Atlantic crossing extended by heavy weather, I have to say that my least favourite port in midwinter was Saint John, New Brunswick in the Bay of Fundy. Most of the time loading was effected throughout a period of intermittent driving snow when, in order to keep the cargo dry, tents were erected over the hatches, great domes of canvas open to the quayside to enable reels to be plucked from covered wagons, swung inboards under the tent and lowered into place in the hold. The predominant colour was grey and my practice was to hibernate for much of the time, once having familiarised myself with the town and what it had to offer. This to my jaundiced memory seemed to consist of one dance hall, two cinemas and a few shops with the rest of the place closed down for the season under its permanent winter snow blanket.

It was during a period of deep depression when anyone wanting my company would have had to winkle me out from behind my book tucked away in my cabin that my immediate senior approached me in a state of some distress. Like most young M.N. officers he was a decent man with no wish to become embroiled casually with random members of the opposite sex, certainly not in Saint John. But he was in a dilemma; "You know my passion for dancing"- he was an expert-"I met an ideal partner at the local hop last night". Ideal she was, but only as a dancing partner.

Apparently she clung to him mercilessly and at the end of the evening he'd had the utmost difficulty extricating himself. He achieved this only after promising to attend again on the following evening which was to be our last in port. What her intentions were is debatable but its effects were terrifying and my poor companion was torn between his passion and naked fear of the aging maiden (?) whom we had already dubbed "the limpet".

He had decided to go only if I were to accompany him as chaperone; I was to take every opportunity to interrupt and interfere generally. I would butt in at every Gentleman's Excuse-me and at whatever other opportunities arose. In short I was to be a counter-limpet.

Earlier I might have refused but at that late stage of our loading program I was in fairly desperate straits and in spite of my lack of enthusiasm for dancing I suppose I needed a break and so I agreed to cooperate.

The dance hall proved to be an enormous wooden barn of a place with the paint peeling off inside and out. It seemed to be lit by a single unshaded 40 watt lamp bulb dangling in the centre. Hundreds of shadowy figures drifted about, released from somebody's nightmare (where had they all emerged from?), and I knew that I shouldn't have come but it was too late now and so I concentrated on the task in hand.

The limpet was a very good if reluctant dancer in my arms. She was also somewhat plain and at a guess high up on the shelf.

She made me work hard to maintain my side of the bargain of which she was certainly unaware initially but surely slowly gaining an inkling, and by the time of the last waltz, a dark suspicion. She tried at that stage to steer her partner to the opposite end of the hall from me but without success in view of his lack of cooperation. The expression on her face when I joined them on their way out of the hall almost made the evening worth while but after a few sulky comments she suddenly capitulated.

"How would you both like to join me in a cup of coffee before going back? There's a café just over the road from my flat" she threw at us.

To say we were taken off guard is an under statement; we were dumbfounded, and bursting with relief we readily agreed.

After coffee she confessed that she preferred to be accompanied to her door as this was not the choicest part of town, but we were not to be deceived and stuck to safety in numbers.

All three trudged across the impacted snow and on opening a door seemingly in the centre of a large house found ourselves confronted by a bare wooden staircase serving flats on either side.

The walls beside the stairs were discoloured and dirty and the stairway itself appeared to have been the route taken by coalmen or someone similar since time immemorial. At all events grit and goodness knows what else grated under our feet as we climbed to the upper reaches of this tenement and I found myself sympathising with the limpet in her desire for company up that ill-lit rising corridor.

At last we reached the top and as the limpet turned the key in the lock,opened the door and allowed the light to flood out, instinct shrieked "step inside to safety" and we gladly tumbled in.

Again we were confronted with generous space, mostly comprised of uncovered floorboards with a wood burning stove smack in the middle, a table and a bed-divan and—-.now was the lady's turn to study the expressions on our faces as, with the door closed firmly behind us and we being too far advanced to retreat, the trap was sprung and limpet mark two crossed the room and immediately glued herself to me.

This one was a lot younger, blonde and quite demented, a condition that can only be respected as indicative of self preservation in consideration of the natural provocation to total madness in that town at that time of year. Just to think of having to live there.

In view of all the stress I had endured up to that moment over a very long period of time, the pressures of youth and a hitherto repressed need to burst forth, what ensued must have been completely predictable to any casual observer.

Limpet mark two attacked me with nail varnish, hair scissors and suchlike to all of which I retaliated in uninhibited and very positive fashion so that in no time at all our behaviour was so outrageous that the dancing partners were forced to flee the room in their embarrassment, into the one remaining room, a bedroom of course.

Thus the knight in shining armour , the gallant chaperone, finally succeeded in forcing his ward inextricably into the position that both had fought so hard to prevent.

I have racked my brain for the best part of fifty years to divine the moral of that story, assuming that there is one, but it continues to elude me.

I took a couple of voyages off in the summer of 1952 in order to accompany Mum and Dad on a visit to Bourges. It turned out to be an anticlimax because Dad was recalled from leave and I was left high and dry in France again.

In retrospect it is clear to me now that this was the time that I started a subconscious search for someone to settle down with and found the next King dynasty.

On the train to Paris I fell in with Jill and her brother and was able to render some assistance as they were newcomers and the association led on to a courtship lasting several months. I was always aware of something missing from the relationship and this eventually resolved itself when I met my second cousin once removed (? Our mothers were cousins) for the first time for over a dozen years.

It took no time at all for me to realise that this was the girl I was waiting for and from then onwards I knew, perhaps for the first time in my life, exactly where I was going.

I had joined "Caxton" as 2nd mate in November, now fully committed and with the seeds of pilotage beginning to germinate in my mind. I would see out my time for master's ticket with Newsprint Supply and then consider my options.

Marion and I had intended to make our engagement official in an anticipated short holiday period in June 1953 when we expected to be at home for the Queen's coronation; a vain hope due to a fiasco played out on the Northern coast of Newfoundland.

It was at the beginning of the season when the pack ice was breaking up and leaving the less formidable field ice for approaching shipping to negotiate. We requested a detailed report from the pilot station serving Botwood at Twillingate and were simply advised by them to proceed but the Old Man remained suspicious because this appeared to be at variance with the general ice reports for the area.

At this stage he made his mistake and went in to St.John's with the intention of picking up a pilot to take us by a coastal route "through the islands".

After waiting three days for the pilot to arrive we were informed that the coastal route was impassable hence we were obliged to take the route that we would have taken in the first place had we accepted the advice of the experts on the spot.

To avoid having to answer awkward questions, when we finally met the field ice the Old Man refused to enter it, preferring to skirt searching for an ice-free route. Failing to find one he anchored in the Northern bay and commissioned a seaplane to survey the area from the air.

By this means he avoided entering most of what proved to be pretty innocuous small ice which would hardly have scratched our sides, but he remained impregnable having "put the ship's safety first".

With the loss of the best part of a week our dream of a brief holiday at home and any sharing of the coronation festivities was dashed.

Trips were averaging about five weeks and I found for the first time that a month or so away was a much longer period than it had ever been before and the annoying part of it was that while it was acceptable to sit alongside a paper mill abroad, waiting while trees were converted into reels of paper, the greatest efforts were now being made to turn us round in the home port in as few as three days. It usually stretched into five, but this gave insufficient time to proceed with any sort of ambitious project.

It was this anxiety of the company to see the back of us as soon as possible that projected our precipitate entry into the marital state in January 1954.

The ship had arrived in the Channel at the end of a six week transatlantic trip, Saint John I suppose, when out of the blue we were informed that arrangements had been made for drydocking.

A frantic cable winged its way home with the query as to the possibility of tying the knot on the following Saturday. As luck would have it the last of our banns had been read just in time and preparations were hurtled forward to enable the deed to be done.

We married 23rd January, just four days after docking and paying off and we were able to take five days away on a snowbound honeymoon.

Such is love.

I don't know if there's a law of averages stating that at least one tragedy must mar every seafarer's life with the attendant shadow crossing the back of the mind from time to time for all eternity.

In Dad's case it was the loss of a shipmate of many years standing who was taken unexpectedly; in my case there were similarities, but the loss was of a younger man.

For what reason I can't recall, my senior whose responsibilities included putting the crew to work, required me to keep a check on, effectively to validate, the overtime worked by the A.B.s

About once a week three of the lads would arrive at my door, enter my cabin and proffer a scruffy hand-written account of dates, hours worked and job description.

I was able to rib their ringleader, a very popular, curly headed young man known universally as Toby (surnamed Jugg) unmercifully over one job description. It appeared that he and his mates augmented their incomes spending a great deal of time "pianting".

Very occasionally we would load in St.John's, Newfoundland and on the voyage in question, I think it was April 1954, we spent several days alongside there completely idle, awaiting the manufacture or delivery of our cargo.

This gave the mate an ideal opportunity to move apace with maintenance work including "pianting" on a stage hung over the ship's bow.

It was after lunch that a group of idle officers in shirt-sleeves, myself included, were passing the shining hour playing darts in the smoke-room when the lamp-trimmer spoilt our party in a state of deep distress. What he said had us flinging on our coats and racing to the fo'c's'le head and look over the side in time to help a soaked and sobbing young A.B. back on board from the pilot ladder. He'd managed to climb it again having jumped into the water in a vain attempt to pull Toby out.

It was bitterly cold on deck and the lads on the stage were clad in duffle coats, seaboots, scarves, woollen hats and gloves. On returning to the stage after a short break, Toby had executed a little dance to keep the circulation going, had lost his footing and somersaulted down, striking his head on the ship's side as he went. The water temperature was 28 degrees F and his clothing undoubtedly drew him under the surface. The blow to his head probably undid any attempt at self-preservation and although he did surface it was only momentarily and the grey-black water hid Toby from us until he was finally drawn out by someone working from a launch nearby.

Whereas Dad reported John Morgan's epitaph word for word, all I can remember of Toby's grave is the wooden cross and the name "Richard Jugg" which has transferred to and is indelibly etched into the fabric at the back of my mind.

Guilty conscience prevents me from working up any enthusiasm for playing darts today.

Harrison, the A.B. who risked his life trying to save Toby, was taken to hospital with hypothermia and shock, made a full recovery and was awarded Lloyd's Gold Medal for his courage.

St. John's never did appeal to me and after that episode I'm grateful that I never have returned there.

CHAPTER TWELVE
DAD'S SWANSONG

Preoccupied as I was with my venture into a new life with Newsprint Supply, I was away from home and ill-informed by a tight-lipped mother when a different type of tragedy struck.

Somewhere in the middle of 1952 Dad suffered that all too predictable breakdown.

In my narrative I have left him on the "Fort Edmonton" in July 1946 still in Singapore long after the company ought to have sent out a relief and while I don't know the date of his return, it must have been early December 1946 as I was completing my last voyage with Ellerman's on the "…Carlisle".

On the 14th December Laura and Ron married with Dad to give her away and me to act as his Best Man. At long last Dad was given a substantial leave, staying home until the end of February.

At that point the "…Tadoussac" came back into the reckoning. She was loaded outward to Bombay and Karachi, supposedly continuing from there to Calcutta to load for home.

I'll let an extract from Dad's letter to his Aunt Em fill in the details of the rest of this trip, things that duplicated my own experience both before and after this date of 31st May 1947:

"For the past couple of months we've been rushed to death in port and rolled to the devil at sea. The most cock-eyed voyage I ever made. We were originally supposed to load home from Calcutta after finishing discharge in Karachi. When I arrived in Karachi I was informed that the Calcutta loading was washed out and so far the Ministry had sent no new orders. Then suddenly I was told to go empty to Lourenco Marques for bunkers, taking enough coal there to carry on – still empty – to Monte Video for orders and then after loading in ports not specified, on to St. Vincent, Cape Verde Islands before re-bunkering. No loading ports or dates given: just a case of "We don't know where you're going, but see that you take enough coal to get there! Somebody else will tell you where to go bye and bye!". The net result is that I've brought an empty ship 9,000 miles before anybody could tell me where I was supposed to go. And at that I was actually within five miles of Monte Video before the Ministry made up their minds: then I got a wireless to go to Buenos Aires Roads – for orders!!

So after punching half way round the world in an empty ship I anchored in Buenos Aires Roads at 2.00am and cheerfully kidded myself that at last I'd get a decent sleep after three weeks with nothing but stray cat-naps. At 3.00am they sent two pilots aboard with orders to come on to Rosario (220 miles further) to start loading.

I don't know if you can imagine what sort of a passage it was – I can't tell you in polite language. A ship of this size, empty and drawing only 10 feet, right on through the South Atlantic winter. Worse than living on a football and I had to nurse her through three nasty little gales on the way. Hadn't had a decent sleep for nearly a month till we got here. But what really gets me is – 9,000 miles with an empty ship and the country crying out for tonnage. At the worst they could have given me a coal cargo in Lourenco Marques to bring here: the freight would at least partly have paid expenses. Good old tax-payer!! But that, of course, is the Ministry. Brains ?

Anyway, there's a bright side to it now. I'm loading here and in B.A. 9,000 tons of grain and food-stuffs for home."

That turned out to be the ship's last commercial voyage. As Ministry property and a wartime build, she presumably became embroiled in the finances of Lease-Lend. At all events Dad took her next from Liverpool to Mobile where she was handed over to the American authorities at the end of August 1947.

Her passing left something of an emptiness after all that she had meant at different times to all the family. She carried an aura of happiness in common with the "..Keelung"; she was a survivor with a colourful history in her short career under the British flag. I suppose she was moth-balled in Mobile and in due course disposed of or broken up.

While speaking of the British flag, in deference to the Old Man who was a devotee of Kipling, I would like to include these lines which he drew to my attention during the war with a great deal of feeling:

"First of the scattered legions,
Under a shrieking sky,
Dipping between the rollers
The English flag goes by."

Very evocative words from a very proud patriot.

Record from 1947 became scanty and I have no joining or leaving dates for Dad's last voyages. I believe the "City of Kimberley followed the "..Tadoussac" and his time on her lasted probably a couple of years whereafter he took over the "City of Delhi" and his last heroic record refers to the rescue of seven survivors of a derelict Burmese dhow.

On 15th December 1951 Derek Curson, 2nd mate and a previous shipmate of mine on the "..Carlisle", spotted an intermittent light abeam at 3.00 o'clock in the morning and decided to call Dad onto the bridge.

The subsequent alteration of course to investigate brought the ship to the badly damaged craft which proved to have been adrift for nine days, having been blown 400 miles across the Bay of Bengal during the passage of a cyclone. The men had been without food for five days and would almost certainly have died but for Derek's vigilance.

I'm fairly sure that Dad's breakdown happened towards the end of May the following year. Derek was still serving with him and when I bumped into him in London some time in the '60s he told me that Dad had gone berserk on the bridge entering or leaving port (Aden?), firing a revolver over the side and generally frightening everyone out of his wits. How the matter was resolved I don't know, but he was brought home and hospitalised, remaining on half pay until the end of December 1952 whereafter he was employed for some time relieving other masters in the home ports.

In the course of the next two years the company reluctantly decided to cut further loss and retire him on a slightly reduced pension seven years early.

Once again I have no exact date but a letter to the Mercantile Marine Service Association dated 14th September suggests that the decision was taken at that time.

Typically, Dad waited until his true retirement date, survived another six weeks and then succumbed to lung cancer.

I fully believe that if he'd not contracted the dread disease, his sense of duty and fair play would have led him to develop and die from some other malady at much the same time.

For as long as I can remember he said that at home Mum was captain of the ship, he merely the mate and he always lived up to that. His last seven years were contented with all the weight of responsibility lifted from his shoulders, giving him the chance to stay put and potter to his heart's content, safe where he wanted to be, under her wing.

CHAPTER THIRTEEN
PILOTAGE?

Those in the know said that there was no point in pursuing a career in pilotage, particularly of the London river, until attaining the age of at least twenty seven. It was also far better to have served in ships plying a regular trade in the river. With these two essentials one had only to wait for the periodic advertisement for applications to be issued, to apply and then sit back and wait for the lists to be closed. In the passage of time successful applicants would be short-listed and called for interview to be placed in order of preference. Thereafter they would be called into the profession in that order as vacancies became available. At that stage a race against time ensued as a further requirement insisted that a man should join the ranks before the age of thirty five; should that birthday arrive before the call, his name would be struck off.

The body responsible for all this is Trinity House. They look after the safety of our coastline by producing buoys and lightships, manning the latter as necessary. They determine the limits of pilotage waters within which local variations of depths and shallows would endanger approaching ships which the pilots effectively take over to bring safely into port.

I was in my twenty eighth year at the time of my marriage and still with Newsprint Supply, filling in time to qualify to sit for master's ticket. Once this was achieved I had a strong challenge for acceptance by the General Steam Navigation Co. which ran what were effectively home trade ships centred on the Thames, mainly at Regent's Canal Dock, but with side-lines to the Mediterranean and from the Bristol Channel to the Iberian Peninsular. A Dutch trade took ships to Felixstowe before the days when containers exploded the place into a major sea-port. One of three troopers serving BAOR taking troops to and from Harwich and the Hoek of Holland was also under their management.

PILOTAGE?

I left the "Caxton" in Tilbury 14th August 1954 and took time off for a proper honeymoon before returning to school; my master's ticket is dated 11th March 1955. By joining General Steam later in that month as 3rd mate I was giving myself six and a half years in which to become familiar with the river, to be accepted and called into the coveted job.

I joined "Whitewing", a vessel of a mere 1100 tons gross and one of very few of the GSN ships to carry three mates; I was even then regarded as something of an oddity as most juniors joined the firm considerably younger, taking 2nd mate's jobs before qualifying as master or, often enough, even as mate. "Whitewing" ran to Antwerp and Hamburg and back to London on a weekly turn-round and I was thus initiated into the madness of home trade.

For three or four days in the week we worked almost non-stop, returning home to collapse and recover in readiness for next week. With three mates life under these conditions was tolerable, but once on two mate ships the tempo bordered on insanity. Daytime loading would be followed by evening or midnight sailing followed by a short spell of four hours on and four hours off before standby to enter port and start cargo work. We used to clock up upwards of 100 hours duty per week.

On the river we kept watch under the master's surveillance, never needing to take a pilot as, because of the frequency of river use, the masters all obtained pilotage licences. They either stayed on the bridge until arrival at the "Sunk" or "Tongue" light vessels where pilots would have completed their operations, or if they were satisfied with their officers' experience and ability, left it to us.

It took the company over nine months to slot me into a 2nd mate's job, this time on "Swift" (Butler's Wharf to Amsterdam) under "Mouth and Trousers" Parkinson.

Parky was a very odd man himself; a very senior master, he would come onto the bridge dressed entirely in civilian clothes but wearing a uniform cap as badge of office. He addressed everyone as "mate" and usually adopted a whinging tone of voice. He always did his own pilotage, whether as a matter of conscience or whether he simply could not trust anyone else, I could never be sure.

His seniority was such that Captain Howgego, the marine superintendent, had been his second mate in the past and was never allowed to forget it! This, I believe, ultimately had very bad consequences for me.

One of the first things Parky did was to complain loud and long on my behalf that a man with a master's ticket should not serve under a senior with a lesser qualification and it was scandalous that I should risk such an indignity. In the course of time he bullied Howgego into seeing things his way with respect to an appointment that was intended for another man and I think this incident sealed my fate and precluded any hope I had of becoming a pilot.

It was August 1956 and the Suez crisis was brewing. Our trooper the "Empire Parkeston" was selected for the campaign for two reasons; firstly she was capable of a speed in excess of twenty knots and secondly she was unusually short and would be able to dock alongside the quay in Famagusta.

Based as she was at Harwich, the crew, all local men, bitterly opposed the idea of being dislodged from their home-every-other-night employment in exchange for an indeterminate period in the Mediterranean.

In particular, 2nd and third mates and the Troop Officer would require replacement and Howgego had earmarked the last of these posts for an obvious favourite who held only a Home Trade qualification.

Buntine was an Australian of undisclosed age whose experiences dated back to a period when some of his shipmates were yet unborn but he had an unhappy knack of telling tales so tall that they were rarely, if ever, believed.

His company was well sought after if only for a laugh and there is no doubt he would have made a very good Troop Officer – the liaison man between the Ship's Commandant (army) and the ship's administration.

Parky talked Howgego into giving me the job and making Buntine 3rd mate.

The job entailed the wearing of three gold bands, equivalent to the mate's, and appeared to involve the responsibility for a very impressive number of keys which permanently jangled on a keyboard beside the bunk.

On Harwich-Hoek service, "Troops" attended pre-embarkation conferences every day together with the ship's commandant, the ship's warrant officer, the army Captain responsible for orchestrating the numbers of officers and other ranks waiting to board and the Sea Transport Officer who had overall responsibility.

Between them they eased some 800 footsore and weary service men aboard, distributing them into appropriate troop decks and allocated cabins to forty or fifty officers appropriate to rank and/or sex. This occurred at the end of what was invariably a long day for them; they were then lectured on safety matters and harangued (all part of Troops' job) about what not to do, settled into place before the ship left the dockside, took them out into a seaway and promptly rolled a goodly proportion into seasickness.

First thing in the morning they were disembarked on the opposite shore and the cleaning gang boarded to clean up and prepare for the next lot to travel in the opposite direction.

Three ships shared this routine, each running non-stop for six weeks before handing the baton to one of the other two so that life was hectic for six weeks and idyllically peaceful for twelve during which time one ship was required to stand by for emergencies and the other could attend to running repairs and such like. Not quite a sinecure but as good as one could hope for in a seafaring context.

When it came to taking the "..Parkeston" off the run, once she had been upgraded in Hull to carry some two or three hundred more troops, the Troop Officer's job became even more of a holiday.

We embarked some 330 men in Southampton and quietly

slipped away, drawing as little attention to ourselves as possible; the campaign was as yet officially undecided and very much under wraps. On arrival in Gibraltar we disembarked our passengers and spent the next six weeks lounging around in the summer sunshine.

We finally took another handful of soldiers aboard and at much the same time suffered a major breakdown of one of our generators. It may be that this caused a change of plan, leading to disembarkation in Malta but it did not have the effect desired by some of forcing our return home!

From Malta we went on to Limassol, Cyprus, where we anchored off and sunbathed for another six weeks while Makarios was making a nuisance of himself on the island. Once a week we went off to Famagusta to refuel, carefully anchoring and avoiding the berth that we were selected to occupy.

Then at last the balloon went up.

The passage of time and lack of personal records have combined to confuse me as to the precise sequence of events, but several remain vividly in the memory.

Primarily I found myself becoming more and more appalled as the realisation dawned that eleven years since the cessation of hostilities were sufficient for us to have forgotten most of what was second nature to us during the war. Flags were back in pigeon holes (some in the wrong ones) and most of those required to handle them didn't know one from another.

A group of ships under naval command coming from Limassol set out to join a convoy from Malta so as to meet head to head. Our group was in the process of making an impressive sweeping turn when whoever was in charge decided that the manoeuvre wouldn't work and aborted in mid-turn. I draw a veil on the ensuing chaos.

The night before the attack on Egypt black-out was ordered; it might just as well not have been, the attempt was ludicrous.

In the morning we anchored off Port Said and I was dumbfounded at the amount of shipping that had come to join in in one way or another. I was hard put to it to find any expanse of blue for the sheer number of ships blocking the view all the way to the horizon which appeared, like us, to be waiting for orders.

Paratroops had been flown in during the night and were joined by commandos landed on the beaches at daybreak; in no time flat they seemed to have taken control without the need of assistance from the accompanying armada.

Our call came at midday; we were galvanised into action, racing towards that old familiar de Lessops statue to propel our troops into action.

In re-designing our troop decks to carry the additional men, the planners overlooked the fact that the army had not yet learnt to travel light. When we embarked our men we also loaded their equipment and with nowhere else to store it, it went way down into the bowels of the ship.

Troop decks are designed for a flow of individuals to enter and leave rapidly by stairways as wide as practicality allows, not for cumbersome wooden cases to be hove about by manpower, the only lifting device available.

Having arrived at our destination point in a blaze of glory in the middle of the day, anchored, and disembarked most of our men into Z craft, we crept away at dusk having finally passed the last of the packages over the side.

We returned to Limassol to pick up Headquarters Brigade and deliver them on the following day and while in the process of returning for more troops a stop was put on our activity. After some further delay we learnt of the unbelievable decision to pull out.

We can argue the rights and wrongs of the campaign until we are blue in the face but there was no doubting the consensus at the time which knew the retreat from Egypt to be a mistake.

History has proved that belief to have been correct and I for one can see no satisfactory conclusion to the consequent de-stabilisation of the Middle East caused by the vacillation of a weak prime minister.

CHAPTER FOURTEEN
HOW NOT TO BECOME A PILOT

On our return from Port Said I was considered as the newly established Troop Officer and for a year I was able to reap the benefits that went with the job. One stipulation was that as a senior officer I was required to sign a two year company's contract.

In December 1957 we went on a periodical trip to Hull to overhaul the engines and carry out routine maintenance work; it was my turn for Christmas leave.

On the day I was to go home a chemist boarded to check and restock the medicine chest. As he had decided to renew some of the stock of cotton wool, I threw some externally soiled or weary packets into my bag – there was always a use for cotton wool in a household with young children. Unfortunately in my haste it didn't occur to me to make mention of these packets on the dock pass which I made out for myself!

Inevitably on this occasion the policeman on the gate required me to open my bag and on sight of the cotton wool he determined that he had caught me in the act of stealing. Slowly it dawned on me that there was nothing I could do about the situation but return to the ship and await events.

The matter was reported to the company who were invited to prosecute and thereby, perhaps, improve the young copper's chances of promotion. Whilst the company declined, they nevertheless were obliged to take the matter seriously and, whether reluctantly or otherwise I can't say, arranged that on 23rd December I found myself joining the "Starling" as 2nd mate as she was sailing from Swansea en route to Lisbon, Leixoes and Spain.

There followed a very pleasant interlude – "Starling" carried three mates and was tucked well away from the prying eyes of the London office. The run was Bristol based and took us finally to Cadiz where we filled up with casks (pipes and hogsheads, mainly) of sherry, a liberal sampling of which always came our way.

After six months of this penance I was reinstated and appointed mate of "Lapwing". She was also Bristol Channel based but with Antwerp, Harlingen, perhaps Bremen and Hamburg also in her orbit. We sometimes docked in Felixstowe or London.

My time on "Lapwing" started in mid-1958 and it was about this time that containerisation of cargo began to threaten the old familiar patterns and practices.

It was also noticeable that German cargoes were becoming scarcer as the post-war re-emergence of their fleet began to challenge ours and set up new competition.

Reading the writing on the wall General Steam had already sent three of their coasters overseas, serving the St. Lawrence seaway, the Gulf of Mexico and the South African coast.

Two events now coincided; pilotage application lists opened for Gravesend/Dungeness and my company contract expired.

Having applied for pilotage I was summoned to the office to see Captain Howgego. He raised the matter of my contract giving me the opportunity to tell him of my application and to argue that in the event of success, I would be obliged to break any contract that I had made. Ethically I was not in a position to renew.

Howgego appeared to understand my position but emphasised that senior officers had to sign contracts; he said that he would give me time to reconsider.

I can see as far through a brick wall as most and I felt that with my luck I would be required to relieve one of the oversea vessel mates the moment I put pen to paper.

Perhaps I should have trusted the man, but either way the fact was that when interviews for pilotage started, Howgego demoted me and packed me off to the "Peregrine" as 2nd mate.

When my turn came for interview I sailed through the initial interrogation without difficulty, feeling that I was making a highly satisfactory impression on the Elder Bretheren, but when the chairman threw the meeting open to his colleagues to ask questions one immediately wanted to know my present rank and then the reason for demotion.

I have to believe that this was not a coincidence, General Steam's office is just across the road from Trinity House and the incumbents were known to one another.

The upshot was a hostile reaction to my explanation. I was told in no uncertain terms that I could not take acceptance for granted and in due course found myself at the bottom of the short-list.

Once the message had sunk in I realised that I was back to square one.

Whether deliberately or not is a moot point; Howgego had successfully smashed my dream and destroyed any chance of pilotage for me.

Now was the moment to re-examine my options and to re-plan my future.

Stephen, our first-born, was already familiar with the "Empire Parkeston" and was fully aware of what I was doing for a living. He was still young enough not to be unduly influenced by the maritime world and I knew that I would have to leave it behind at the earliest opportunity.

I suppose I waited long enough to be absolutely sure that there really was no possibility of pilotage before handing in my notice.

Would you believe that in an effort to retain my services the company offered me a mate's job on the "summer boats" ("Royal Sovereign" or "..Daffodil") with no strings attached?

I declined and came ashore with sufficient money to keep the family going for six months in February 1960, while I sought alternative employment. Within the time I had allotted to myself I found compensation by way of occupation in the world of marine insurance. At least I had at last become a committed landlubber.

CHAPTER FIFTEEN
FULL CIRCLE

Twenty-nine years later and a little less than three years short of normal retirement age I found myself unexpectedly unemployed and in need of the means to keep body and soul together.

The gods were friendly, sending a guardian angel to point out to me an advertisement inviting men of my background to apply for officers' positions on "Cutty Sark".

At that time she was manned as nearly as possible as a seagoing vessel with a master, a chief officer and three 2nd officers as well as a sizeable crew under a bosun, with shop assistants in lieu of catering staff.

Rather to my surprise my application was accepted and on 1st January 1990 I set out for my first day's work on a sailing ship!

As I approached I fell in with a colleague-to-be, Alan Moore who had previously been, of all things, a Thames pilot! Together we discovered that while the uniforms were suitably nautical, the work had little in common with seafaring, our major responsibility being one of collection, counting and banking of money.

The atmosphere and companionship were right enough and in this regard I have to say that familiarity with the ship has blurred the impressions gained on boarding at the time of my initial visit several years earlier.

The ship is entered through a hole cut into the side of the 'tween deck which, with all the exhibits and the shop enclosed, gives some sense of Santa's grotto, nautical style. This is not to suggest that it doesn't have an enormous effect of welcome and warmth and whatever my initial reaction was, I cannot cross that gangway now without feeling that I am coming home.

"Cutty Sark" was preserved for the nation in 1953 and in hindsight it seems clear to me that, though with the best intentions, a double blunder was made at the time.

She was brought into a purpose built dock in Greenwich, sealed off from the river and then the supporting water was pumped out in order to show off her beautiful lines in their entirety. Moreover her keel was settled on a horizontal plinth.

Naturally she attracted vast numbers of visitors, upwards of 400,000 per year at the time of our joining, and it follows that there was a regular routine washing down before the public boarded. This influx of people and water had two undesirable consequences; because of the removal of external support, new stresses were suffered and with so much internal water used percolation over the years was causing unseen damage.

When Alan and I joined, Captain Bell was in the process of retiring, to be replaced by the present master, Simon Waite. Once installed, Simon did something which had probably not been done for a long time – he donned a boiler suit.

The very thorough investigations that followed brought appalling, indeed frightening, facts to light. Because of the even keel placement of the ship, water had penetrated beneath the permanent cement ballast covering the wooden keel. This was found to be rotting, severely in places, the metal lower masts were rusting through, side and deck planking required replacement, internal metal support structure was rusted to the degree that some of the jointing had been forced apart, the rigging (ropes, wires, blocks, chains etc.) required overhaul and/or replacement and –but I think that's enough to be going on with.

A very modest estimate of £2,000,000 was arrived at for the cost of perceived requirements and it was clear that stringent economies were called for.

The first casualties included many of the crew whose loss materially affected the impression given to the public and a great deal of thought went into ways and means of compensating and introducing new methods of attracting custom. These included inviting youngsters to become "a seaman for a day" and join in a truly hands-on experience.

It is fair to say that at least some of the need for remedial work pre-dates the ship's arrival in Greenwich as a quick look at her history will indicate.

Too much has been written about the glories of "Cutty Sark" in her heyday for me to attempt to add my two penn'orth, but there are relevant facts in respect to her condition which should be borne in mind.

She was built at a time when steel hulls with engines were beginning to threaten traditional sailing ships and she came into commission in the same year that the Suez Canal was built. This indicates the cut-throat spirit of competition abroad at the time and indeed "Cutty Sark" was designed specifically to out-race the opposition.

She held her own for seven years on the very lucrative China tea trade, straining every fibre to be amongst the first arrivals each season and thereby to reap the highest profits for her cargoes. One voyage was sufficient to repay her building costs.

Forced out of the trade by steamers, the ship virtually tramped for the next five years before the Australian wool trade opened up.

For another twelve years during which time she set up enduring speed records and made a name for herself that was never rivalled, the gallant but aging lady was effectively flogged to death. By 1895 she had become uneconomical to run and was sold to Portuguese owners whose treatment of her remains a mystery.

They appear to have built the after companionway which truncates the master's cabin-cum-chartroom and leads into the officers' saloon. They managed to put her ashore (and refloat her) in a Gulf of Mexico hurricane. They also lost a mast at sea during the first world war.

By the time she was spotted by Captain Dowman in 1922, bought by him and taken to Falmouth for restoration, she was pretty much of a wreck, and "restoration" must be a relative term.

She was subsequently used as a training ship and was given to the Thames County Training College in 1938 by his widow on Captain Dowman's death.

She doubled for H.M.S."Worcester", the pre-eminent London based training ship during the war which, I think, is when the portholes were cut in the 'tween deck used at the time as a dormitory.

She does not look particularly prepossessing in photographs taken on her arrival at Greenwich and a great deal of work must have been done then but nothing compared with what has been done recently.

This started with painful removal of the cement ballast followed in due course by dismantling of the yards and attendant rigging to allow removal of the metal lower mast sections which extend to the keel. These were replaced with steel for iron replicas and suspect or downright dangerous rigging was replaced in the process of re-establishment. Decking, side planking, lifeboats, "gingerbread" were all being worked on when my time expired in October 1991 and I was put out to grass, also partly as an economy!

I didn't leave without a struggle, returning for a while to relieve some of the remaining incumbents when their holidays became due.

Nowadays I drop in from time to time to keep an eye on progress and make as big a nuisance of myself as I can, but I have to concede that I am still received with the greatest courtesy.

Long may it continue.

CHAPTER SIXTEEN
REFLECTION

It is as easy as it is pointless to speculate on what might have been; I came ashore to break a vicious circle, the existence of which I took for granted.

In retrospect I find myself doubting very much whether Stephen would have followed me to sea had I stayed afloat. He is very much more his own man than ever I was.

I do believe that our relationship is an improvement on what mine was with my father and there is no doubt that Stephen's relationship with his son, Andrew, is better still. Had I stayed at sea I would have had the dubious pleasure of witnessing the depletion, the decimation, of our shipping thanks to the advent of containerisation and with it the transformation of the life-style in terms of the length of stay in ports built more remotely from the city centres than in the past. It would appear that today's officers are employed far more in office work at which they slog unremittingly for long periods before being relieved and given lengthy spells of leave in compensation. But where is the interaction, the familiarity with the places at home and abroad that they visit so fleetingly?

Surely the short sea trade was to be preferred to this; it had advantages that I was not truly aware of at the time. Certainly I had the privilege of being on hand when each of my children was born and at a time before fathers were regarded as anything other than a necessary nuisance. I was only summoned to hospital after the work was done, and probably just as well too! At that time conditions and attitudes in hospitals were an absolute disgrace; they would cause something of a riot if reintroduced today. This father might well have had something to say had he been invited to attend when our babies arrived.

Stephen came at the right part of the week when I was serving on the "Swift" so that I was able to see him within the hour.

I was on "Empire Parkeston" for Lesley's arrival which she

timed to coincide with Denis Brain's untimely death. I like to think that some part of his spirit transferred itself to her such is her affinity with wind instruments. Once again I was waiting at home for the call.

Cathy had the sense to wait until I was established ashore.

I think, in the event, I was able to make a fuller contribution to the foundation of our branch of the dynasty than Dad achieved.

And pilotage? I really am not sure whether it would have lived up to the dream; the work was absolutely right, but then chain survey was great fun in the days of working for the Ordnance Survey, and that proved to be no good.

I wonder if the pilots' closed shop with its protocols and hierarchy might have been too claustrophobic for me, or whether I'm grasping at straws, looking for justification for an alternative way of living? As I said, speculation is pointless; what is done is done.

EPILOGUE

I have seen palaces and I have seen hovels and met and talked to the people who live in them.

I have worked with people of many different nationalities, colours and creeds all over the world.

I have seen the sea at night lit from horizon to horizon by phosphorescence produced by countless millions of organisms.

I have seen the night sky stretching to infinity, lit by millions of blazing stars, scarred by any number of shooting stars.

I have watched St. Elmo's fire dancing across the rigging.

I have seen a whale leaping clean out of the sea and heard the rifle shot sound of its return to the water.

I have steered a ship at 2o'clock in the morning in a tropical sea of glassy smoothness with all doors and windows open, cooled by the air moved around me by the ship's movement through the stillness of the warm night, lulled by the rhythmic protest of the sea frothing and falling back on itself as the ship's bows sliced it apart.

I have smelled the breath of wood fires drifting out to sea from the Corsican coast.

I have been enveloped, almost grasped, by the smell of a pine forest when entering the straits leading from the Pacific into the Puget Sound.

I have witnessed the majesty of the albatross and heard the raucous chorus of the hungry, wheeling gulls.

I have responded to the intoxicating liveliness of Portuguese music and participated in the more disciplined measures of the Victor Sylvester style of dance.

I have missed making acquaintance with the ancient civilisations of western South America or of the East beyond India or indeed of the bulk of the Pacific Ocean and these are all very big misses.

I have set out to collate and preserve my father's records and in the process have, for better or for worse, produced a book of sorts.

I have signally failed to achieve what I set out to do by way of describing and recording the passing skills connected with our brand of seafaring, the old-fashioned methods of cargo handling, navigation by magnetic compass, chronometer and sextant, manipulation of heavy packages by ropes, manpower and shanty chanting and so on ad nauseum, but, after all, does it really matter?

APPENDIX

To C.F.W.

When sea and sky in darkness blend
And the curtain of night comes down,
On a path of dreams, that has no end,
Fly my thoughts to a dear home-town;
Dreams of days that are past and gone,
And hopes for the years to be;
The whispering breezes waft them on
O'er the surge of the restless sea.

Instinctive Action ready stands
But memory is far away,
Borne by the space-destroying hands
Of a love that shall not decay:
Duty and training keep their watch
O'er the heaving stretch of blue,
But my thoughts are back on the homeward track,
To rest awhile with you.

H.M.T. "Karroo", May 1917.

The End of Christmas

Two nights ago was heaven on earth – laughter and love and
    wine;
Crackers and jokes and Home's delight, the cheerful log-fire's
    shine:
Chatter of children's voices. Lord, how a few hours tell!
Two nights ago was heaven on earth – tonight is merely hell.
Tonight I sit in my room alone, no laughter, nor jokes, nor fun;
And dream of that lost two nights ago and the holiday that's
    done.

221

No sound of children's voices, no echo of Christmastide;
No crackling fire to drown the moan of the wind and rain
   outside.

Oh Lord, I know I can't go back to that lost two nights ago:
I do not ask for that night again, and the mirth and the fire's
   warm glow
Christmas has gone and I'll wait for its joys till Christmas
   again may be
But, Lord, give back to my arms the wife who shared that
   night with me.

New Moon

The footlights' glow, the magic spell of instruments in time;
Love scenes by a tropic sea, beneath a silver moon:
Fair pageantry of former days, valour and beauty bright.
The pleasure of an evening whose memory is delight.

The power of perfect acting has enthralled us for a while;
Has roused a lover's sympathy, called forth a lover's smile.
We shared each blissful moment, we felt each stab of pain,
And knew the lover's ecstasy in sunshine after rain.

And I, whene'er I dream afresh that evening's happiness
Shall know again your lips' delight, the joy of your caress;
Shall hear your whispered tenderness and know afresh the
   charms
Of Love enriched with Passion's fire, enfolded in your arms.

And I shall know, whatever play awhile our hearts may thrill,
That always our own story has a greater splendour still.
No acting e'er can rouse me as your touch has power to do;
For the play is only make believe – but you are really you.

APPENDIX

The Prayer

Gone is the day and the day's share of labour,
Evening draws on and the light fades away;
Thus too the evening, so steadily passing,
Soon will have vanished, to follow the day.
Then in my bed, while soft slumber comes creeping,
Turn I at length, to extinguish the light;
This my last thought, betwixt waking and sleeping,
My Wife and the Kiddies, God bless them tonight.

s.s."Kasenga", Middlesbrough, 22.3.23

Incomplete

There's a nice new cloth on the table spread,
And a soft new mat on the floor;
The curtains round the ports and the bed
Look neater than ever before.

The shaded light shines softly down
On the pictures around the walls:
The clock on the shelf ticks steadily on
As the tropical evening falls.

It's quite an inviting little room,
With a cheerful sort of a gleam,
And it's calling me now to settle down
To a quiet smoke and a dream.

It would almost seem as cosy a den
As ever you'd wish to meet;
But – we're both of us waiting, the room and I,
For the touch that makes it complete.

For we both of us know, the room and I,
That it's not quite all it might be;
That there's bound to be something missing here

As long as the ship's at sea:
That I might strive for that final touch
Of cosiness in vain,
Till Her step sounds again in the doorway,
And I see her smile again.

To the Lady whose presence transforms a comfortable little
    cabin
into a cosy little home.

s.s."Rialto", 13.12.27

Dear Love

I cannot find words to speak, Dear Love, the things that my
    heart would say,
For the thoughts that are born in my inmost soul in silence
    seem hid away:
But this I know, though the spoken word seems vain betwixt
    you and me,
You have wakened a song in my heart, Dear Love, that never
    will silent be.

I dream of the sound of your voice, Dear Love, and I see your
    dear eyes shine;
I feel again the clasp of your arms, the touch of your lips on
    mine:
I think of the sacred hours we have known, the joys we have
    shared, we two,
And the song springs afresh in my heart, Dear Love, and
    sweetens all life anew.

Ah, soon we shall meet again, Dear Love, the ages of waiting
    past;
And I shall hold you close in my arms, my lips on your own at
    last:

And you will know in that instant sweet that ends the hours
    apart,
The things that my tongue cannot speak, Dear Love, the song
    you have taught my heart

s.s."Rialto", August 1927.

Ten Years

Ten years! How endless ten years seemed –
Those years whose span seems now so short –
Love was our all: we neither dreamed
The love ten wedded years have taught.

Ten years ago! When life seemed all fair weather,
Warm as the sun that blessed us on our way;
Bright as the hope that bound our paths together
Ten years today.

Ten years have passed with changes rife –
Ten years whose hours seem all too few –
Teaching us Love that laughs on Life
And blooms each year to love anew.

Ten splendid years! And I who knew their glory,
Of future years would make no other claim
Than that our love endure, throughout life's story,
Ever the same.

s.s."City of Khartoum"

Letter to Dorothy May

at sea near Panama
27ᵗʰ June 1930

Dear Dorothy May,

I'm sure you think that Daddy's very slow
In sending you the letter that he promised long ago.
But really the reason is that my lazy little brain
Just simply wouldn't work to make some proper verse again.

I promised that some verses for your birthday I would send.
They started very nicely, but they somehow wouldn't end:
The proper words just wouldn't pop into my silly head,
So now I'm going to send you a letter rhyme instead.

I hope you'll like it just as well, because it would be wrong
To disappoint a lady when I'd made her wait so long.
So now I'll stir my lazy brain, and, if it really tries,
I'm sure you'll get a letter of a quite enormous size.

First, thank you for the letter that you wrote some weeks ago.
I was so pleased to get it, and I'm sure you'd like to know
That, when I saw the writing on the envelope so plain,
I said "That's come from Dorothy" – I knew your hand again.

Of course I bought some postcards, as I promised you I would:
Some pictures of skyscrapers – but they don't seem very good.
I'm sure the folks in England who make postcards could do
    better
Than the chap who made the pictures that I'm sending in this
    letter.

We'll soon arrive at Panama, or rather Christobal:
That's the small town at the entrance to the Panama Canal.
You wouldn't like to live there, though it's quite a pretty spot,
For it's often very rainy there and always very hot.

And after leaving Panama we've twenty-seven days more
Before we'll have another chance to take a walk ashore

226

That will be in New Zealand, where we'll need our coats, I'm
   told:
For its winter-time down there just now and really very cold.

But I shan't feel the cold, I hope, for I'll be able there
To find a nice warm fire and have a comfortable chair,
And spend some pleasant evenings (won't that be nice for me?)
For Mummy has some cousins there, whom I shall go to see.

Now soon you'll have your holidays. Of course I know you'll be
Delighted to go down again and paddle in the sea.
And later on I know that I shall have some photos sent
Of Laura, Bernard, and yourself, on holidays intent.

Now, Daughter, I must finish off these little lines to you,
For I must write to Mummy now, and to your Grandma too.
If you will write to me again I shall be very glad.
Goodbye, with heaps of kisses, from Your ever-loving Dad.

To Laura on her Birthday

Somebody's got a birthday, somebody's fast asleep –
I know I'd see nothing but bedclothes if I could come and peep –
I ought to write her a letter, if I only knew what to say,
For somebody's got a birthday, and she's seven years old today.

But there's nothing for me to tell her that Laura would like to
   know.
There's only the sea all round us, and the little winds that blow:
Only the weather to talk about, and the weather seems all
   wrong,
For nobody wants to think of rain when birthdays come along.

So I'll just have to write this message, for the English mail to take;
That Daddy thought of her birthday before she was awake:
A tiny little letter, to come to her and say
 "With love and kisses from Daddy, Many Happy Returns of the
   Day".

Mediterranean Magic

The white moon rises slowly from the bosom of the deep,
Light zephyrs from the eastward stir the air
The wavelets softly murmur, half awake and half asleep,
And the evening fills with magic rich and rare.

In the south the town lights twinkle to the wanderer passing by
With a glow of friendly welcome in their gleam,
While the stars that stud the night-sky dance and shimmer in
    reply
To the brilliant flash of Caxine's warning beam.

The moon-tracks silver radiance on the sleepy ocean plays,
Kissing gently every wavelet in its net:
A rugged outline darkens in the soft horizon haze,
Where the mountain peaks of Africa are set.

Then the call that stirred your boyhood with its sweet insistent
    strains
Seems to echo in the balmy evening scent;
And you set your shoulders squarer for the tingle in your veins:
And you know a wanderer's peace, and are content.

s.s."Rialto" off Algiers, 6.11.27

A Ballad of Beachy

Said a sub to a ship in the Channel one day
"I'm pleased to see you coming this way
For I'm out to tickle such chaps as you –
It's the pleasantest job I can find to do".

"My four-point-one has a nice little song,
Just list to the chorus – it won't take long;
I am far too kultured to make you wait –
So here's the first chord of our hymn of hate."

Then the song commenced with a shrill little squeal,

And the spray danced away from the falling steel.
But his shots all missed, as they sometimes will,
And the total increased on the Kaiser's Bill.

Said the ship "That's a song I have heard before;
I was stung last time, but this time I'll score:
And you're rather raw at this sort of fun,
So I'll show you the right way to use a gun."

Then we sent him our love in a good strong dose,
And the sub protested "That's far too close;
I think I'll skip while there's time to run."
But he stopped one shell – and that stopped his fun.

H.M.T. "Karroo" off Beachy Head, 24.5.17

Two Ships

Masts almost invisible, canvas dimly white;
Every star a diamond in a purple velvet night:
Memories which never fade – full of charm to me –
Of a "windbag" drifting on a silent tropic sea.

Beauty marred by derrick-posts, ne'er a sign of sail;
Engines driving endlessly through tropic calm or gale:
Just a cargo steamer, nothing lovelier than the rest,
But she was the first I knew, so I loved her the best.

It may be that hereafter, on some deep celestial lake,
I'll find again good ships to sail and passages to make,
And if I'm bound to follow then the call on earth I knew,
Lord, give me first a windbag, and second the "Karroo".

s.s."Karroo", November 1925

From a Merchant Seaman to a Good Friend

It sometimes happens that two men meet, firm-friendly from
    the start;
And they seem to be kindred spirits, though their callings are
    far apart.
They sit and talk of a thousand things and, at the evening's
    end,
When they say "goodnight" and go their ways each feels he
    has found a friend.

And I hold that no blind chance controls such meetings of man
    and man,
For the God who made man and friendliness ordained it part
    of his plan:
Though friends might part, nor meet again until the journey's
    end,
Each holds that added treasure and joy – the memory of a
    friend.

Lament of the F.S.S. 29.10.41

Don't think we're wandering sailormen;
We know darned well we're not:
We're just a flock of little lambs
They penned and then forgot.
Stuck solid in a spot from which
We cannot seem to part:
For other blokes propellers kick
But ours will never start.

Lost little lambs out in the cold
Who bleat and baa in vain;
And all of us are growing old
And most of us insane.
Our bones are chilled, our fleece grows thin
We'll fall to pieces one day –

And it blows like hell and rains as well
Each Wednesday and each Sunday.

The ships come in and rest awhile,
Then leave – but we do not:
'Twould need a blooming earthquake now
To shift us from this spot.
We're growing solid to a place
From which we'll never sever;
For ships may come, and ships may go,
But we remain for ever.

Midsummer Madness

Once in the dear dead days beyond recall
While the village blacksmith danced around his stall
Out of the mudpies, silent and intense
Love built a dustbin on the backyard fence:
And in the beer that trickled from the vat
I found a porcupine without a hat.

Just a pink and blue cat with a purple tail.
Beechams Pills are sweetest in a southwest gale.
If your corns are hurting and your braces short,
Grab the nearest curate and make him snort
The way you think he ought.

Still we shall hear that apple tart of yore
Squealing in the bedroom, papering the floor.
Dogs may go bankrupt, postage stamps may crack,
Still we shall find that a raincoat can't hit back.
And in the dusk with onions round your waist,
Shirt fronts and sawdust make the best tooth-paste.
Just a piebald monkey in a saffron suit,
If his name is Henry wears a worn-out boot.
Take the dustman's baby, dear little lamb,
And hide him carefully underneath his pram.

The Village Burglar

Under a spreading goose-gog bush the Village Burglar lies-
The Burglar is a crafty bloke, with whiskers on his eyes,
And the muscles on his brawny arms keep off the little flies.

He goes on Sunday to the church, to hear the Parson shout:
He puts a button in the plate and takes a shilling out-
And when he reaches home again he smiles, without a doubt.

When coming home one winter night he spies an open door
An overcoat hangs in the hall – he creeps along the floor.
A moment later out he comes and the vile deed is o'er.

He proudly gazes on his prize, and holds it out a-stretch:
Then down the lighted street he goes, and Ah! The crafty
    wretch!
He takes it to a pawn shop to see what it will fetch.

Burgling, boozing, borrowing, have told their dreadful tale.
Now in the Village Clink he lies, with many a mournful wail:
Something attempted, something done, has earned him six
    months gaol.

To F.A.N.

There's a fellow called Frank, a bit of a swank
And around the "Karroo" he does toddle;
Kilowatts and megohms in his brain-pan find homes:
There's a small wireless world in his noddle.

If you happen to roam to his small cabin-home
And find him intent at the table,
He roars viciously "Now don't make such a row.
How the —- can I hear in this Babel?"

As he strolls through the streets all the ladies he beats
At their own game of shop-window-staring:
He'll walk into a shop, and there he will stop,
While you loiter outside, wildly swearing.

Of girls, too, he's fond, both brunette and blonde,
Though he tells us his thoughts are above 'em:
And if you watch his eye when a maid passes by
You will never need ask "Does he love 'em?"

Now taken all round, this Frank that we've found
Is an average sort of a blighter.
Though he's easily vexed, he's as good as the next,
So here's wishing him luck, from the writer.

H.M.T. "Karroo", 1917

To Two Karroosters.

Sing a song of Leghorn;
A bellyful of wine:
Two chaps carried back on board,
Feeling fresh and fine.

Hung 'em on the aerial;
Pegged 'em out to dry:
Lectured 'em on evils
Of drinking on the sly.

Full of wine Italian;
Awful sort of muck:
Yet they both imagined that
They'd had a stroke of luck.

Luckily the pair of 'em
Very soon were broke;
Otherwise it might have been
A paralytic stroke.

Oh, the darling innocents!
Really it is sad:
One's a dirty drunkard, and –
The other's just as bad.

H.M.T. "Karroo", 1917

Scares

It is the noble ship "Karroo"
That sails the western seas,
Manned by a gang of hard-case knuts
Who scorn luxurious ease.

Ah! What is that awful, quivering crash?
Are we now our fate to meet?
But it's only the Captain's punchball
Shaking the bridge-deck under my feet.

There! The report of a heavy gun!
Watch where the shot shall fall!
But it's only a mule that has dined too well
Dancing around in his stall.

Hark! That's a fog-horn very close!
And I'm deadly scared of wreck!
But it's only a sick horse blowing his nose,
In the depths of the dark horse-deck.

And now we're in it at last, my boys!
There's horror and death on the deep!
But it's just that lobster I had for lunch,
Returning to wreck my sleep.

H.M.T."Karroo", 1917

The Lies of Ancient Rome
(being the truth that Macaulay forgot to explain).

Quoth brave Horatius to his pals "Now how long must we wait
For our blinkin' buses homeward? – today's my wedding date
And a Special Dinner waits me, a little tete-a-tete:
But first we've time, I really think,
A foaming glass of beer to sink –
We'll go and have one little drink,
Just one, to celebrate".

234

They drank one drink sedately, but one led on to more,
Till suddenly Horatius, with air perplexed sore,
Cried "Lord, my Anniversary, it's very nearly o'er."

Thus counselled him Herminius, a brain-wave in his eyes,
"You'll have to tell your Missus the usual pack of lies:
How press of work has kept you in –
And though it may sound Rather Thin,
She can't prove otherwise."

Then answered him Horatius, payer of tax and rate,
"It's seven-fifty-seven now and Dinner's on at eight,
And how can I roll homeward, with beer soaked tie and vest,
And staring eye and wine flushed mien,
And tell my wife that I have been
Detained by business unforeseen
And work I never guessed?"

Then up spake Spurius Lartius – an artful bird was he –
"I had to meet my girl at six and take her out to tea.
But women they must understand
Work don't go always as it's planned:
We'll come and stand at thy right hand
And tell the tale with thee."

Now meanwhile Ma Horatius, she paced back and forth,
And glanced full often at the clock in fierce and gathering wrath,
And while she mused, with thoughts not nice,
On Burnt-up Fowl and Ruined Rice,
She heard at last the gate creak thrice
And heard the steps of three blind mice
Come staggering up the path.

She flung the front door open, and on the Three she rushed,
Wielding the family copper-stick with expert cut and thrust:
Straight at Horatius she did fly –
She banged his crown and bunged his eye.
His pals let out a doleful cry
To see his topper bust.

Then on the twain she rounded, and treated them real rough:
Then back to poor Horatius and grabbed him by the scruff.
She quickly yanked him through the door
And banged him down upon the floor –
His pals departed sad and sore, for they had had enough.

For now Self-preservation their valour did abate,
And both were for the roadway, and none was for the gate,
They fled away to brood at length
On Woman's unexpected strength
And cares of married state.

And as for poor Horatius, long after he is cold
By his children's children's children, oft shall the tale be told
How he his Wedding Day did wreck,
And brewed of Trouble, many a peck,
While three men got it in The Neck
In the brave days of Old.

Supper

Dorry bought some fish and chips on her way home tonight,
They packed 'em in a tiny bag and packed 'em in too tight.
She was loaded up beforehand with packages and things
And the fish-bag dangled cornerwise, the way a limpet clings.

She scuttled up from Brownhill with our supper in her charge:
The bag, you know, was very small, the chips were very large.
She turns around the corner and past the police-box trips,
The policeman gave a sudden cough – and bang went all the
     chips.

They tumbled right side up by chance – the paper underneath –
And some stuck to the paper, by the skin of a tater's teeth.
The streets are muddy, the night is wet, there's misery in the air:
She grabbed up the paper and some of the chips – the rest are
     Lord knows where.

We've had our supper of fish and chips, before I started to
   write.
We've had our supper of fish and chips, all we shall get
   tonight.
I'm holding my pants up extra tight, for fear my waist belt
   slips
For we've had our supper of chish and fips – but minus half
   the fips.

Amateur Aquatics
or The Ballad of the Bewildered Boat

Three little London Gals went and found a river:
Tried some rowing exercise – splendid for the liver.

One little London Gal showed the others how:
Said "You try it, Dorothy, my arms are tired now".

Second little London Gal went and took the oars:
Splashed all the river up and bounced off both the shores.

Twisting and turning, made an awful show:
The others murmured wearily "Let Auntie have a go".

One little London Aunt rowing – more or less:
Tearing pieces off the banks – what a mess!

Hundreds of picknickers ran to see the sight:
Thought it was a comic turn and cheered with all their might.

Scores of kids a-paddling, having lots of fun:
Boat turned and rushed at 'em and then there were none.

First little London Gal feeling very wild:
Went and grabbed the oars again - then the others smiled!

One little rowing boat pulling out of view:
Picknickers all glared and said "Time they hopped it, too!"

The Pathetic Ballad of THE TOMATO SCOFFER

Now all you market-gardeners who complain that trade is dying
Just choke your sighs and dry your eyes and have another try;
Grow nothing but tomatoes and you'll set the bawbees flying –
There's a person up in Aberdeen will keep you till you die.

This tall tomato-slaughterer once visited a steamer;
They called her the "Rialto", of the Bucknall Cargo Line:
And this translated into Banff, means "Big Tomato-garden,
Where they flourish by the hundred and are always ripe and
      fine".

Now, judging by its sad effects, the gorging of tomatoes,
Though all right in moderation, is most dangerous in excess:
For it turns the shyest maiden to a cool and crafty plotter,
And the quiet obedient lamb becomes a roaring lioness.

And so this silent girl developed soon into a scrapper
Who would dare to sit and argue with her master and her lord!
While the others at the table sat and shook with apprehension,
And the Steward dreamed tomatoes while his grub-rate daily
      soared.

When she'd scoffed her tenth tomato she would murmur so
      politely
"No more now, thanks; I've eaten two, that's quite enough for
      me".
Then she'd flash a winning smile at some misguided youth at
      table,
Who would promptly pinch the rest for her consumption after
      tea.

Her Husband fair, with auburn hair, - a handsome lad and
      youthful –
He did his best to guide her in the proper wifely track;
But the Spirit of Tomatoes just stepped in and spoiled his efforts,
And she actually had the sauce to answer back.

She would cheek her lord in public, in a manner most outrageous
Until even the tomatoes wore a sickly blushing look:
She confessed a youthful passion for a shy young lad of sixty,
Yet brazenly declared she learned her courting from a book.

Her Husband had a friend, a meek and harmless little fellow;
She tickled him until he wriggled helpless on the floor:
Now he wonders if his wife will ever quite believe the story
That those dents upon his ribs were printed by a lion's paw.

Her favourite form of welcome to her Husband's male
    companions
Was to artlessly entice them to a comfortable seat;
Then, with hair behind her streaming and her eyes with fury
    flashing,
She would drench them with cold water, while they struggled
    to retreat.

And the natural conclusion to be drawn from this sad story
Is that Man must have for ever this excuse for secret mirth –
It's a good thing Mother Eve was only tempted with an apple:
If she'd tackled a tomato, she'd have wrecked the blessed earth.

Sent to Mrs. McD. after her holiday on board s.s."Rialto",
July 1927

Our Team

We 'ad a game in Pirie, in a friendly sort of way;
Some blighters found a football and they asked us out to play:
So we scrounged a team together, proper motley sort of crew,
All as blazin' 'ot as pickles, and as mixed as pickles too.

There was rigs of all varieties of colours, shapes and sorts,
From football shirts and under-pants to vests and khaki shorts:
We was slippin' down the gangway when the Fourth began to
    roar,
"Hey! Shorty! Stitch these pants for me before we go ashore!"

We waited for a tramcar at the corner of the street
But the trams 'ad knocked off runnin' so we 'ad to use our
    feet;
And when we'd walked a hundred miles, and wasted all our
    vim,
We met 'erbert in a taxi, so we bundled in with 'im.

At last the game got started, at a devil of a pace;
It didn't seem like football, but a bloomin' Derby Race!
The fastest game of football since this weary world began;
And them that couldn't kick must run – so everybody ran.

Our 'erb streaked round like lightenin' in 'is little shorts and
    shirt,
And 'alf of 'im was sweat and steam, the other 'alf was dirt.
Don Pedro 'e was chargin' round as savage as a snake,
A-lookin' out for ears to chew and collar-bones to break.

Joe King was puffed and blowin', doubled up and lookin'
    green,
A-cursin' all the fags 'e'd smoked since 'e was seventeen;
And when the ball bounced past 'im 'is share of work was
    done,
For 'is lungs was burstin' through 'is legs and so 'e couldn't
    run.

John Connell, in the back line, kept a-bouncin' on the grass
And 'owlin' at poor Shorty "After 'im you silly ass!"
The Fourth and Fifth on either wing was both defendin' fine,
For every time they got the ball, they 'oofed it o'er the line.

Young Opium Joe was runnin' 'ard – 'e did a lion's share –
But mostly when the ball arrived poor Opium wasn't there.
And Leo stopped some lovely shots, 'e wasn't much to blame;
But if 'e'd saved four more then we'd 'ave won the bloomin'
    game.

We was sweatin' there like porkers, fairly stickin' to the job;
All runnin', kickin', tumblin', in a puffin', pantin', mob:
And I'll bet the sound of shoutin' bust the skies from pole to
    pole
When a bird from the "Kentucky" scored our only bloomin'
    goal.

The way they put it over us, it really was a sin,
But since they owned the football – well, we 'ad to let 'em win;
And if they'd got one goal the less it wouldn't 'ave been right,
For we might 'ave scored another three – I only say WE
    MIGHT.

Now we ain't a fancy football team, with colours and reserves,
But still we like to give a ball the kickin' it deserves:
So send your fancy teams along – we'll see the blighters
    through –
When the Gods send down a football to the boys of the
    "Karroo"

*After losing a football match against a team from the
s.s. "Anglo-Chilean", in Port Pirie, South Australia, November
    1925*

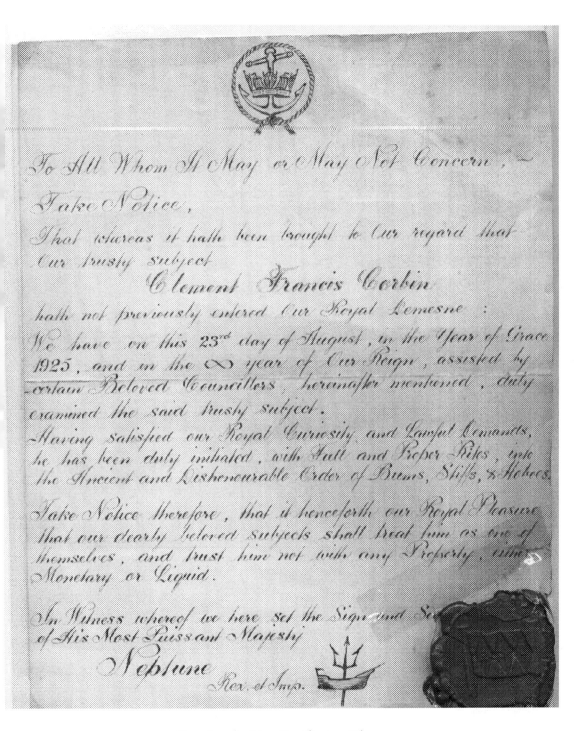

To All Whom It May or May Not Concern, —

Take Notice,

That whereas it hath been brought to Our regard that Our trusty subject

Clement Francis Corbin

hath not previously entered Our Royal Demesne :

We have on this 23rd day of August, in the Year of Grace 1925, and in the ∾ year of Our Reign, assisted by certain Beloved Councillors, hereinafter mentioned, duly examined the said trusty subject.

Having satisfied our Royal Curiosity and Lawful Demands, he has been duly initiated, with Full and Proper Rites, into the Ancient and Dishonourable Order of Bums, Stiffs, & Hoboes.

Take Notice therefore, that it henceforth our Royal Pleasure that our dearly beloved subjects shall treat him as one of themselves, and trust him not with any Property, either Monetary or Liquid.

In Witness whereof we here set the Sign and Seal of His Most Puissant Majesty

Neptune
Rex. et Imp.

Crossing the Line Certificate - Obverse

244

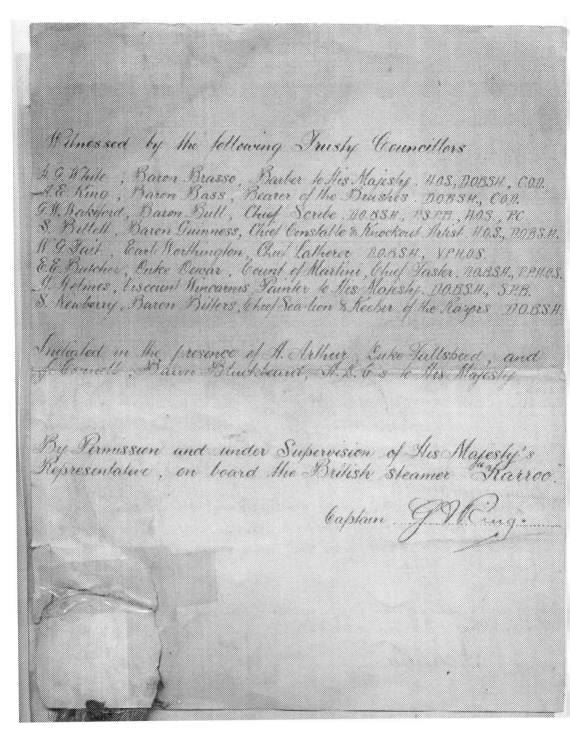

Crossing the Line Certificate - Reverse

EXTRACT FROM THE "DERBY DAILY DIGEST" 19th September 1927

THE TRAINING OF WATCH DOGS FOR HOME SERVICE

IN THE FIRST PLACE, YOUR DOG SHOULD BE BLACK, IN ORDER THAT AT NIGHT AN INTRUDER MAY FALL OVER HIM BEFORE SEEING HIM, AND THUS AWAKE THE HOUSEHOLD.—

IF NOT NATURALLY BLACK, PAINT HIM BLACK: ALSO PROVIDE HIM WITH A PAIR OF SMOKED SPECTACLES, IN ORDER TO PREVENT THE UNTIMELY GLEAMING OF HIS EYES IN THE DARKNESS

FROM HIS PUPPYHOOD HE SHOULD BE CAREFULLY TRAINED, AND MADE TO UNDERSTAND THAT IT IS FAR BETTER TO BITE OFF A BURGLAR'S HEAD IN SILENCE THAN TO FRIGHTEN HIM AWAY — AND ROUSE THE WHOLE NEIGHBOURHOOD — BY BARKING. FOR THIS PURPOSE HE SHOULD SPEND AN HOUR EVERY DAY LOCKED IN A ROOM WITH A BOWL FULL OF INFURIATED GOLDFISH, IN ORDER THAT HE MAY THOROUGHLY STUDY THEIR HABITS, AND ACQUIRE, — BY OBSERVATION, THE NECESSARY TRICK OF SILENT SAVAGERY. AT INTERVALS EVERY EVENING PROD HIM IN THE RIBS WITH A COBBLER'S LAST COVERED WITH AN OLD SOCK. THIS WILL GIVE HIM THE NECESSARY ANTIPATHY TOWARD THE ANKLES OF DUSTMEN, POSTMEN, AND ALL THE OTHER PEOPLE WHO DISTURB YOUR MORNING HOURS, AND THEN COME AND HOLD OUT THEIR HANDS FOR PENNIES AT CHRISTMAS TIME. BE SURE, HOWEVER, THAT THE SOCK IS NOT A SILK ONE, OR HE MAY MISTAKENLY CHEW THE ANKLES OF THE GIRL NEXT DOOR, AND SO WRECK YOUR DEAREST HOPES

EXTRACT CONTINUED

TAKE HIM OCCASIONALLY FOR A VISIT TO A FIREWORKS FACTORY:
HE WILL BE ABLE TO STUDY THE HABITS OF CATHERINE
WHEELS, AND SO LEARN THE CORRECT METHOD — INVALUABLE
TO A GOOD WATCH DOG — OF WINDING
HIMSELF UP.

ALL WATCH DOGS SHOULD HAVE GOOD
MEMORIES, SO ARRANGE IF POSSIBLE THAT
HE SHARES HIS KENNEL WITH AN
ELEPHANT. YOU WILL PROBABLY HAVE TO
BUY ONE, AS THEY ARE AWKWARD THINGS
TO STEAL, BUT I BELIEVE THEY ARE REASONABLY CHEAP
AT MARKS & SPENCER AND WILL SHORTLY BE PROCURABLE
AT WOOLWORTH'S. THIS MAY SOUND AN EXPENSIVE ITEM,
BUT IF YOU CAN GIVE YOUR DOG, FOR A PLAYMATE, AN
ELEPHANT WHO NEVER FORGETS,
YOU WILL BE SURPRISED AT
THE WAY HIS OWN MEMORY
WILL DEVELOP. THERE ARE
MANY BREEDS OF DOGS, BUT
I CONSIDER THE BEST WATCH
DOG IS A DACHSHUND (CANIS
SAUSAGEORUM). OPINIONS ON
THIS SUBJECT VARY, BUT
WHEN IT COMES TO LOOKING FOR BURGLARS, INCOME TAX
COLLECTORS, AND OTHER SOCIAL MENACES, THERE IS NO
GETTING AWAY FROM THE FACT THAT A DACHSHUND
CAN LOOK LONGER THAN ANY OTHER DOG.

CANIS SAUSAGEORUM

"BLOTTO"

B.N.3

Suez - Bombay   5th - 19th September 1940

Commodore   Vice-Commodore
{ Captain O.C.Hare R.N.   { Captain A.P.W.Collister
{ Captain A.E.King   { S.S. "Beaconstreet"
{ S.S. "City of Keelung"

01	02	03	04
11	21	31	41
"British Fusilier"	"Beaconstreet"	"City of Keelung"	"Planter"
12	22	32	42
"Priestman Prince"	"Captain A.F.Lucas"	"British Union"	"Mahsura"
		33	
		"Felix Roussel"	

Escorts :-
H.M.S. "Leander"
H.M.S. "Carlisle". H.M.S. "Clive". H.M.S. "Grimsby" H.M.S. "Auckland". H.M.S. "Kingston"

Signals at parting — H.M.S. "Leander" to "City of Keelung" : "It has been a great pleasure to work with you. Wish you good luck and pleasant voyages." ...... S.S. "City of Keelung" to H.M.S. "Leander": "I and the whole convoy thank you for your signal and your escort, and wish you always the best of good luck & good hunting".

A grand convoy, fine weather, a good passage, and no excitement except that some blighter tried to bomb us as we left Suez Bay; he didn't get away with it. The first I've been Collister since 1909! "Brownhill for ever"!

Convoy B.N.3

Father, Son and Unholy Trinity

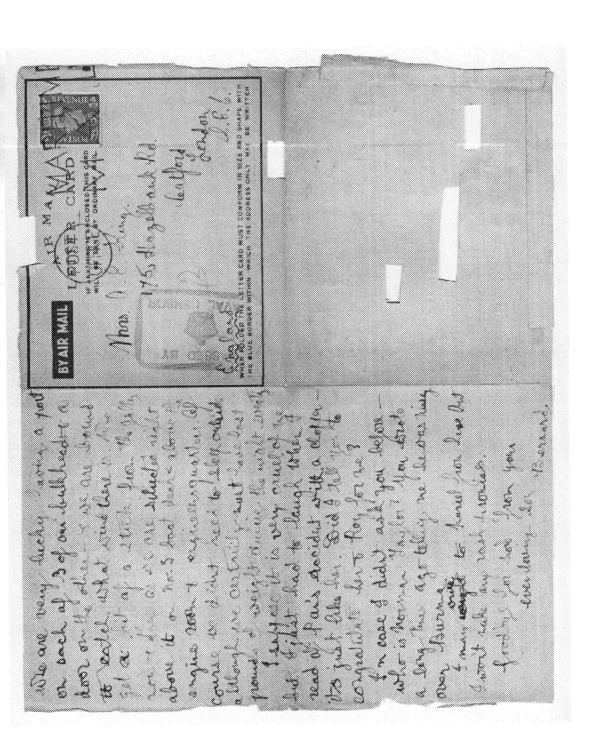

AIR MAIL
LETTER CARD
BY AIR MAIL

Mrs. A. Young.
175 Hazellbank Rd.
Catford,
London
S.E.6.

We are very lucky having a flat
on each of 3 of our halls—but a
door on the other. We all stated
to realise what wind there is. Now
I sit in a tub bed—really
I'm sitting up in a little bed. Really
we did & Guy's but silence ring
about it on — Pa's had black wound
engine work — explosion again. (?)
Couric and but near to his child
I thought he certainly but he —
hands of weight. Since the night time,
I said it is very cruel of us
but I first had to laugh when I
read of Pa's accident with a duffer —
It's just like her. Did I tell you to
congratulate her? hey for me?
In case I didn't ask you before —
who is your ...?
a long time & getting ... there lucky
dear Laura.
& many ... to hand from dear Pat
won't ask any ...
freely for us from your
ever loving dau. Bernard

250

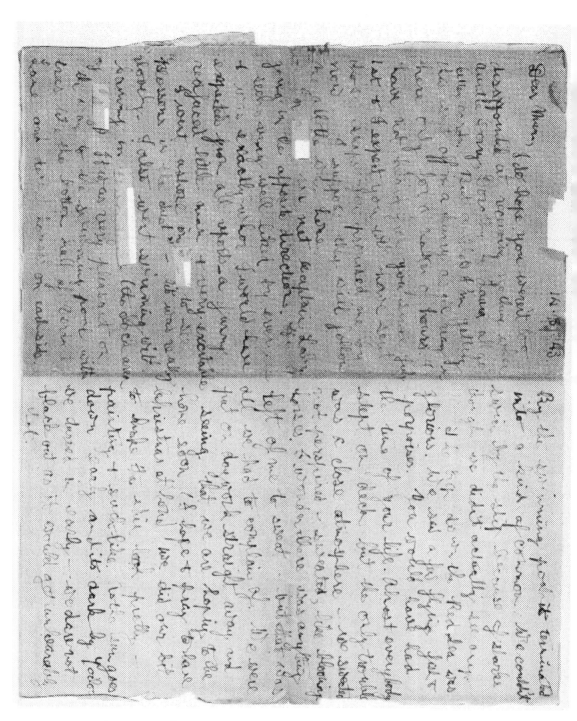

The Censor objected to the inclusion of port names in this Air letter;
Suez and Port Tewfik are not too difficult to guess!

1. "City of Carlisle" at Birkenhead 1946
2. "Paraguay Star" at sea 1948
3. "City of Canberra" in Durban Harbour 1945

Victory Parade.

DIEU ET MON DROIT

Official Programme of the VICTORY. CELEBRATIONS 8th June 1946

Twopence

HIS MAJESTY'S PROCESSION

The King, accompanied by the Queen, the Princess Elizabeth and the Princess Margaret, will drive in a State Landau. The Royal Carriage will be escorted by a Captain's Escort of the Household Cavalry with Standard.

ROUTE

Buckingham Palace	10.10
Marble Arch	10.19
Oxford Street	10.25
Charing Cross Road	10.35
Northumberland Avenue	10.40
Bridge Street	10.46
Whitehall	
The Mall (Saluting Base)	10.57

CHIEFS OF STAFF'S PROCESSION

The Chiefs of Staff at VE Day and VJ Day, together with the Supreme Allied Commanders, will precede the Mechanised Column, leaving the Clarence Gate in Regent's Park at 9.15 a.m. and arriving at the Saluting Base at 10.20 a.m.

MARCH PAST

The Mechanised and Marching Columns will follow the routes given below, joining at Parliament Square and passing together up Whitehall, the Mechanised Column leading. Between the arrival of H. Majesty at the Saluting Base and the commencement of the March Past, the Massed Pipes of Scotland and Irish Regiments will march and counter-march in The Mall. The head of the joint Column will pass the Saluting Base at 11.30 a.m. At the conclusion of the March Past, Squadrons of the Royal Air Force, together with Squadrons of the Naval Air Arm, will fly past the Bloc.

MECHANISED COLUMN

ROUTE

	a.m.
Regent's Park	9.11
(Clarence Gate)	
Park Square West	9.18
Marylebone Road	
Euston Road	
Pentonville Road	9.28
City Road	
Old Street	
Hackney Road	
Cambridge Heath Road	9.45
Whitechapel Road	
Whitechapel High Street	10.04
Aldgate High Street	
Minories Street	
Royal Mint Street	
Tower Hill	10.11
Tower Street	
Eastcheap	10.14
King William Street	
London Bridge	
Borough High Street	10.19

ORDER OF MARCH

Police Motor Cycle Patrols
Despatch Riders of the Royal Navy
* ALLIED COMMANDERS
* ROYAL NAVY COMMANDERS
Despatch Riders of the Army
* ARMY COMMANDERS
* ROYAL AIR FORCE COMMANDERS
Despatch Riders of the Royal Air Force
Despatch Riders of the National Fire Service

* ROYAL NAVY
Amphibious Jeeps
Weasels
DUKWs
Mobile Wireless Telegraphy Units
Aircraft Refuellers
Mobile Sick Bays

* ROYAL AIR FORCE
Reconnaissance Cars
Radio Vehicle   Special Ambulance

Light Ambulance
Van
Refuelling Van   Pre-warmer Van
Freighter   Aircraft Refueller mounted on
                     10-ton Tender
Despatch Rider Letter Service   Signals Van
                     Fire Crash Tender
Foam Tender

MARCHING COLUMN

*ARMY

Household Cavalry
Band
Life Guards and Royal Horse Guards

ROYAL ARMOURED CORPS

Band
1st King's Dragoon Guards
The Queen's Bays
3rd Carabiniers
4th/7th Dragoon Guards
5th/6th Royal Inniskilling Dragoon Guards
The Royal Dragoons
The Scots Greys
3rd Hussars
4th Hussars
7th Hussars
8th Hussars
9th Lancers
10th Hussars
11th Hussars
12th Lancers
13th/18th Hussars
14th/20th Hussars
15th/19th Hussars
16th/5th Lancers
17th/21st Lancers
1st Royal Tank Regiment
and Royal Tank Regiment
3rd Royal Tank Regiment
4th Royal Tank Regiment
5th Royal Tank Regiment
6th Royal Tank Regiment
7th Royal Tank Regiment
8th Royal Tank Regiment
Royal Armoured Corps
North Irish Horse
Royal Wiltshire Yeomanry
Warwickshire Yeomanry
Yorkshire Hussars
Northamptonshire Yeomanry
Staffordshire Yeomanry

followed by

1st and 2nd Derbyshire Yeomanry
1st and 2nd Lothians and Border Horse Yeomanry
1st and 2nd Fife and Forfar Yeomanry
Westminster Dragoons
3rd and 4th County of London Yeomanry
1st and 2nd Northamptonshire Yeomanry
1st ... Riding of Yorkshire Yeomanry
The Inns of Court Regiment
40th and 46th Royal Tank Regiment
41st and 47th Royal Tank Regiment
42nd and 48th Royal Tank Regiment
43rd and 49th Royal Tank Regiment
44th and 50th Royal Tank Regiment
45th and 51st Royal Tank Regiment
107th Regiment Royal Armoured Corps (King's Own)
116th Regiment Royal Armoured Corps (Gordon Highlanders)
2nd Reconnaissance Regiment
43rd Reconnaissance Regiment

ROYAL ARTILLERY, ROYAL ENGINEERS AND ROYAL SIGNALS

Royal Horse Artillery
Royal Artillery

Royal Artillery Band

Royal Engineers and Royal Signals Band

Royal Engineers
Royal Corps of Signals

MARCHING COLUMN

*NAVAL FORCES

ROYAL NAVY

followed by

Seamen
Engine Room Department
Band
Miscellaneous Branches and Reserve
Royal Marines

Queen Alexandra's Royal Naval Nursing Service and V.A.D.'s
Women's Royal Naval Service

MERCHANT NAVY

FISHING FLEETS

LIGHTHOUSE SERVICES

COASTGUARDS

PILOTS

ROYAL NATIONAL LIFEBOAT INSTITUTION

*CIVILIAN SERVICES (FIRST CONTINGENT)

POLICE

Metropolitan Police Central Band

Civil Police
Admiralty Civil Police
War Department Constabulary

followed by

Air Ministry Constabulary
Railways and Docks Police

FIRE SERVICE

National Fire Service
Salvage Corps

CIVIL DEFENCE SERVICES (FIRST PART)

followed by

Rescue Dog Handlers and Dogs
Civil Defence Reserve
Wardens

Rescue Service
Report and Control Service

CIVIL DEFENCE SERVICES (SECOND PART)

followed by

American Gift Ambulances (Great Britain)
Ambulance Service
First Aid Post
Civil Nursing Reserve
Nurses in Voluntary and Public Hospitals

Midwives and District Nurses
War-time Nurseries
Leg Stretch of Hospitals
Medical Auxiliaries

NURSING SERVICES

Joint War Organisation of British Red Cross Society and Order of St. John of Jerusalem
St. Andrew's Ambulance Association

WOMEN'S VOLUNTARY SERVICE

AGRICULTURE

Women's Land Army and Timber Corps
Farm Workers

256

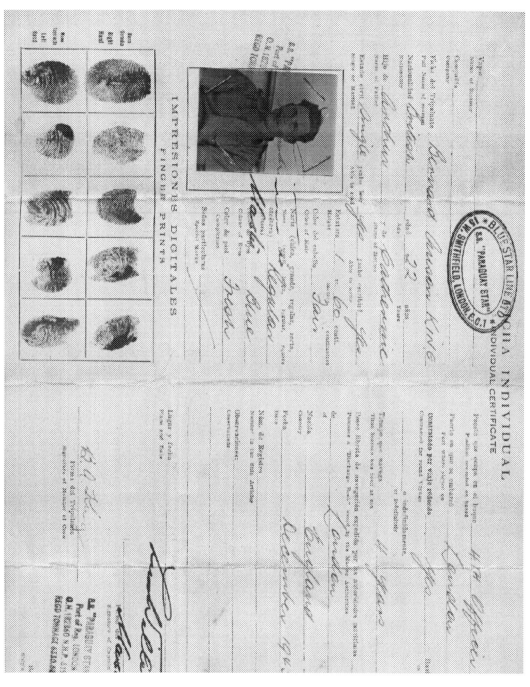

Dock Pass - Buenos Aires

Aspirant 2nd mates King Edward VII Nautical College, London E14. (Who's not wearing a tie?)

Courting Couple - Connaught Rooms London 1953

JOHN STEWART & Cº

SHIP OWNERS
AND
SHIP & INSURANCE BROKERS.

TELEPHONE AVENUE 1480.   TELEGRAMS "STENOGRAPH, LONDON.

CODES: Scotts (1906) Watkins (1901) A.B.C. (5th edition.)

"WILLIAM MITCHELL"	1885	TONS REG
"FALKIRK"	1882		
"KINPURNEY"	1887		
"MONKBARNS"	1771		
"CUMBERLAND"	1710		
"KILMALLIE"	1519		
"GALGORM CASTLE"	1267		
"EDINBURGH"	1409		
"AMULREE"	1330		

26/28 Billiter Street

London March 27th 1916
E.C.   49

W.T.King Esq.,
192, Ardgowan Road
HITHER GREEN.

Dear Sir,

        "A M U L R E E"

    We have yours of to-day enclosing Bank Notes for £2 account
your Son A.E.King, Apprentice on this vessel, and which amount
we are crediting to his account, and are advising Captain
Cooper of same.

        Yours faithfully,
        John Stewart & Co.
        Geo. H. Young

Telephone No. 10472 Central.
Telegram: "Stenograph, London."

MEMORANDUM.

London, 20th. January 1913.

From
JOHN STEWART & Co.,
3, FENCHURCH AVENUE.
E.C.

To
Mr. W. T. King,
192, Ardgowan Road,
HITHER GREEN. S.E.

    "AMULREE". In reply to yours of yesterday, this vessel has
been delayed in Newcastle N.S.W. by a strike at the Colliery,
and has not yet sailed for Taltal (Chile). She should be
sailing shortly now, and the next address is simply :-

        barque "AMULREE"
            care The Lautaro Nitrate Co.,
            TALTAL. Chile.

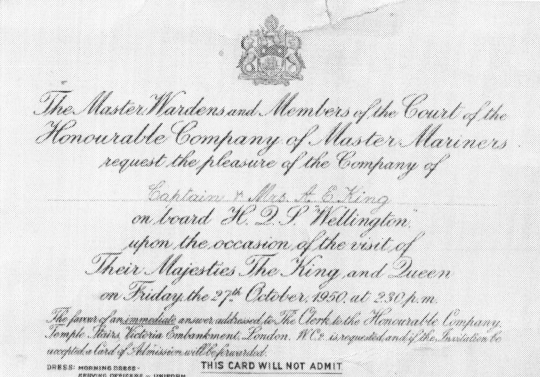

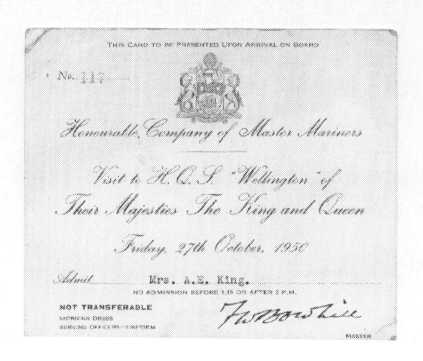

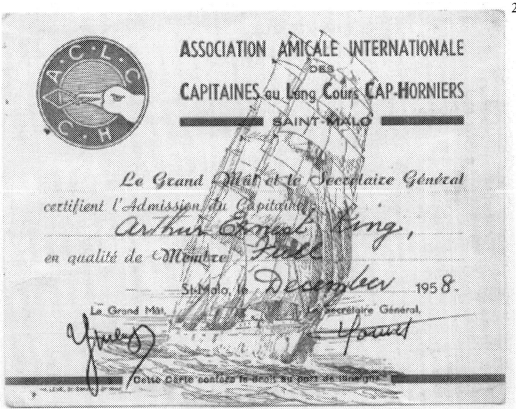

Cape Horner Certificate

S.S. "City of Evansville" (survivor of the octane convoy)
Dressed overall in post war colours.

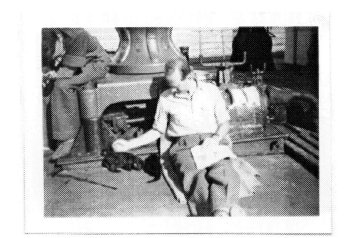

Doc. Heron and R.A.M.C. Sergeant with kittens born
aboard "Empire Parkeston" in Malta.

Suez D-day off Port Said
Fellow trooper "Empire Ken" at bottom right.

264

Time was

In pursuance of

His Majesty's Commands

that Third Officer Arthur Ernest King,

of the S.S. Karoo

be commended for zeal and devotion to duty shown in carrying on the trade of the Country during the War.

The Lords Commissioners of the Admiralty

hereby certify that

Third Officer Arthur Ernest King,

was duly commended for his good services in the London Gazette dated 13th May 1917.

By command of Their Lordships

Dated 2nd September 1920

THE WATCH DOG AT WORK

HAVING WISELY TRAINED YOUR DOG ON THE LINES
INDICATED IN MY PREVIOUS WORK, YOU MUST, OF
COURSE, THOROUGHLY TEST HIS CAPACITY FOR HIS
INTENDED VOCATION BEFORE YOU CAN SAFELY
SNATCH A FEW HOURS SLEEP AND LEAVE HIM
TO LOOK AFTER THE HOUSE. AS SOON AS YOU
FEEL THAT HIS EDUCATION IS, OR SHOULD BE,
COMPLETE SEND HIM AWAY TO THE COUNTRY
FOR A THOROUGH REST, FIRST GIVING HIM
CLEARLY TO UNDERSTAND THAT THE MID-TERM
EXAMINATIONS WILL COMMENCE AS SOON AS HE
RETURNS. AT THE END OF A WEEK BRING HIM
BACK AND PROCEED WITH THE EXAMINATION.
THE FIRST DAY SHOULD BE DEVOTED TO WRITTEN
SUBJECTS ONLY, LEAVING ORALS FOR THE
FOLLOWING DAY. YOU MAY SEND HIS PAPERS TO
ANY COMPETENT EDUCATIONAL COMMITTEE FOR
MARKING, THOUGH PERSONALLY I RECOMMEND
COLNEY HATCH UNIVERSITY. IF HE PASSES THE
MATRICULATION STANDARD YOU MAY REST
ASSURED THAT YOU POSSESS A REALLY UNIQUE
DOG. IF, HOWEVER, HE ONLY PASSES 'GENERAL
SCHOOLS' IT WOULD BE WISE TO RE-EXAMINE
HIM. POINT OUT TO HIM IN ADVANCE
THAT FOR EVERY MISTAKE HE MAKES
HE WILL SPEND A WEEK WITHOUT
ANY SORT OF FOOD EXCEPT AN
OCCASIONAL SAUCER OF SODA WATER,
SENTENCES TO RUN CONSECUTIVELY.
ANY INTELLIGENT DOG WILL
QUICKLY REALISE THAT IF HE MAKES
A MESS OF HIS HOMEWORK TWICE
IT WILL MEAN NO GRUB FOR A
FORTNIGHT. EVEN SUCH SLIGHT

PUNISHMENT AS THIS WILL CERTAINLY SHARPEN HIM UP. OF COURSE, IN THE CASE OF A DULL DOG, IT MAY POSSIBLY SHARPEN HIM OFF ALTOGETHER; EVEN SO, DEFUNCT DOG IS VERY GOOD FOR THE RHUBARB OR VEGETABLE MARROWS: AND YOU SHOULD HAVE HAD SENSE ENOUGH IN THE FIRST PLACE TO BUY A DECENT DOG ANYWAY.

NOW, ASSUMING THAT HE HAS PASSED AS A FULLY COMPETENT WATCH DOG, HOW WILL YOU SET HIM TO WORK? MAKE HIM UNDERSTAND THAT HE WAS BOUGHT, TRAINED, AND CERTIFIED, FOR A WATCH DOG, AND IS THEREFORE EXPECTED TO WATCH EVERYTHING WATCHABLE. HE CAN WATCH THE PAPERS FOR THE RESULT OF YOUR FOOTBALL COUPON ENTRIES: WATCH CAREFULLY TO OBSERVE WHEN THE SUN GETS OVER THE FORE-YARD: WATCH THE CLOCK FOR KNOCK-OFF TIME: AND WATCH THE EXPRESSION ON YOUR WIFE'S FACE WHEN SHE SEES MRS. BROWN IN THE FROCK SHE JUST MISSED GETTING FOR HERSELF AT THE SALES. WHEN YOU AND YOUR WIFE — I ASSUME, YOU WILL NOTE, THAT YOU CAN AFFORD A WIFE AS WELL AS A DOG — GO TO THE THEATRE HE CAN WATCH THE BABY. HE CAN PATROL THE WASP ROUTES IN THE BACK GARDEN, TO KEEP THE FLYING ZEBRAS FROM SHARING YOUR STRAWBERRY JAM WITH YOU AT BREAKFAST TIME. ARM HIM WITH A FLY-SWATTER FOR THIS JOB. YOU NEED NOT BUY

ONE TILL WOOLWORTH'S PRICES COME DOWN A BIT, AS THEY ARE VERY EASILY MADE. GET A FEW BITS OF WIRE AND A POT OF GLUE, AND THEN ASK THE BLOKE NEXT DOOR HOW HE MAKES HIS. THERE IS ONE JOB EVERY WATCH DOG SHOULD BE GIVEN, WHICH

WOULD MEAN MUCH SAVING OF TIME AND TROUBLE TO A HOUSEWIFE. HOUSEWORK SUFFERS FROM MANY INTERRUPTIONS EVERY DAY, AND IN ADDITION IT IS VERY EXHAUSTING FOR A WOMAN, WHEN SHE IS BUSY UPSTAIRS DOING A SPOT OF DUSTING, TO REPEATEDLY HAVE TO THROW DOWN THE NOVEL AND RUSH DOWN TO SEE WHETHER THAT'S THE BAKER OR THE COALMAN OR ONLY THAT BLOOMING MRS. JONES COMING TO BORROW ANOTHER JUMPER PATTERN. ARRANGE THAT YOUR DOG DECIDES WHETHER OR NOT A CALLER SHOULD BE ALLOWED TO CALL. THE ARRANGEMENT IS SIMPLE. NAIL A CHURCH BELL, WITH A LONG LINE ATTACHED, TO YOUR BEDROOM CEILING: PASS THE END OF THE LINE OUT OF THE WINDOW AND DOWN TO THE DOG. HAVING DECIDED THAT THIS ONE IS A LEGITIMATE CALLER

AND NOT ONE OF THE INFERNAL NUISANCES, HE SIMPLY PULLS THE LINE AND TOLLS THE BELL. ALL YOUR WIFE NEED DO IS TO GIVE THE DOG THE LINE, GET ON WITH HER WORK, AND LEAVE HIM TO GET ON WITH THE WATCHING. BUT - EXPLAIN THAT TO HER VERY DISTINCTLY. OTHERWISE SHE WILL CERTAINLY SWEAR NEXT MONDAY EVENING THAT YOU YOURSELF TOLD HER TO GIVE THE DOG THE LINE AND LET HIM GET ON WITH THE WASHING.   I THINK I HAVE NOW COVERED FAIRLY COMPREHENSIVELY THE WORK OF AN EFFICIENT WATCH DOG. IF HOWEVER YOU HAVE YET OTHER WORK FOR HIM IN MIND, AND WISH TO KNOW IF THIS IS PERMISSIBLE UNDER HIS UNION RULES, FULL AND DEFINITE INFORMATION MAY BE OBTAINED BY DIRECT APPLICATION TO ANY RELIABLE MANUFACTURER OF DOG WATCHES.

"BLOTTO"